THE LIFE AND
ADVENTURES
OF MR. WIL

The Life and **ADVENTURES** of Mr. Wil

John Wilcox

To order additional copies of this book, contact:
Xlibris
1-888-795-4274
www.Xlibris.com
Orders@Xlibris.com
553549

Contents

Marine Corps Years 26
Yellowstone Years...84
Real Life..222
One Final Note 229

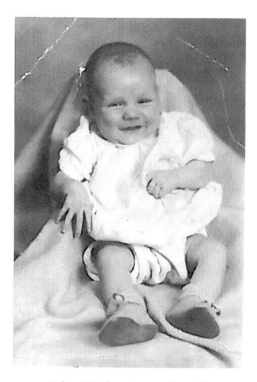

John Wesley 3 months old

In all of my sixty-plus years, I have few regrets; however, I have always wondered what my grandparents were like—what their lives were like and what stories they could tell. My father would seldom talk of his dad or what he was like. I only met him one time, just before he died, and I was only four or five years old. So, I guess my reason for attempting to write my story is for my grandkids. With me being the age I am and them being the age they are, there is a good chance we will never get to know one another. So, this is for you, any of you kids that might be interested.

I am the youngest of five children born to Norman and Marjorie Elliotte Wilcox on April 12, 1947, in Mulberry, Arkansas. My brother, Don, and three sisters, Norma, Mary Ann, and Glenda, were all born in Texas while my dad worked as a pusher on a derrick crew for Sinclair Oil. We lived in Odessa, Texas, until I was school age; however, I remember very little of Texas except getting caught in a dust storm and being rescued by my oldest sister, Norma Fay (Wanda, which she wanted to be called), who was in high school at the time. I also remember a big cactus at the rear of the house that I managed to get into several times a day.

In about 1953, we returned to Catcher, Arkansas, where my father had bought a small country store, The Catcher Store, down in the Kibler bottoms, not far out of Van Buren. The store was great fun; everyone gathered there. I remember people gathering on the porch of an evening and playing music and singing. The store was a typical country store of that time with a high porch across the front, a lean-to shed on the south side for feed and seed, and an ice house next to that. There was one gas pump and a pump for kerosene. The store itself was a true general store, which carried a wide range of products besides groceries.

Glenda and John

Our house was set a good ways behind the store and was an old frame house with a steep-pitched hip roof and a porch across the front— no indoor plumbing either. I don't remember much else about the place, but I do remember it snowed so much that winter that the snow was level with the front porch.

Dad bought an old pickup of some kind, put a coke box in the back, and would load it up with sandwich stuff and snacks. Then he would visit the fields where people were working to sell them lunch. I often got to go along on these trips and had a ball. Dad had a good business but was too soft-hearted and extended too much credit. Dad was one of the most honest men I had ever known, and his word was his bond and thought so of everyone else. Needless to say, Dad didn't last too long in the store business. He had thousands of dollars out in credit that he was never able to collect. I remember Mom complaining to Dad about extending credit to certain people because they would not or could not pay. Dad would just respond that he was sure they would eventually pay, which most never did.

Mom was the opposite of Dad, standing just barely over five feet, cautious and skeptical of everyone, and possessed a fiery temper. She suspected everyone would try to take advantage of you. Mom was thrifty to the extreme, as most people of that generation were, having gone through the Great Depression. Mom threw nothing away and found a use for every scrap, no matter how insignificant. Mom would sacrifice of herself and endure anything for us kids but would not mind giving a good old-fashioned beating with whatever she happened to have in her hand at the time when you pushed her too far. She would whip you from your ankles to the top of your head, just wherever it happened to land. Her thrashings, as we called them, might have hurt when we were young, but as we got older, we would scream as if she were killing us and then laugh about it afterward. Dad seldom whipped us, mainly because he didn't have to. We just knew not to mess with Dad, and it was too hard to make him mad. He would tell you something once and then swat you once with that big hand if you forgot.

After closing down the store, we moved to the farm on Georgia Ridge, where I still live today. My grandfather, Ben Wilcox, acquired the farm in about 1907 and lived there with my grandmother, Ann Inman Wilcox, until they separated. Grandpa evidently had an affair with the wife or daughter of a neighbor, who lived across the creek from us. I guess Grandpa was plowing more than corn when he would go down to the creek. I don't really know any details since none of the family ever talked about it. I think Dad was still pretty young when the split happened, so being the oldest son, he had to drop out of school in the eighth grade to work the farm. Dad always regretted not getting his diploma; however, I think he was more educated than me with all my diplomas.

Dad built his house on the farm in 1947, the year I was born, but never finished it. It consisted of six rooms: living room, dining room, kitchen, and three bedrooms. There was no bathroom or hallway, just the typical shotgun style house of that era. I still live in the house today, after having added on and remodeled, but the original house is still there, as are the memories.

Grandma lived in a little old two-room shack next to us for years. The original log house had burned several years before, and Uncle Herbert had moved this little shack from elsewhere on the farm. Uncle Herbert had built the little shack when he and Aunt Edna were first married but soon moved to Texas to find work in the oil field. Neither house had indoor plumbing or electricity when built. Grandma had an old black wash pot set up right behind her house where she and Mom would do laundry and hang it over the fence to dry. She also made her own lye soap in that pot and a dozen other projects as well. I usually got the jobs of fetching water out of the rain barrels to fill the pot and gathering wood to keep the fire underneath the pot burning.

Mom always resented that Dad had made her move from Texas to Arkansas. She really loved west Texas; I guess it was more like where she was raised in western Oklahoma. She was always talking of how much she hated the heat, humidity, and about anything else you can think of about Arkansas. She would never admit it, but I think she got to where she loved to go down under the hill into the woods and look at the wildflowers.

Electricity did come to the ridge in about 1949 or so. We drew our water from a well, used an outdoor toilet, and raised most of our food. We milked from two to six cows, depending on the year. Mom sold the cream in Mulberry, and most of the milk was fed to the hogs along with slop and a ground corn called shorts. To feed such a large family, we had to raise a big garden and orchard. In the garden, we raised a wide variety of vegetables, tomatoes, corn, beans, peas, cucumbers, squash, eggplant, popcorn, peanuts, sweet potatoes, Irish potatoes, strawberries, and many other things; so we had a wide variety of food if the weather had been favorable.

Since we raised most of our food, there was always work to do. I don't ever remember just being able to sit and listen to radio or watch TV. We were always having to shell peas, snap beans, shuck corn, or something. We did not get TV until the late 1950s but would listen to the radio programs while we worked. I remember the whole family walking to a neighbor's house one summer evening to see their TV. Neighbors from all over the ridge had come to see the TV, the first of its kind anywhere around.

Norma(14), Mary(12), Mother, Don(7), Glenda(4), and John(2)

The small TV, about twelve inches, was in a huge wooden cabinet, and the picture was so snowy that it was hard to see the picture. I remember that what we watched was a program called the *Louisiana Hay Ride,* and one of the performers was a newcomer named Elvis Presley. I was not much impressed with my first exposure to TV and spent most of the evening chasing fireflies out in the pasture with the rest of the wild little boys.

Since we lived in the country and rarely went to town, my brother, Don, and I, along with the Pannell boys, Dickey, and John David, spent most of our free time in the woods under the hill from the house where Mulberry Creek runs through our farm. Dickey and Don are four and five years older than John David and I, who are of the same age. We would fish, swim, and camp every chance we got. We camped in the woods at the far eastern end of "The Long Hole," as we called it. At that time, that little bit of bottom land there was cleared and in cultivation. One year, one of our neighbors, Charlie Kenny, raised a watermelon patch down there. Life could not have been more perfect for a bunch of boys who were always starved to death. A good campsite, a fishing hole, a swimming hole, and a watermelon patch all in the same place.

That campsite has always been one of my most priceless memories, and I am sure it helped set a course for the rest of my life.

In the fall and winter, we would hunt and trap. Each one of us had our own trap line that we would check in the dark before school, but on weekends, we would all get together and check everyone's trap line. We also spent a lot of time learning to identify the plants and animals of the Ozarks, a love I still have today. I was never the trapper that Don and Dickey were; I have always been so soft-hearted that it hurt me to see the animals in traps. I would much rather see them wild and free.

We had so many great adventures, many of which I dare not mention, all of which were great times. We did not have tents to sleep in, so we read how to build a lean-to shelter out of limbs with brush piled on top. We worked for days building the lean-to, and as soon as it was completed, we spent the night. Would you believe it? It rained hard all night! We quickly realized there was a major flaw, not in our design but in our material selection. Cedar boughs just funnel the rain in. We spent a lot of cold, wet, hungry nights on these trips over the next several years.

I remember the times when the fishing was great, and we ate our fill of half-burned, half-raw fish, but no fish has ever tasted better. Most times, pork and beans were our standby or whatever we could scavenge from a garden or the wild. We ate about anything that was in the food chain, from snakes, turtles, and fish to squirrel, opossum, and raccoon seasoned with a variety of wild plants, many of which gave us the shits. After more than fifty years of adventures, we still get together as often as possible for new adventures. Our cooking and equipment have greatly improved, as evident by our girth, but the adventures are never as sweet.

We tore apart one of the wooden rain barrels once to get runners for sleds we were making so we could slide down the side of the hill. The place we picked for this activity was a very steep slope covered with loose shale. It was a wonder we did not kill ourselves. Dickey was the first to try it since he had the best sled; he was always the best builder of the group. He went down that slope like Chevy Chase in *Christmas Vacation;* luckily, he had the good sense to abandon ship really quickly. The sled hit a tree on the way down at about fifty miles an hour and flew into pieces. The adventure was sure not worth Dad's wrath over the destruction of the barrel.

On one occasion, we decided to build a raft out of logs, a real Tom Sawyer–type thing. We worked all week cutting logs with a double bit ax and then dragging them to the water where we lashed them together with grape vines. When we launched it, Don was standing on the raft, which quickly became a Tom Sawyer submarine.

Don and John

Another incident that comes to mind happened when we were a little older. Dickey, Don, and I had gone coon hunting one cold, winter night and had taken my old dog, Red. He was what is known as a Red Bone hound, which is a cross between a blood hound and who knows what else. Normally, Red was always good for running a couple of coons a night, but on this particular night, we had no luck. After a couple of hours of nothing, we found a good spot sheltered from the wind, so we built a good fire and settled down around it to have a smoke and wait for the dogs to come in. Dickey and I were on one side of the fire, sitting on a log, while Don was laid out on the other side of the fire, about half-asleep. So here we were, all comfortable around the fire, smoking, telling lies to each other, and just enjoying the night.

Don had just bought a new rough out leather hunting coat, which really had a strong leather smell. While he was reclined there with his head propped up on his hand and elbow, Old Red came into camp behind him, sniffed his coat up and down, and then proceeded to hike his leg and piss all over the back of the coat. This was more than Dick and I could stand. We both fell off the log; we were laughing so hard. Of course, Don had no idea what we were laughing at, and we gave Old Red plenty of time to get away before we told him.

The community I was raised in was very typical for Arkansas during this time period, very rural with a small town of less than one thousand people about every ten miles or so. Arkansas, like the rest of the South, was decades behind the rest of the nation economically. There was very little industry or anywhere else to work. A combination of factors led to the economic conditions in Arkansas and the entire South. The severe restriction during Reconstruction after the Civil War, the Great Depression, and the Dust Bowl all contributed to the conditions.

The year I was born had been hot and dry for so long that the creek was dry. All of Dad's crops failed, and all of his livestock died, so we picked up and left Arkansas for Texas, where Dad could always work the oil field. All during this time, Arkansas continually lost population each year. Most of them headed for California, particularly Glendora, which had so many Mulberry people that it was known as the Mulberry of California.

Most people around the Mulberry area lived in the country on a small farm where they had no running water or indoor plunging. We were in this group as I have already mentioned. Since everyone in the country lived under these conditions, it did not seem strange. Our living conditions were essentially the same as had existed in the rest of the country at the turn of the century instead of the 1950s and 1960s, but when this is all you are used to, it seems normal.

On Saturdays, most everyone headed to town, which meant Mulberry. We would take what extra produce we did not need, load it into our 1950 Chevy coupe, and sell it in town along with cream and eggs. Mom would buy what little supplies she needed, mainly salt or flour, and then stay and visit while we kids went to the movie in town. Dad never came to town; as a matter of fact, he rarely left the mountain at all for any reason.

Mulberry was the hub of what little resources there were in the area. It had a bank, two grocery stores, at least two dry good stores, three hardware stores, a doctor, a drugstore, a four-lane bowling alley, and a movie theater that showed a double feature on both Thursday and Saturday nights. For 25¢, you could see both features and get a bag of popcorn and a coke. There were also about a half dozen places to eat, though we never ate there since we did not have any money.

There was also a two-story hotel down by the train depot. I guess it was a good hotel in its day, but Mulberry was already in its decline since it peaked at about the turn of the century. An old lady named Tommy Green owned the hotel. About all I remember about her was that she wore an old red wig that looked more like a coonskin cap than a wig, and she had about a hundred cats, so the whole area around the hotel smelled of cat shit. Yes, Mulberry was quite a town during this time. The streets and sidewalks were so crowded that you could scarcely get around.

Around behind Main Street was the city water trough where those families that came to town in a wagon pulled by a team of horses or mules could water their stock and tie them under a big Mulberry tree. There were not that many families who still came to town this way, only about a dozen, mainly the old-timers. An hour or so before dark, you could see them headed out of town so they could get home by milking time.

All week, I would walk up and down the dirt road looking for empty pop bottles to sell in town on Saturday. I could sell them for 2¢, unless it was one of those big 16 oz. pop cola bottles, which were worth 5¢. Money was hard to come by, but it also went a long way. You could buy a hamburger, fries, and a coke for 25¢. A gallon of gas was around 18¢ to 20¢.

During this time, the social center for males was the Anderson Brothers' pool hall on Main Street. It was an old sheet iron building with a potbellied stove near the back where all the domino tables were located. There were at least six or eight domino tables, each with its own spittoon. On Saturday and in bad weather, all the tables would be full with four players each and another bunch watching and waiting to take on the winners. Those guys were so good that after each one placed a couple of "rocks," as they called them, they all knew what dominoes each other was holding. You could see some real strategy played out; it always amazed me to see the good ones go at it.

The front part of the building was taken up by two pool tables and one snooker table. Most of the younger men and boys played snooker or pool until they were asked by the pros to play dominoes. The pool hall went out of business in the early 1990s. All the old men died off, and the younger generation was just not interested. I wish I would have taken the time to take pictures of the pool hall and the men that frequented it. It was a part of our history that is long gone and never to be seen again. The old men were the real story. Their winkled, weathered faces alone told volumes. Their clothing, mannerisms, and interaction with other men told still more. Good times, bad times, love, war, respect, or no respect—you could read it all in these men.

In the front half of the pool hall were the two pool tables and one snooker table. Most of the younger men played pool or mainly snooker. There was no shortage of outstanding snooker shooters in town, and on Saturday, they were all there. The table was always so busy that you would have to wait for hours for a chance to play. Pool was a nickel a cue, and snooker was a dime a cue. Even bad shooters could shoot all day for next to nothing.

On the north wall of the pool hall, there was a trap door about one foot square that opened into a small cafe in a lean-to building that just kind of hung on to the side of the pool hall. You could order something to eat, pick it up, and pay for it all through this window and never have to leave the pool hall or your game. Wives could also yell at their husbands through this window since women never entered the pool hall. This was, of course, a cause for much good-natured joking among the men when a wife would call her man outside.

For the most part, the pool hall was a real good place for young men to hang out. No alcohol was served and not too much consumed. Anyone who did come in drunk was always taken care of so they didn't get into trouble or arrested. The man that ran the establishment most of the time was named Red Riggs, and he had an older brother named Doc. About once a month, Red would get so drunk someone would get his nail apron, in which he kept his money, and take care of business. He would either sleep it off in the corner, or Doc would take him home. But other than this, it was just a bunch of men having a good time playing, smoking, dipping, and socializing. Most were farmers, and a lot of business was conducted over the domino tables. Wealthy, poor, young, old—there did not seem to be any social barriers in the pool hall.

Down at the south end of Main Street was the train depot and cotton gin. I used to like to walk the couple of blocks to the depot and watch the train come through. Several old steam locomotives were still operating on that line, and there was still passenger service, though I remember very few passengers ever getting off at Mulberry. They would just hang the mail bag out on a hook, and the train would highball right on through, grab the mail sack, and throw out a mail bag onto the platform.

I do remember taking a school trip on the train to Little Rock to visit the State Capitol and zoo. We caught the train long before daylight, were gone all day, and arrived home late evening. All the schools in the area went, so we stopped at every little town from here to there. The zoo was kind of depressing; I hated to see the animals caged up like that. They were not in natural settings like they are now. They were in small cages in which they just paced back and forth.

The four-lane bowling alley I mentioned was owned by A.G. and Robert Benham. When I got old enough, I would set pins for 10¢ a game on Saturdays. Some days, I could make a dollar or more. Each alley had an automatic pin setter, sort of, but you had to gather the pins by hand after they threw the first ball and put the pins in the pin setter, then get the ball and put it in the ball return. After they threw their second ball, I would repeat the process and pull a cord on the pin setter, which would lower the pins into place. Then I would get out of the way because some of the big, strong guys could throw so hard that pins would fly over the barricade we hid behind. I always liked it when there were not enough pin setters and I got to work two alleys at the same time. You really had to hustle, but the time went much faster, and you could make more money. The bowling alley went out of business sometime in the late 1960s or early 1970s while I was gone from Mulberry.

John hard at work at Bowlin Drug Store

There was a drugstore on the opposite side of the street from the pool hall that was bought by Larry Barber around 1962 or 1963. His store was the typical old drugstore, soda fountain and all. It was also the only place other than the bank that had air-conditioning. Larry kept the store open until sometime in the 1980s when he retired, moved to Alaska, and worked part-time at a pharmacy there for several years before returning to Mulberry in the early 1990s, where he died in 1997. Larry and his wife, Gwen, became very active members of the Mulberry community during the years they ran the drugstore.

At the end of summer, right after Labor Day, the Crawford County Fair was held in Mulberry on a lot near the north end of Main Street, where it crosses Highway 64. In the late 1950s, its location was moved to its present day location on Highway 215 at Kirksey Park. The fair is the only reminiscence of the world I grew up in. Fair time was always a busy time for young and old alike, and most everyone attended and had something entered. We boys would have 4-H chickens, a calf, hog, or all of the above entered for judging. Many times, we would borrow chickens from the neighbors to enter, sometimes with their knowledge but most times not. We would always bring their chickens back, but seldom the same ones because we could not remember where we got what. The real reason we entered so much stuff was that we got out of school to take care of our animals. The more animals you had, the longer you could be gone.

There was and is a parade on Saturday morning during the fair, and each class at the high school entered a float in hopes of winning a cash prize for the best. I don't know how much money we are talking about since my class never won, but it was great fun getting together in a secret location to create our masterpiece on a borrowed trailer. We spent about as much time trying to find out the location of the other classes' floats and their themes as we did working. It was a real lesson in life and your niche. We had class members who were creative, those who were leaders, scroungers, and even a few workers. Me, I was the spy. I could locate the other float and find out its theme, no matter where they hid; I was a pretty good scrounge, and I could build. The classes no longer build floats due to lack of interest, but the parade still goes on each year. Some years, it is better than others, but it is still a great small-town event.

Every year at the fair, there is a beauty contest open to high school girls and a little princess contest for preschool girls. I think now they have added a junior high age group. This is probably the single event that the whole county participates in. All the girls ride on a fancy or classic vehicle in the parade. My sister Glenda, "Nellie," won the title of Miss Crawford County in 1962 or 1963. Mom and Dad didn't have the money for her to run, but Gwen and Larry Barber paid her entry fee and bought her an evening dress to wear while Dad's brother, Uncle Clarence, and his wife, Aunt Eva, paid for her swim suit. Nellie was a looker in her younger days and very outgoing. A few weeks later, she competed in the Miss Arkansas pageant at the State Fair in Little Rock. She did not win but had a real good experience, and it did a lot for her self-esteem.

It was during this time period that I met the Barbers, Gwen, and Larry. Glenda, my sister, was working for Larry at the drugstore after school and on Saturdays. Larry is the one that hung her with the nickname Nellie, which most people still know her as today. The drugstore had sponsored her entry into the queen's contest. Gwen had helped her with her makeup, clothing, all that stuff. I began working for Larry, mowing the lawn, chopping hedges, waxing the store floor, and just doing whatever he needed. Eventually, I was spending most every day with them, doing whatever needed to be done.

The Barbers opened my eyes to a whole new world that I knew existed somewhere but that I had never witnessed. They were young, active, and enthusiastic. They also had money to spend on things other than the bare necessities. They were always traveling somewhere: Dallas, Houston, Memphis, Oklahoma City, or Little Rock. Most of the trips were business related, so I would go along to watch their three young kids while they were busy. We would stay in nice motels, dine out at fancy restaurants, and see all the sights. Over time, I became like a member of the family, and we were inseparable.

I began to spend more nights with them than at home. I never had any problem getting along with Mom and Dad, and I loved and respected them both; I was just ready to leave home and start my life. There was really nothing else for me at home after Nellie left home. Being the youngest, I was always used to a house full of kids and a lot of commotion. I was always so close to Nellie all my life that when she left and it was just me, Mom, and Dad, the place was so dead.

It eventually got to the point that I came home to visit, but long before I was out of high school, I was living with and working for the Barbers full-time. Larry and I became closest friends, a relationship that lasted for more than forty years until his death in 1997. Of Larry Barber, all I can say is that he was the biggest character I have ever met, and I have had a lifetime of associating with characters; it's as if I attract them. The Boss, as we called him, was #1 on the all-time character list with #2 not even a close second.

For over forty years, the Boss and I did everything together, good and bad. We camped, canoed, hunted, fished, worked, and traveled together. He was moody and could either be the most enjoyable person to be around, or you wanted to kill him. Gwen had a knack for being able to put him in a foul mood faster than anyone. On canoe trips, we would split them up into different canoes; it was either that or kill them both, for together, they were unbearable.

I can think of nothing during that part of my life that did not involve the Barbers. From my years in Vietnam to Yellowstone, to my marriage and the birth of my children, Gwen and Larry were always there. After Larry's death, either Gwen or I changed for we could not seem to get along. I really hated it, but it got to where I just stayed away, and it was at a time when I should have been more sympathetic and patient with her.

Another event that was always looked forward to in Mulberry was the arrival of a traveling skating rink. It was not very large but had a hardwood floor covered by a big tent. Mr. Kelly ran the rink and would hire some of us boys to help set it up. We would work all night to have it ready for the next day. The rink was always set up in what was then a vacant lot across from Tommy Green's Hotel where the city complex is now. We were paid 50¢ an hour to help and got a discount on skating, so it usually worked out about even by the time the rink left town. The skating rink would do a good business for the first couple of weeks but then slow down until Mr. Kelly would pick up and move to another town.

Most of my education came from the Mulberry school system, except that I attended my first grade in Oak Grove Elementary near Van Buren and that I spent the last half of my second grade and all of my third grade years in Glendora, California. I have few memories of my school days in Glendora except for being made fun of because of the way I talked and because I wore patched jeans. I do remember going on a school fieldtrip to an Indian museum, which really impressed me. I can still picture the exhibits today, over fifty years later. I guess this may be the reason I like to take my classes on fieldtrips now.

Dad had gone to California ahead of the rest of us in search of work and a place for us to live. We all followed a few weeks later. We had a room in the Glendora Hotel when we first arrived, but we eventually found a place to rent across the street from the school. 512 East Lemon was the address, and it was surrounded by an orange grove on three sides. I really liked living in the hotel though; it was right next to the train depot and only one block from downtown. Every morning, the fog or smog would be so thick you couldn't see anything. It was like a scene from a Sherlock Holmes story. I do remember having a lot of animals when we lived on East Lemon. I know we had a large desert tortoise, all kinds of chickens, a pet gopher, and many other kinds of animals.

It was while living in California that Dad developed his respiratory problem, due partially to the smog, but mainly to many years of pipe smoking. Eventually, we were forced to leave California due to Dad's health and returned to Mulberry and the family farm. We should have stopped in the desert of Arizona or New Mexico since Dad's breathing cleared up while we were in the desert. The climate in Arkansas was not much better than that of California, but at least, we did not have the smog. This was in the mid-1950s, a time when the air pollution in California was so bad that you could rarely see the mountains, and on some days, many people of risk, like Dad, would die due to the pollution. His breathing was a little better in Arkansas but not much. It was difficult to watch him struggle to make it to the table for supper or to do anything else for that matter. To me, a little boy, Dad had always been this towering giant of super strength, and to see him struggle for every breath was hard to take. Dad took a job at a furniture factory running a saw, which allowed him to sit down and work. I don't guess he ever missed a day of work in all the years he worked there. The job didn't pay much, but Mom was thrifty, so we got by all right.

I was in the fourth grade when we moved back to Mulberry, and I was sure glad to be gone from California. Glendora was most likely a nice town, but I had never lived in a town before and haven't since, and I guess it's just not my niche. Living on a farm five miles outside of a town of about one thousand people is more to my liking.

As I said before, I was in the fourth grade when we returned to Mulberry. My teacher was a nice old lady named Mrs. Cartwright, who lived right across the street from the school. She was a very good teacher, worked us hard, and didn't put up with any crap. I think it was in the fourth grade when we boys got caught smoking grape vines under the science room of the high school. The smoke drifted up through cracks in the floor, and Mr. Bruce, the science teacher, thought the building was on fire and called the fire department that came rolling in and found nothing but a dozen or so little boys smoking grape vines. We sure got our asses busted for that. Other than that, the fourth grade was pretty dull, except that when Mrs. Cartwright was out of the room one time, one of my female classmates raised her shirt and showed all of us her little titties, which were just beginning to swell. Hell, I wasn't even sure what I was supposed to be looking for.

Our fifth grade year was more of the same. Miss Lillian Winfrey was my teacher, another older woman, but an ex-WAC from WWII, another excellent teacher who did not put up with much, and it was a good thing because we sure put it out. Not much of interest happened that year except I had a girlfriend. I was too timid to show any interest because this was during the time period when little boys sure would not be caught showing any affection to girls for fear of what their friends would say.

My sixth grade year was just more of the same, except Mrs. Perrier was my teacher, and boy, did she pile on the work! Mrs. Etta Jordan was my seventh grade teacher. She had taught for years at a one-room school just north of where we live, Pope School House, which still stands. It's a large rock building where Thell Morris lived until just recently. It's located at the junction of Cattlemen's Road and Chastain Road. Mrs. Etta used to ride a big white mare to school and back each day, a distance of about five miles each way. She did not learn to drive a car until her husband Smith died. She drove his pickup but not very well. Everyone would watch for her and just get out of the way, but she never got over 15 mph, so you had plenty of time to avoid her. Dear, sweet, old lady and a good teacher.

It was in the seventh grade that I started playing basketball for which I developed a real love and developed a fair amount of talent. From this point on, school was all about playing ball. Being a small size, I learned that I had to do things better than the bigger boys and had to be meaner and tougher also. I also developed one of a few close friendships that I have had in my life. Roger Benham and I had been classmates since the fourth grade, but basketball, hunting, and fishing have forged a friendship that has lasted to this day. Roger's dad, A. G. Benham, was a high school history teacher, a business man, and an outstanding person that had a lot of influence on my life. I consider myself lucky to have known so many great men during my childhood.

In those days, Mulberry was a basketball power in Arkansas, with most of its teams going to the state tournament year after year and winning three state titles in four years in boys' basketball: 1960, 1962, and 1964. I played on the 1962 team and was named All State that year. I started to get inquiries from several different colleges. Up to this point, I had not even been considering college. I was planning on going into the Marines like my brother, but I thought it would be good to play ball for a couple of more years.

The college I had hoped to attend was Arkansas A&M at Monticello, which had the only forestry school in the state, and that is what I wanted to major in. Their coach was very interested in having me play for him, so I went down there and toured the campus. He told me that I had the scholarship and he would send it to me the next week. I was to send him a copy of my transcript. I sent him a copy of my transcript as soon as I got home and never heard from him again. Evidently, my grades were not up to his expectation.

I eventually took a scholarship that was offered to me at Fort Smith Junior College; today it's the University of Arkansas at Fort Smith. It was rather ironic that I went to college to play ball, but after I got there, I really liked college but did not care for college ball. The coach at FSJC was the old Springdale High School coach that we had played against several times and had always beaten. He was a real good man but just not the coach that Cotton had been. I never really got into it since I had a chemistry class that conflicted with the first hour of practice.

This was during the time when there was a big buildup of the military for service in Vietnam, and you had to maintain a two-point average to keep a draft deferment. I had let myself get so far behind in high school due to my own stupidity, since I had as fine a group of teachers as could be found anywhere, that I was unable to keep my grades up and lost my draft deferment. After my third semester, I joined the Marine Corps since I didn't want to serve with a bunch of draftees. This ended my childhood and began a period of my life, though often painful to remember, that made me a stronger person.

Marine Corps Years

I left Mulberry on a Trailways bus headed to Little Rock for my induction into the corps in early April 1967, with more than a little apprehension about what lay ahead. I was not totally ignorant about what I was in for since my brother had served in the Corps a few years earlier during the Cuban Missile Crisis of the Kennedy administration.

I reported to the induction center, which was right downtown. In those days, downtown Little Rock was a pretty shabby city, with old run-down hotels and businesses. The hotel they put us up in was terrible. Not only was it old and shabby, but there were also old prostitutes working every floor. This was not my first encounter with such things as I had traveled a fair amount to Dallas, Kansas City, Houston, and many others, but the prostitutes I saw in most of these places were a little more appealing than the ones I saw in Little Rock. Most of them looked as though they were about one or two years from being eligible for social security.

We spent all day getting our physicals and paperwork in order and flew out the next day, which was my first time on a plane. We had a long layover in Dallas, which put us in San Diego sometime after midnight. There were about six or eight of us on the flight, so we banded together as big, bad Marines. Waiting at the terminal for us was a gunny in undressed blues. We walked up to him, and one of us asked (and I am sure glad it wasn't me), "Are you who we are to report to?" The gunny went ballistic. "Do I look like a f—ing ewe? Do I smell like a f—ing ewe?" And all of this at the top of his lungs.

I guess they are used to it in San Diego because there were all kinds of people walking by, and they hardly gave us a glance. The ones that did gave us a look that said, "You poor s.o.b.s." The gunny fell us into formation and left us standing at attention for what seemed like a couple of hours. Every so often, another flight would come in and bring more "poor s.o.b.s" like us.

This went on until we had a bus full. We made the trip from the airport to the Marine Corps Recruit Depot (MCRD) in just a couple of minutes, since it's just across the runway, and were met by our drill instructors who mounted the bus yelling and screaming at us to get our asses off their Marine Corps bus since we maggots were not worthy to ride their bus.

We were hustled into a supply building with the DIs yelling, screaming, and kicking us in the ass all the way. Once in the building, we stripped naked and boxed up all our belongings to be sent home. One of our DIs told us to put our dicks in the box too because we were not going to be needing them for the next twelve weeks. Then they started to issue our gear. First came underwear, then our utilities (pants and shirts), then boots and socks. When it came time to issue the web belts, they just grabbed a handful of them and threw them into the floor yelling and screaming that we had better get a f—ing belt, but of course, they had not thrown enough belts for all sixty-five of us, so the fight was on. Thank God I was quick; I got one, though it nearly cost me my life.

This is the way the rest of the night went until we finally had our issue, and they fell us in on the yellow footprints out front of the building with a sea bag full of everything. They marched us to our barracks, which was an old Quonset hut left over from pre-WWII, and put us to bed about 0400. Reveille sounded at 0500. I don't think anyone slept a wink, even though we were all exhausted. I have spent many sleepless nights during my life, but that first night at receiving barracks was one of the longest.

Day one was just a blur of yelling, screaming, cursing, and constant exercise, with more paperwork and physical exams mixed in. My first meal was an experience. It was breakfast, and you just side-stepped down the line, and the mess men put on your tray what the drill instructors told them to. Being a skinny kid, I got loaded down, but the fat kids got nothing but vegetables. I could hardly get it down and hoped I could keep it down. After that first day, I was not quite so hard to please and would eat anything and as much as they would put on my tray.

We were kept hard at it all day, from 0500 in the morning until after taps at nights with not a minute to relax, except Sunday when we would be marched to the non-denominational chapel for services. After church, we were given a few minutes to write a letter home before we had to participate in organized athletics, which usually meant Marine Corps football, which was more like the assault of Iwo. There would be about thirty or so men on each team and about that many in reserve for when the others got drug from the field injured or unconscious. I don't remember ever hearing any rules except kill the guy with the ball and anyone that stands in the way. I don't remember anything that was illegal except touching a drill instructor, which were walking all over the field. I have been in many battles where there was less bloodshed and fewer casualties than our Sunday afternoon games.

Head calls were another memorable experience. Sixty-five men had, at the most, five minutes for the three S's (shit, shower, shave). I didn't have a bowel movement for the first two weeks we were there. Then after that, we could wait until after taps and straggle to the head on our own. It was almost the cause for a celebration, our only freedom, freedom to take a dump. Boot camp routine was very predictable: up before 0500, fall into formation in front of the duty hut. We were given no more than a few seconds to roll out of our racks, make them, and fall into formation outside in our skivvies and be marched to the head.

After head call, we would be marched back to our Quonset hut to get dressed in our utility trousers and a bright yellow sweatshirt with a big red Marine Corps emblem on it. The guy that slept in the rack below me would get into trouble every morning because he would panic and could not open the combination lock on his foot locker. So one morning, as soon as my feet hit the floor, I asked him for his combination. He just looked at me for a second and then told me what it was. I would unlock his footlocker for him every morning after that. Since we were not allowed to talk, I knew nothing about him except that his name was Williamson, S.J., which I could read on his shirt. After that, we became close friends, which was strange since we were total opposites.

Willie, as he was called, was a short, stout built guy from Tacoma, Washington, a city boy that was about as home in the woods as I was in the city. Hot humid weather just killed him, and he could not stand to be dirty or sweaty. He was high strung, and almost anything would send him into a panic so bad that he could hardly function. I think this was one place where having played ball paid off. I guess I had played in so many big games that I was used to dealing with pressure and always appeared to be very laid back even though I might be scared to death. I have seen Willie stand and tremble when a DI was chewing on his ass.

My old basketball coach had been an old Marine from WWII and had fought all over the Pacific and could give a good Marine Corps ass chewing, so I was used to it. As a matter of fact, I got into more trouble for laughing at some of the crap the DIs would say or do. They would get right up in my face because I just could not keep from smiling at their antics. I have always had a good sense of humor and have been accused of being a bit of a clown myself, but some of the DIs would make good standup comics when you were not the one they were chewing on.

After getting dressed and policing up the barracks, we would fall in again for our five-mile run every morning, just to warm up before chow. Mess call was quite an experience also. If we happened to get there a little early and another platoon was still in line to go in, our DI would find some infraction that had been committed by one of us, or not, and they would put us down on our faces doing push-ups until it was time for us to go in. Once you got your chow, you set your tray down on the table and stood at attention until everyone was at the table. Then the DI would give you a command to sit. You all had to drop your ass onto the bench at one time and sit at attention until you were given the command to eat. If everyone's butt did not hit the bench at the same time, you would have to do it again, and if you did not do it right this time, you were given the command to pick up your trays and get out. When this happened, which it did quite often, you would have to eat all your food standing up in line waiting to rinse out your tray. And you could not throw away any food, so you had to get it all down in about a minute.

After chow, the rest of the morning would be spent in class where we learned about different weapons, Marine Corps history, military tactics, obstacle course, or close order drill on the main grinder, which was a large asphalt lot in front of the headquarters building. We drilled for many hours every day, rain or shine, daylight or dark. We marched in formation everywhere we went so we were constantly being drilled, and of course, when we did not do it right, we were down on our faces doing push-ups or something. It went this way for the first eight weeks and then we were loaded onto busses and taken to Camp Pendleton for firearms training.

Camp Pendleton was quite a change from San Diego and MCRD. We ate better and were not punished as much or at least without a reason, unless you had problems shooting, then you were in a world of trouble. One guy in our squad just could not shoot and caught all kinds of punishment. I can't remember his name, but the DIs put me to working with a guy in the head after taps since I had been shooting expert since the first day. He showed enough improvement that he was shooting well enough to qualify as a marksman, which is the lowest level of qualification, until the day we had to shoot for our actual qualification.

I think he would have made it if they had not got on him so hard, but as it was, he just fell apart and did not make it. But I can't say much because I missed expert by three points after shooting expert with at least twenty points to spare. I took a gamble and put five rounds on his target to try and help him qualify when I saw he was in trouble. Even without those five rounds, I still would have made it, but I had a bad time at the three hundred meter sitting position. I don't know if I put the wrong windage on my sights or what I did, but I had always shot the max from three hundred meters. The Marine Corps takes tremendous pride in its marksmanship, so not qualifying is about the worst thing you can do. I guess things worked out well for him though. All of the rest of us that qualified were put into the infantry as grunts, and he made a cook.

After we finished at the rifle range, we returned to MCRD for our remaining two weeks, and we started to be treated a lot better, even by Sgt. O'Donnell. He was the toughest badass of all the DIs at MCRD. It was just my luck to be in his platoon. He knew ways to inflict pain on us that would make the strongest of us break. One of his favorite tortures was to put us down in the push-up position on our knuckles on the grinder, which was asphalt. He would give us the command of "push-ups forever" and then would call cadence. He would say, "One," and we would push up and say, "One." Then he would say, "Two," and we would go down and repeat his command, and all the time we were on our knuckles. It was not at all unusual for us to do over one hundred push-ups this way, and if he was really pissed off, he would leave us in the up position for a long time between commands. If you let your back sag, he would walk up and kick your arm, which would scrape your knuckles across the asphalt and tear the hide off the knuckles. The worst part was the next day when your knuckles scabbed over and you had to get down on them again. The pain, at first, was unbearable, but O'Donnell would force us to take our minds off the pain, and we learned that we could endure tremendous pain if we did not think about the pain and concentrate on something else instead. I would usually force myself to think about home or how I planned to kill O'Donnell if I ever had a good chance.

O'Donnell was the picture-perfect Marine, a little over six feet, about 190 pounds or so, handsome, and tough as they come. He had already been to Vietnam once, so he had a lot of personal experience to share. Every time he had the duty at night, he would have us out on the company street in front of our Quonset hut, sitting on our buckets fieldstripping our M14s in the dark by feel alone. Sometimes, he would light the smoking lamp and just talk to us about what we needed to know to stay alive in Nam. During these times, he almost seemed human, but the next day, he would remind us once again that he was actually sent from hell by the devil just for us. I don't know what kept him from getting busted because he did not hesitate to knock you down with his fists if you gave him cause, and it did not take much to give him cause. I remember one time when we were having trouble mastering a particular movement while doing close order drill. O'Donnell halted us in formation, walked up to the first man in formation, and screamed, "What was the f—ing command?" and the guy would give the command, "Step pivot step." O'Donnell would then knock the guy down with his fist and then repeat the same thing all the way down the squad. It was real hard to stand there at attention and wait for your turn, but we endured, and the next time we were given the command "step pivot step," we executed it perfectly. O'Donnell had a way of getting his point across.

Almost every evening, we would take practice tests over the Uniform Code of Military Justice, Special Orders, or Marine Corps history, and if you did not score 100 percent on the tests, you would have to report to the duty hut and answer to guess who? Sgt. O'Donnell. After one session with him, guys that could not even read or write became Rhodes Scholars. I made sure that I scored well enough that I did not have to report to the duty hut, so I don't know and don't want to know what was done to them.

In the Marine Corps, when you salute, your thumb is laid flat next to your index finger, not sticking out. A lot of guys had trouble remembering this until O'Donnell got their attention, which he would do by placing their thumbs inside the chamber of their M14 rifle and letting the bolt slam shut, which would mash their thumb. Blood would fly everywhere, and of course, the thumb nail would come off in a few days. He would do the same thing to guys who could not remember their left from their right.

Our other DIs were tough and competent, but when we were having trouble mastering something, Sgt. O'Donnell was the man that could get the point across. Our platoon commander, Sgt. Fisher, was a lot older than O'Donnell, who was a buck sergeant. Fisher was just as tough but not as mean. He reminds me of Gunny Ermy, an old Marine that has made several movies and has a series on the History Channel. He was the one I got into trouble with for laughing at some of his antics. I never laughed at anything O'Donnell did; I knew he would have killed me for it or made me wish I was dead.

Physically, boot camp was not a problem for me since my coach in high school conditioned us like we were Marines, but mentally, they could sure screw with your mind. I don't care what we were doing; they could find a way to be mentally conditioning us to carry out commands given to us without a second thought. I remember several times when a Marine from another platoon would walk between us and our DI when we were in formation. Instead of telling the Marine not to do that, O'Donnell would order us to attack and beat him, which we did without hesitation. When we did bayonet or hand-to-hand training, you had better try to kill your opponent or at least make them think you were going to kill him, so they would have to drag you off him. Everything we did, we had better leave our opponent bleeding, and they really liked it if we were both bloody. Guys that did not fight hard enough would be singled out to fight four or five guys at the same time, and of course, he would get beaten severely. Many times, they would have to be taken to sick bay. A friend of mine from Colorado got hit in the nuts so hard that his nuts swelled to the size of volleyball and turned as black as a boot. He was on sick call for only a couple of days, and then he was right back with us.

The last couple of weeks of boot camp, the DIs quit calling us pukes, maggots, and slimes and actually started calling us Marines. We starched our utilities, spit-shined our boots, polished our brass, and bloused our trousers. When we marched, we were really sharp, everyone in step and aligned in all directions. It felt good to see the results of all our hard work. On Memorial Day, we were bussed downtown to march in a parade, along with the Navy recruits. There was no comparison between the way we marched and the way the sailors marched. None of them were in step, head bobbing up and down, and very little alignment in any direction. We marched as if we were one person, everything perfect.

It was at this parade that I got the first glimpse of what was happening in the outside world. Being from a small, conservative town, I had no idea about what the attitude of the rest of the country was like. Vietnam had really been heating up for the past several months, and protests were starting to occur on several college campuses. We all knew we were headed to Vietnam since we already had our orders and were gung ho to go, but I wasn't ready for the reaction of the American public to us when we marched down Main Street of San Diego that beautiful spring day looking as sharp and well-trained as any military unit ever did; and I guess we had the image of how well troops were received during WWII, so it was more than a little disturbing when we were booed by the American public that was gathered to watch the parade. It was just a glimpse of what was to come.

After boot camp, we went to Camp Pendleton in California for our infantry training. We were to be there for four weeks, but we got quarantined for two additional weeks because of a meningitis outbreak. I went home for a thirty-day leave before having to report back to Camp Pendleton to staging battalion for thirty days of advanced infantry training before going overseas. It was here that we were trained specifically for service in Vietnam, and we received training with the M16 rifle.

From staging battalion, we flew out of L.A., via Hawaii and Guam, to Okinawa, where we were given base liberty for the night. We all proceeded to try to drink the island dry, but just about the time we all got good and drunk on all that 10¢ beer, we were sent word to muster at the barracks. Four hours later, we were landing in Da Nang, Vietnam.

It was early morning when we approached Vietnam that early September day, and as I looked out of the window, my first impression of Vietnam was that it looked just like home from the air. When we landed, we grabbed our sea bags and were hustled away from the air strip since they were always taking incoming artillery when a plane arrived. The heat and humidity were stifling, mud was everywhere, and everything was shot to hell. There were Marines walking around everywhere, dirty, nasty, and unshaved, and the look in their eyes was something I will never forget. I can't even describe it—not fear, not surprise, just a look.

From Da Nang, which was the Third Marine Division HQ, we were assigned to our units. Willie, me, and several others from my platoon in boot camp went to the Ninth Marines. Willie and I both went to Echo Company of the Second Battalion while several of the others went to Fox, Golf, and Hotel Companies. Our battalion headquarters was at a place called Dong Ha, a lovely tropical paradise of mud, bugs, and continual artillery fire since it was well within the range of the guns from North Vietnam. We were flown there by C-130, sitting on the floor holding onto a cargo strap on takeoff and landings and hoping that the jeep and other gear that was with us stayed in place. As we were landing, artillery shells were exploding on the runway both in front of us and behind us. The C-130 did not come to a stop but kept rolling while we were hurried off the plane and all the gear kicked off while the plane continued its taxing down the runway, turning around, and taking off without ever stopping. The whole process took less than a couple of minutes.

The Marine Corps base at Dong Ha, which was just outside of the city of Dong Ha, was a sand-bagged tent city, muddy or dusty, depending on how long it had been since the last rain, and since this was at the start of the monsoons, it was nothing but mud. The tents were riddled with shrapnel holes; water poured in when it rained, which it did every afternoon. In front of the rows of tents was a boardwalk made of empty wooden crates that artillery shells came in. Outside each tent was a trench with sandbags around it, and often, the trenches were covered with the same type of ammo crate that the boardwalk was made of, except that they were filled with sand to form a makeshift bunker.

The tents had a wooden floor in them, but the mud was so thick on the floor that every day we had to scrape it off with a shovel. The mud had a type of clay that was extremely slick and sticky. Vehicles did not really sink down into the mud but would just sit and spin, and when they tried to stop, they would slide a long ways before stopping.

It was the middle of the afternoon when we got checked in at the company HQ, got assigned to a tent, and checked in at the company supply to get all our combat gear, better known as 782 gear because that is the number of the form that it is all listed on. When we entered the supply tent, there were piles of all kinds of equipment, all of which were muddy, bloody, and hard-used. I assumed this was gear that was to be thrown away—was I mistaken! When we gave the supply sergeant our paper work, he pointed at these piles and told us to rummage through the piles and find the best stuff. Nearly all of it was covered with blood and mud. From a pile of M16s, I found one that looked pretty new, but the bolt was jammed shut. When I told the supply sergeant that, he said, "Take it anyway. They all jam." I started going through the pile of helmets and found one with a bullet hole in it and someone's brains on the inside of the liner, or at least that is what I thought it was. Either way, I knew I didn't want that helmet. Another had a bull's eye drawn on the back of its cover—culled that one, too. I finally found one that had no issues that concerned me, except being muddy and smelling of sweat; so I took it. It was almost as difficult to pick a flak jacket as a helmet. Same problem, too many bullet holes, blood, or targets drawn on them, and the smell of sweat was overpowering. We really had no idea what all we needed, so we just took whatever they had; consequently, we ended up with a lot of stuff that we had no use for, like a gas mask. We got all our gear back to the tent and spent the rest of the afternoon and evening getting it cleaned and ready to go since we were going to be flown out to our unit the next day. That evening, we went to the mess hall. I don't remember what we had to eat, but I do remember that it was pretty bad.

That evening, after we were asleep, an artillery round from the enemy had hit in the main ammo dump at Dong Ha, and everything started exploding. This ammo dump supplied all the infantry, artillery, and helicopter units in the entire I Corps area, so there were millions of rounds of all different kinds of ordnance in this ammo dump. Things exploded continually all night and were still exploding the next day when we flew out. We all spent all night sleeping, or trying to sleep, in a trench just outside the tent. I don't know how many days the dump exploded, but I heard it was over a week.

The next morning, we had a breakfast of powdered eggs, fried spam, and toast. The toast was real good since the mess hall baked its own bread. The bakery became one of our main targets to raid when we ever got back to the rear area. After chow, we were taken by truck to the LZ (landing zone) and were put aboard choppers. The choppers were remnants of the Korean War, CH-47s I think, better known as "shuddering shitters." There were about a half a dozen of us, a heavy load for this type of chopper. We all had so much gear that we had to be helped onto the chopper. There were no seats on the chopper, so we just squatted on one knee and tried to keep balanced as the chopper took off. I was the last in, so I was kneeling in front of the opening on the right side where the door would have been located when it had a door. We took off, and the pilot turned to the right, which kind of laid the chopper on its right side, which put me kind of looking right down at the ground from about a hundred feet up. We flew in a northwesterly direction for about ten minutes, right up to the DMZ (demilitarized zone), which separated South Vietnam from North Vietnam to a place called Con Thien.

Con Thien was the first base built along the DMZ as part of what was to be known as McNamara's Wall. McNamara was the Secretary of Defense under both Presidents Kennedy and Johnson and proposed building a series of bases along the entire length of the DMZ to prevent the enemy from crossing over the border into the south. I guess it slowed them down by forcing them to come around to the west of Vietnam and enter the south through Laos and Cambodia. Con Thien was still under construction at this time, and my unit, Echo Company Second Battalion Ninth Marine Regiment, was assigned the task of keeping the base secure form being overrun by the North Vietnamese Army while the engineers worked. Just before I arrived in the country, there had been a terrible battle for control of the area along the DMZ, and in many ways, it was still going on when I arrived.

As we approached the LZ at Con Thien, which was just a small clearing in the jungle just outside of the wire perimeter, mortar rounds were falling all over the LZ. The pilot did not set the chopper down but ordered us to jump out quickly as he hovered the chopper about a foot or two above the ground. With all the weight we were carrying, we hit the ground like a rock and rolled over into a small depression in the ground that had been created by an exploding artillery round some time earlier. As soon as the chopper took off, the shelling stopped, but Willie and I did not have a clue as to where we were or where the perimeter was located. After a few minutes, we spotted a couple of Marines just inside the jungle west of the LZ, so Willie and I started hustling in that direction. Before we got to the jungle, four Marines came running out of the jungle headed to the LZ, struggling with a poncho, which appeared to be loaded with something heavy. When they saw us, they yelled for us to give them a hand with the poncho, so we dropped our gear and grabbed hold of the poncho. I had no idea what was in the poncho until I grabbed hold and looked in. Inside the poncho was what was left of a Marine that I guess had received a direct hit from an artillery round, probably one that had been fired at our chopper as we were coming into the LZ. I was shocked numb. I looked at Willie, who was on the other side of the poncho from me. He looked back at me; the color and expression on his face, I will never forget. I saw that look many times after that on different men's faces. It was the same look you see on the face of the dead, as if they are just an empty body. A dust off (medical evacuation) chopper was coming in to pick up the dead and wounded, which brought more artillery fire, which caused more casualties, which brought in more choppers, which brought more artillery, etc. I think you get the idea what it was like at Con Thien.

Willie and I had not been in the bush but a couple of minutes and had already encountered the horrors of war. Neither of us spoke much until that evening while standing watch in our foxhole and sharing a cup of coffee. I cannot remember which of us said it though, but I will never forget what was said, "It's going to be a long thirteen months."

We were both assigned to the same four-man fire team in the Second Squad of the Third Platoon of Echo Company, except we were the only two men in the fire team besides the team leader, Lieutenant Corporal Kelly. The squad, platoon, and even the company had been pretty well wiped out at Con Thien, so BNG (brand new guys) were coming in on every chopper, and many of them going out in a poncho on the next. How Willie and I ever survived long enough to finish our tours, I'll never know. Somehow we did. The first couple of days at Con Thien, we did not do any patrolling or much of anything except watch our perimeter since we did not have enough men to function as a combat unit. The morning would start bright and sunny. The mud would start to dry. We would bail the water out of our foxhole and lay things out to dry in between artillery barrages and incoming choppers. Every time we would get hit with artillery, Willie and I would dig our hole a little deeper, which would mean that when it rained, we had more water to bail. And it rained every afternoon, a little earlier every day; until by the end of October, it was always raining. After the first few days, we finally had enough men to start functioning as a unit. Every third day, we would have a platoon-sized patrol somewhere around the base, and one of our three squads would fade into the jungle along the way. This squad would then set up an ambush along the trail and stay there until daylight the next morning. The rest of the platoon would continue on patrol and return to the perimeter before dark.

The other two platoons in the company would man the lines of the perimeter during the day, have work details, clean their weapons and gear, and do anything else that need to be done. At night, everyone manned the lines. We all dug two-man foxholes around the perimeter, and one man would stand watch four hours while the other slept there beside him, and then they would trade places. The squad leader and his radio man would have a foxhole a short distance behind the squad on the lines, and they would take turns manning the radio all night.

One fire team from each platoon would be assigned the task of setting up an LP (listening post), about two hundred yards or so out in front of the lines, to listen for any enemy movement and give an early warning in case of an impending attack. The NVA (North Vietnamese Army) would rarely attack in force but liked to probe our lines at night and look for weak spots to infiltrate and kill a couple of men if they caught the men asleep. Staying awake on watch was a problem for everyone since we never got more than about four hours sleep. LPs were scary since it was just two or three men alone out in front of the lines with a radio. Not only did you have to worry about the enemy, but you hoped that your own men knew where you were in case you had to return to the perimeter before daylight.

The squad that had the ambush would stay where they had been dropped off until just before dark and then move to the site of the ambush. I would usually set up my men in a line along the trail close enough to touch each other. I would let every other man sleep for four hours, but you had to wake them up if they started to snore, so we had to stay in close contact with each other. I had a man by the name of Brady that was very good at setting booby traps with grenades, so I would have him get the extra grenades that we all carried, and he would go about fifty yards behind us and booby trap the area so we could not be snuck up on from behind. He would do this in total darkness. Brady was very good at it, but he was always messing with grenades, no matter where you were or what you were doing. I don't think he was all there most of the time. I lost Brady in a battle a few months later, so after that, I would have to assign a fire team to cover our rear.

Just after first light, we would break up the ambush and return to the perimeter. This was always dangerous when you entered our perimeter after an ambush. The guys on the lines were drowsy from lack of sleep, so they were not very alert. We would have a prearranged signal using pop-up flares to let them know we were coming in. We would pop three different colored flares in the predetermined sequence as we approached the lines. When we were challenged by the men guarding the lines, we would have to give the correct password that was changed daily and tell him how many men were coming in and then be counted off as we entered. After we got back to our foxholes, I would drop my gear and report to the Command Post (CP) and make my report to the platoon commander. We would then eat something, have a cup of coffee, and grab a few minutes sleep. Many times, the entire company was getting ready to move out, so we got no rest that day. We never got enough rest. Sometimes, we would go for days without any rest.

This was the usual routine, day after day and night after night, for the entire thirteen months of our tour. Most patrols and ambushes were routine, no contact or enemy sighted, but every once in a while, we would make contact with the enemy or be discovered and get mortared. Usually, we would just find an abandoned bunker complex. They would usually leave a man or two behind to snipe at us and slow us up until the rest of them slipped away into the jungle. If we were lucky, they would have left a lot of supplies behind, but we would have to crawl through these tunnels to check them out. You never knew who or what you might find in these tunnels that seemed to go on forever. We always carried C4, a plastic explosive, with us to use for blowing up these bunkers and supplies.

The NVA had already learned that they could not stand and fight us but had chosen instead to hit us with a few men, usually by setting off an antipersonnel mine at our point element and then snipe at us as we tried to rescue our wounded. We would call in artillery or air support and then assault their position. We would usually find a few enemy bodies after the battle, but rarely did you actually see them during the battle.

The man that walked point was going to get wounded or killed when you made contact unless he was very perceptive and alert. As a squad leader, it was a tough decision as to who you would put on point. I would rotate it between my fire teams, but I would usually walk point for whichever team was the point element. I was not supposed to be on point, so I would wait until we were out of the perimeter before I assumed the point. Many squad leaders would put new guys or their shit birds (guys that are always screwing up) on point, but to me, this was just murder. I just couldn't do it. I had some real good men that would volunteer to take point many times to keep me off point. My radio man Calvin, a black kid from D. C., always complained to the platoon commander, Lt. Carson, when I walked point because he had to be right with me wherever I went, and he was afraid I was going to get him killed.

While we were at Con Thien, I was just a rifleman in a fire team made up of team leader, Kelly, Willie, and me. My squad leader was a short timer named Walley. A short timer is someone with less than a month left in their thirteen-month tour. Walley was good-natured, experienced, and smart, but he was not going to take any chances, so we were very cautious on patrol. I guess it was probably a good thing as it kept me alive long enough to learn some things from him before he rotated out of country. The thing I remember most about Con Thien was the near constant shelling from North Vietnam, day in and day out, thousands of rounds a day.

It was while we were at Con Thien that something happened that I will never forget. I was away from my foxhole on the lines for some reason, a work detail or something, when we started to take incoming artillery. I ran to the nearest hole and jumped in, and another Marine fell in on top of me just before a shell hit the edge of the hole. When I looked up, the guy that had fallen in on me had blood running out of his mouth, eyes, and ears. I started to yell for a corpsman, who it turns out was in the next hole from us. The corpsman yelled back to see if the injury was severe enough that he needed to come right over or if it could wait until the shelling stopped. I told him the guy had blood running out of his mouth, ears, eyes, and nose. The corpsman yelled back, "Is it gurgling?" I yelled back and told him it was not. The corpsman said he would be all right, and I looked at the guy again and thought to myself, "He may be, but I'm not sure I am."

We were at Con Thien for about a month, mainly because we did not have enough men to function as a combat unit. That was the main reason we were sent there, to get replacements enough to bring us up to at least minimal strength. Sometime during October, we were marched from Con Thien to Dong Ha, where we were picked up by trucks and taken to Camp J. J. Carroll, an army artillery base just a few miles west of Dong Ha. Camp Carroll was on a hill overlooking Route 9, a major supply route for all our bases on the west side of the country.

Camp Carroll sat on a flat-topped, treeless hill overlooking Route 9 and the river—I have forgotten the name of the river—just a little west of the village of Cam Lo. It contained a couple of batteries of 105 and 155 howitzers and one battery of eight inch howitzers. There was a tent-covered mess hall with a trench that you lined up in because of the constant threat of incoming artillery that served two meals a day when they could. There was also a shower tent (cold water only) if you wanted to risk your life trying to take one. It seemed as though every time I tried, we would get shelled.

Our positions on the perimeter were not too bad. We had sand-bagged bunkers for sleeping and aboveground sand-bagged bunkers for fighting positions. Being aboveground kept the bunkers from flooding when it rained, which it did almost every day. The base was surrounded by a triple strand of concertina wire, which was located just outside of our fighting positions. From the wire, it was about one hundred feet to the jungle, so we had a strong defensive position.

As soon as we got to Camp Carroll, we got a new company commander, Capt. Sams. He was a Marine's Marine, a real hard charger. Sams had been an enlisted man and had then gotten his commission, so he was not your typical CO. He was tough, but fair, and had good common sense. He knew what things to be petty about and what things were not worth the trouble. Shortly after he arrived, he held formation and presented medals to all of those that had been wounded or recommended for other medals. He fell us into formation, and then he had those receiving medals step a few steps forward and do an about face so they were facing us. About 90 percent of the company was receiving a Purple Heart, so many were receiving more than one. There were a few guys getting the Bronze Star and other medals. The only guys not getting a Purple Heart were those of us that had just gotten in the country. As I watched them receiving their medals, I could not keep from thinking that the prospects of me living through the next thirteen months were not very good. I always tried to avoid thinking about getting wounded or killed, but under the circumstances, it was hard to ignore the possibility.

John at Camp Carol, Vietnam 1967

We spent most of the next couple of weeks guarding the perimeter all night at Camp Carroll and training all day on navigating with a map and compass, running patrols, setting up ambushes, and LPs. By this time, the company was getting enough men; even though we were not up to full strength, we could function as a full company. One morning just after chow, we were given the word to get all our gear ready, draw at least one thousand rounds of ammo, extra grenades, and rations for five days because we were moving out at midnight. I was not prepared for the amount of weight we would be carrying. Ten C-ration meals, one thousand rounds of ammo, fifty rounds of 45 cal. ammo, and six grenades were a pretty good load, but we all had to carry extra ammo for the M-60 machine gun, usually five hundred rounds, which was two bandoleers. We would also be carrying smoke grenades, willie peter (white phosphorus), grenades, pop-up flares, mortar rounds, light antitank weapons (L.A.W.s), C-4 plastic explosive, claymore mines, and who knows what else. I have done a lot of backpacking since then, carrying fifty to seventy pounds, but nothing near what we had to carry then.

We pulled out of Camp Carroll on a pitch-black, drizzly night round midnight. I had become a team leader by now, even though I was still a private first class and was outranked by a lance corporal in my fire team. My years of prowling the woods, camping, and night hunting made me better prepared than most for being able to function as a leader. I have always had exceptional eyesight, especially at night, so anytime we had a night operation, I was always the point man. It was so dark that I could not see a thing. I had to follow the trail by feeling with my feet. The men behind me had to be able to touch each other to stay in contact.

We headed out of Carroll on a trail that went south for a ways and then curved around to the east until we were headed to the north. We crossed Route 9 and the river at first light, which was right on schedule. My squad was relieved from the point for the rest of the day, which was good. From here on, we hacked our way through the jungle, staying off the trails trying to avoid an ambush. Our course was north by east until we were inside the DMZ. I am guessing we were just west of Con Thien because we could hear their artillery.

We sloped along through the jungle for more than a week, seeing little in the way of action except for an occasional mortar barrage ever so often. The weather was so bad that we could not get resupplied with food or anything else. I went five days without food and some guys longer. I had been supplementing my rations with whatever I could find, pineapples, oranges, bananas, and grapefruit, but most of it gave me the shits; I guess because of the acid content. Then on the 10th ofNovember, which is the Marine Corps birthday, the sky cleared, the sun came out, and the choppers came in. We set up a defensive perimeter in an abandoned village (a forced abandonment) and waited for the choppers. On the first chopper was a birthday cake carried on a pallet slung underneath the chopper, and then came C-rations, mail, and our beer ration. Life was good for a little while, but just for a little while as it started to rain just before dark.

This was the way it went for the next week or so until November 20. We had set in the night before on the edge of the jungle and a flooded rice paddy. That morning, we headed across the rice paddy to the jungle on the other side when the NVA opened up on us with small arms and mortar fire. We were in the point position and were caught out in the middle of the rice paddy with no place to go but under water.

Fox Company, which was the last company in the column, was sent around the rice paddy to attack from the south. When Fox Company opened up on the enemy, we were to attack them from the west, which we did. We got out of the paddy to the jungle's edge, and all hell broke loose. Bullets were flying so thick that banana trees were being cut off as if with a machete. Mortar rounds were falling all around; we were taking many casualties, and I had yet to see the enemy. The battle raged for what seemed to be hours, but I am sure it was not that long. We did have to call in medevac choppers and resupply for more ammo, but the weather was closing in fast, so we were not able to get all our causalities out in time.

Sometime during the battle, the enemy had withdrawn to the north, leaving my company, Echo, and Fox Company to fight it out. Somehow during all the confusion, we were now fighting with Fox Company, but who could tell? You could not see anyone; we were just firing blindly into the jungle in the direction of the sound of gunfire. The AK-47 that the NVA used had a different sound than the M-16 that we used, and someone finally noticed that the only shots being fired were from M16s. It's no easy task to stop Marine Corps units when they are engaged in a battle, but somehow, the battle stopped.

It took the rest of the day to mop up after the battle, gather the dead and wounded, and set up a secure perimeter. The weather had turned bad—heavy rain, strong winds, and ground fog. The night was one of the worst, if not the worst that I have ever experienced—cold, wet, hungry, no smokes, and the wounded lying all around you moaning and crying. We did all we could to comfort them, but we had little comfort to give. I spent most of the night holding a wounded friend face up out of the water listening to him talk, which was more an incoherent rambling, until he died sometime before daylight. He was the first out of my platoon in boot camp to die. He was from somewhere in Ohio, was married, and had a little girl. I can never forget the feeling of his blood between my fingers when I changed his battle dressings that had become soaked nor the sounds he made as he died. Thank God I could not see his expression. It was while lying there, thankful that I was still alive that I began to ask myself, "How in the hell did I end up in such a predicament?" I finally came to the conclusion that if I would have just studied in high school, I would still be in college. It was at this point that I made myself a promise that if I lived through Nam, I would return to college, get a degree, and make something of myself.

We eventually ended up on the DMZ at a place called Gio Linh, another base of McNamara Wall. We were located across a rice paddy to the north of the base and were to be the first line of resistance for the base. The base received near constant shelling, not as bad as Con Thien, though. We were far enough north of the base that we were not affected by the shelling; however, our perimeter was probed nightly. Most of the time, we were just cold, wet, and hungry as usual.

The NVA had one of the bunkers on the base zeroed in so well with their artillery that only volunteers were used to work on it. The bunker was the first one south of our position, so we watched it all happen. Eventually, they could not get volunteers on the base to finish the bunkers, so they came to us. We had been on near starvation rations for over a month now, and they promised us each a case of C-rations if we would come over each day and work on the bunker. I find it hard to believe now, but the whole squad went, and, would you believe it, we did not take a single round of artillery.

It was at Gio Linh that I spent my first Christmas away from home, inside the DMZ, miserable, and homesick, but we endured. Lying there in the mud in a foxhole, we would tell each other of our homes, families, and friends. I don't know if it made us feel better or worse, but you sure got to know each other well. I guess that was one of the things that was so tough about watching them die, you remembered too much. After several months of watching guys die, I tried to keep from getting to know the new guys, but it didn't work. When all you have is a shared cup of coffee, a cigarette, and conversation, it's hard to keep from getting to know someone.

Most of our conversations were just typical male bullshit lies, the fastest cars, prettiest girlfriends, worst fights, best drunks, etc. But sometimes, we talked from the heart about family, friends, and what we were going to do when we got back to the real world. We never talked about the war or politics. For one thing, we knew nothing of either. The war consisted of where we were at the time, and the only news we got was in letters from home, so we knew nothing of the political turmoil and war protests going on at home.

Sometime between Christmas and New Year's Eve, we were pulled back to Camp Carroll because the weather had gotten so bad we could not be supplied where we were and enemy action had dropped to nothing. It was good to be out of the mud and rain, if only for a little while. We still had to stand lines and set up LPs and ambushes, but the rest of the time, we were under a tent with a wood frame and floor. Even the floor was covered with mud.

New Year's Eve was a memorable occasion for me. We had received packages from home shortly after arriving at Camp Carroll, and a dear friend of mine had sent me a fifth of whiskey disguised in a box of oatmeal. Several of us spent the evening drinking, eating junk from home, and just having a good time. At midnight, we all went to the nearest ammo bunker and broke out cases of pop-up flares and started shooting them off. Other guys from other units at other bunkers joined in the fun. The mortar and artillery crews even joined in and started to fire illumination rounds all above the perimeter. The officers let us have our fun for a little while before putting a stop to it but not before we had fired hundreds of rounds.

It was while we were at Camp Carroll that I had an encounter with God that was to affect the rest of my life. I had been raised in the church by good Christian parents who always practiced what they preached, so I had a belief in God and his power, or maybe it was that I had heard about his power but didn't really believe. One night while standing lines by myself, I started to think, which has always caused me problems. I had been in country long enough that I had become the first team leader in the second squad, and I guess I was worried about how I would react or make decisions in a combat situation. I was scared, depressed, cold, wet, and just generally at wit's end. I had run out of answers, or resolve, or whatever you want to call it. This was something new for me; I have always been confident of my abilities to handle whatever situation comes along. But not this time. Most of the experienced men had finished their tours and had gone home or had been wounded or killed. Whatever the reason, we had a large turnover in personnel, and I was one of the more experienced men that was depended on, and I had been in country only a few months. The war was continuing to escalate, and I was having the feeling that we had not yet seen the worst of the fighting.

For whatever reason, I was really down emotionally, physically, and spiritually. As we all tend to do when we are in situation like this, I started to cry and asked God for help because I had nowhere else to turn. All of a sudden, I had this feeling come over me like nothing else I have ever experienced before or since. It was as though I could feel life flowing back into me, warm, confident, and a feeling that I would be all right and that I had a future. In a matter of seconds, it was as though I had been reborn and given a new lease on life. In the back of my mind came the thought, "Okay, I will save your ass, but you had better prove you are worth it." Ever since this encounter, I have tried to live an honorable life and be worthy of his favors.

A few days later, we (Third Platoon) left Camp Carroll and hiked a few miles to the south and east, by my recollection, to an old French fortress called Delta 5. D5 was located down in the flatlands just south of a village, maybe Cam Lo, but I am not sure. There were a lot of abandoned plantations of some type in the area just south of D5. Many of the buildings were still standing, though most were badly damaged. There was enough left to see how beautiful they had been. The country was much more open than the mountainous country to the west that was all rainforest.

The fortress of Delta 5 was in the shape of a triangle, made from dirt mounded up like a pond bank, with covered bunkers dug into the bank. There was an open air mess hall with a thatched roof in the center of the fortress, but it served little purpose since we had no cook. We survived by eating C-rations supplemented with whatever we could scrounge. There was a road that ran south out of the vill in front of the west side of the fortress and continued on south somewhere.

Stationed at the fortress was a platoon of South Vietnamese soldiers, ARVNs, half of which I think were VC, so we had little faith or trust in them when we had to operate with them. Going on an operation with them always reminded me of going camping with a bunch of boy scouts. There were about the size of twelve-year-old boys and were always jabbering and carrying on. I remember one time that two of them were carrying a pig hanging by its feet from a stick between their shoulders. Another time, one of them had a live goose with its neck sticking out from his pack, squawking and carrying on. This could have been one of the reasons we saw so little action at D5; there was no way we were going to surprise anyone, and the only way we ever made contact was when we caught them by surprise or they caught us by surprise.

Delta 5 was good duty in that we saw very little action. We continued to run patrols each day, send out LPs, and send out ambushes, but for the most part, it was quiet. The only action was when we set up ambushes on a trail leading into or out of the vill. There was a curfew in the village. Everyone had to be inside after dark, and if they had to come out for any reason, they must carry a light. We would go into the vill, split up in groups of three or four men, set up on several of the trails, ambush whoever came by, and then fade into the jungle without even checking our kill. We might do this a couple times during the night before linking up with the rest of the squad and returning to the camp. For the most part, I am sure our kills were mainly VC and NVA, but there were probably some civilians also.

Most of our days were spent rebuilding the mess hall that I accidentally burned down one morning while coming in from an ambush. Stationed at D5 in the position next to mine was an Army tank crew and tank. The tank was pulled right up to the south wall of the fortress with its turret sticking up above the wall. All night, one of the tank crew kept watch while setting up on the turret. We were constantly giving these guys a hard time and playing practical jokes on each other. They had won the last round, so it was payback time.

We had been out all night on a routine ambush, had seen nothing, and were returning to the perimeter at first light. We were approaching D5 from the south, and just as we broke out of the jungle, I got the three flares to signal our arrival. I could just barely make out the outline of the tank with a man on top. I shot the first two flares straight up as usual, but the last one I decided to shoot at the tank and make the tank crew scatter. I overshot the tank and hit the grass-thatched roof of the mess hall. It burned to the ground in a matter of minutes, along with a lot of C-rations and other supplies. Luckily, all our ammo was in a protected bunker. As punishment, my squad got to rebuild the mess hall in our off time.

Conditions at D5 were pretty plush by the standards we were used to. We had dry bunkers to sleep in, and we traded with the villagers for candles. Usually, we had to make our own candles using those little rolls of toilet paper that came in C-rations soaked with insect repellant, but they would not burn for very long and put out a foul-smelling odor. The worst thing about D5 was the rats, which grew as large as cats or a good-sized opossum. They would come right in the bunkers where we were sleeping and rummage for food or anything else they could find. Many would come in while you had a candle burning, but most would wait until the light was out then they would just walk right over the top of you.

I remember one time the whole squad was sleeping on the floor in a concrete bunker. I don't remember where we were or what we were doing there, but one of our new guys, upon seeing his first rat, drew his 45 cal. pistol and shot at the rat. Most of us were asleep and pretty jumpy anyway. Well, the sound of that 45 going off in that small enclosed place sounded like a howitzer, and the bullet ricocheted around in that bunker for what seemed to be a couple of minutes. How the bullet missed everyone I will never know since we were packed in there almost shoulder to shoulder.

Several men had been bitten by rats during our stay at D5 and had to be evacuated back to Dong Ha to get their shots. It got to where many of the guys would scratch themselves with a can opener for C-rations, a p-38, so they could get out of the bush and war for a couple of weeks. I don't like shots that well, so I never even considered it. I preferred to make a game out of it. I would lure them in with food and see how many I could snare, trap, or kill with a bean flip or sling shot I had made from a forked stick, a rubber strap, and a piece of leather. I tied each end of the rubber strap to the forks on the end of the stick. Then I tied the piece of leather in the middle of the strap, which was used to put a small pebble in. I would pull back on the rubber straps, holding the leather with the rock in it, and then let it fly. We used to make these all the time when I was a boy, so I was a pretty good shot with it. I can't remember what my record was for a one night kill, but it was over a dozen.

It was at D5 that we got the word that Dr. Martin Luther King had been killed. The black Marines we had with us, which were considerable, made jesters that they were going to cause trouble, but I guess they thought better of it when they realized that we were all heavily armed, that we had not killed Dr. King, and we were not going to put up with any crap either. Personally, I felt he was a great man, teaching non-violence to achieve social change Even though I had been raised in the South where I saw the prejudice and segregation, I had been taught that it was not right and to respect the person for who they were or did and not for the color of their skin. There have been few since him that I could admire; most of them are like Jesse Jackson or Al Sharpton, who I feel have just exploited the racial situation for their own benefit and keep tension stirred up.

For the most part, racial problems in the bush were very few. We needed each other more than we disliked each other. I became real close with several of the blacks in the platoon. One of my radio men when I was a squad leader was a black kid from Mississippi. I have forgotten his name because all we ever called him was Hose Nose because of his huge nose. He was a great guy and a good Marine but was killed during Tet.

The time we spent at D5 was not only quiet, but like an old western movie, it was too quiet. Several of our LPs started to report movement of large numbers of troops during the night, but they chose not to bother us for some unknown reason. Then toward the end of January, we could not get out of the perimeter without contact. I was even afraid to go to the outhouse, which was located just outside the front gate. It was the same at all outposts and bases in the area, lines being probed every night and increased enemy movements over the entire area.

We were pulled back to Camp Carroll near the end of the month to strengthen their perimeter and to provide added security for the convoy that traveled each day from Dong Ha to Khe Sanh and supplied all the bases in between, including Camp Carroll. In the past, convoy security had been pretty good duty, and I always kind of enjoyed it, sitting up on top of a 6 ' 6 with a 50 cal. machine gun mounted on a turret and just blasting away at anything that you wanted to. While going to the other bases, I would usually run into someone I had gone through training with and hear the fate of many others.

Just about the first of February, everything started to go really bad. The convoy, which was many miles long, was getting ambushed continually along Route 9, which was little more than a one-lane, muddy road through dense jungle. The jungle was so thick in most places that you could touch the trees on both sides of the truck.

We were headed out of Khe Sanh one morning; leading elements of the convoy got ambushed severely to the point that the road was impassable. As they began to try and turn all of these vehicles around, we started getting sniped at and mortared along the entire length of the convoy. I fired so many rounds with the 50 cal. that the driver of the 6 ' 6 was sitting ankle deep in brass shell cases. I was getting sniped at from so many different locations that I eventually had to crawl down from the turret and find a little more cover.

The 6 ' 6 behind us was trying to turn around, which was difficult on this narrow jungle road because a 6 ' 6 takes a lot of room to turn around. There was a man walking beside the 6 ' 6 when it hit a land mine at the edge of the road. He was blown almost ten feet in the air and all the way across to the other side of the road. Three or four of us rushed to him, but it was of no use; he had been killed instantly. When we tried to load his body on the back of our 6', it was as if he were a rag doll; there did not seem to be a bone in his body. His head flopped back against his back, and his limbs were limp as a rope. A tank that was directly behind the 6' that had been blown up pushed the disabled 6' from the road; we turned round and returned to Dong Ha for the night. We could not even get back to Camp Carroll.

The next day was more of the same. We boarded trucks and headed down the road toward Khe Sanh again. We did have air support this time, but it did not seem to make a difference. The lead elements of the convoy got hit again, and the convoy was stopped dead in its tracks. We were a little farther back in the convoy this time, just a mile or so west of Cam Lo, when the convoy got hit. We were still down on the flatland and not in the jungle yet. There was a small hill on each side of us covered with elephant grass, so our vision was very restricted. The front part of the convoy was getting hit hard with artillery, rockets, and mortars that were located just north of our position judging from the sound, but we could not see the exact location because of the hills. My platoon commander, Lt. Carson, sent my squad up to the top of the hill that was on the north side of the road. We found a good trail through the elephant grass, which led all the way to the top.

On top of the hill was an abandoned perimeter complete with sandbagged bunkers and a triple strand of wire surrounding it. It looked like an ARVN perimeter that they had abandoned very recently; a Marine unit would never have left it intact. We would have filled in all the holes and blown the wire.

We were able to see where the muzzle flashes were coming from and call in artillery that quickly knocked them out, or at least it silenced them. We could not see our part of the convoy from where we were, but we could see that the front part of the convoy was moving again. We stayed there, calling in fire missions for a long while, when we noticed that the tail end of the convoy heading up the road west of us, which meant that we had been left behind out here in Indian country.

Our platoon commander could not believe that the truck that we were on had abandoned us out in the middle of nowhere. He suggested that we get back on the road, hike back to Cam Lo, where there was a small unit of Army Special Forces, and see if we could spend the night there. We were able to sneak along the road and arrived at the Special Forces perimeter by late afternoon.

The Cam Lo perimeter held only a small handful of Special Forces troops that were there to work with the civilian population. They were not a combat unit. They were guarded by a platoon or so of ARVNS in an old French perimeter like Delta 5, except it had a concrete building in the middle, which served as a mess hall and command post (CP). Meals were prepared by a couple of Vietnamese mamma-sans and served family style at big tables. It was the best meal we had eaten in month.

The Army was glad to have us as it gave them more security. Perimeters everywhere had been getting hit almost nightly, and some had even been overrun by the enemy. The officer in charge (OIC) assigned us to guard the north wall for the night or until arrangements could be made to pick us up.

After a fine meal, we took our positions along the north wall just before dark and received our watch schedule. I had last watch from 4:00 a.m. until daylight. There was a game of bridge going on at the CP, and I had practically majored in bridge in college, so I sat and watched until one of the players had to leave, then I took his place. We smoked, drank whiskey, and played bridge until about midnight when I left to get a little sleep before standing watch.

I lay down as usual on the bare ground, fully clothed with my boots still on my feet and nothing but a poncho for cover. I used my flak jacket for a pillow, my M-16 cradled in my arms like a woman. I had made the mistake one time of laying my weapon down near me. We got hit that night, and I had trouble finding my weapon in the dark. I was not fully asleep when they hit us first with artillery, rockets, and mortars. They pounded us with everything they had for what seemed to be an hour or more. Camp Carroll also started to fire illumination rounds over our position. Then, under their own artillery barrage came the ground troops.

At the first round, we had all taken up fighting positions on the dirt bank of the fortress, but this left us exposed to the shrapnel from the artillery. When I looked out across the triple strand of wire and the mine field beyond, all I could see were many hundreds, or maybe even thousands, of enemy soldiers crawling through the mine field like it did not exist. I put my M-16 on fully automatic and began to just spray the area with bullets. I then realized that one thousand rounds of ammo would not last very long like that, so I switched back to semiautomatic and started to pick my targets.

Our M-60 machine gun had been firing almost continuously since the start of the battle and was beginning to run low on ammo. I had noticed an ammo bunker, which was located a good distance farther down the lines, so I made a run to the bunker for ammo. We were still taking a lot of artillery at the time but not nearly like it had been a little earlier. I was only able to get a couple of thousand rounds of M-60 and M-16 ammo because there were other guys there for the same purpose.

When I returned to my position with the ammo, I started to fasten together the belts of ammo for the machine gun team since one member of the three-man machine gun team had been wounded and was out of action. Before I got the ammo belted together, I was knocked down and felt a sharp, burning pain on my right side just at the bottom of the rib cage. I was instantly sick at my stomach and threw up. We had no corpsman with us, so we had to do our own first aid. I was not sure how bad I was hit because I could not see the wound, but it felt like a tiny hole, and I was not losing much blood, so I figured it wasn't too bad. I did feel light-headed and dizzy. I patched myself up the best I could and returned to the fight.

A short time later, a good friend of mine named Larry from Bald Knob, Arkansas, was wounded pretty severely. I drug him down from the bank and patched him up. I don't think his wounds would have been fatal, but he was out of this battle. When we first got to Cam Lo, I noticed a difference in it compared to D5. At the bottom of the bank was a narrow ditch about a foot wide and deep. I remember wondering what the ditch was for since it was not wide or deep enough for a fighting position, but I put it out of my mind at the time. After I had dressed Larry's wounds, I eased him down into that trench as much as I could to protect him from the artillery.

I had just resumed my position on the bank when a ChiCom grenade came flying over the bank and rolled down the bank. At that instant, I knew what that trench at the foot of the bank was for; it was a grenade sump. The grenade rolled right into the ditch and exploded. The grenade had landed by Larry, and when it exploded, it removed half of his head, killing him instantly. I was protected from injury by the grenade sump.

I was out of grenades, so I got one from a buddy of mine, George. George was always afraid of the pin in the grenade being pulled accidentally by vines or brush in the jungle, so he always taped the spoons down on all his grenades. I knew this, but in the heat of battle, I had forgotten. I pulled the pin and just rolled it over the top of the bank to where it would roll down the other side. In just a second, the grenade came rolling back over the bank right to me. I panicked until I realized I had not untapped the spoon, and I guess the gook on the other side of the bank didn't either. I rolled it over again. This time, it did not come back.

By this time in the battle, our perimeter had collapsed along the entire south wall, and there were as many gooks inside our perimeter as there were outside. The few of us that were left took up two-man positions with each man back to back and cut down anything that came at them. George and I had moved to the extreme northeast corner where there was an old, water-cooled 30 cal. machine gun. I fired the machine gun facing out, and George covered my back.

I guess whoever was in charge figured that if we were going down, we were going to take as many with us as we could, for about this time the artillery fire from Camp Carroll, which had been hitting just outside our wire, started to fall inside our perimeter. We were at least partially protected from the artillery while the gooks were fully exposed. This action may have been the only thing that saved us from being wiped out totally, but as the sky started to gray in the east, as quickly as they had come, they were gone.

At daylight, reinforcements arrived and relieved us. While the relief force was busy evacuating our severely wounded and checking out the NVA for any wounded, I took time to take it all in. I had seen a lot of death and destruction in the few months I had been in Vietnam, but nothing could match what I saw as I walked down the lines checking on my friends. We were extremely lucky; Larry was the only man killed in our squad, but George was the only one not wounded at least once.

As I peered out past our lines, I could see hundreds of dead NVA. They were everywhere you looked, in the mine field, tangled in the wire, and lying all around us inside of our perimeter. I thought to myself, "How is it possible that anyone lived through this night?" At that instant, I remembered that night at Camp Carroll when I asked for God's help. I remember giving him thanks, but at the same time, I was thinking, "Couldn't you have been a little easier on me?"

An incident that I was not a party to nor did I see, happened early that morning after all the fighting and artillery had stopped. I guess a small group of ARVNs had spent the entire night holed up in a bunker, safe and sound. When they came out of the bunker, which was not a bunker you could fight from, all fresh and unscathed, my squad leader, whose name I will not mention, opened up on them with his M-16 and killed all five or six of them. I don't guess anything was ever mentioned of the incident except among those of us that were there. There was a saying in my unit, "When in doubt, kill them all and let God sort them out."

I went out on one of the later choppers, the same one that carried Larry's body along with several other KIAs. The chopper was another "shuddering shitter" and was so heavily loaded that it could hardly get more than tree top high. The pilot followed the road all the way to Dong Ha, just barely clearing the tops of the 6's on the road until we reached Delta Med, which was located next to the air strip.

Delta Med was basically like a MASH unit except it was not really mobile. The buildings had metal roofs, the sides were open on the top half, and they had concrete floors. The building where they treated all of the casualties had a trough down through the middle of the floor that a corpsman or medic would sweep and hose blood, chunks of flesh, and everything else.

There were no operating tables, but instead there were saw horses; when they would bring in a wounded soldier on a stretcher, they would flop it up on the saw horses. Doctors and nurses would descend on the stretcher and attack. Pieces of uniforms, boots, battle dressings, meat, and limbs were hitting the floor everywhere while blood was pouring through the stretcher. At first, I thought that they were just finishing up what the NVA started, but as I sat there watching the staff work, in just few minutes, they had the wounded Marine cleaned up, patched up, and headed out the door to a waiting plane or chopper headed to a hospital in Japan, the U.S., or to the hospital ship *Sanctuary* stationed just off the coast.

As I watched all the wounded coming in and the choppers landing about seven minutes apart loaded with the wounded, I felt guilty for being a crybaby, as I saw how badly many of them were wounded—severe burns, missing limbs, you name it. I watched for several hours and was truly amazed at the medical staff. Their professionalism was outstanding while standing there in the blood and gore, their scrubs soaked with blood from floor to almost the knees. A doctor would finish with a patient at one stretcher, strip off his gloves and gown, turn around to the stretcher behind him while being gowned and gloved, and step up to the next patient. It was a sight to behold.

I never got to see a doctor; they were just too overwhelmed to be concerned with guys like me, the walking wounded, so we just sat. Finally, a corpsman came over and inspected my wound, went over and consulted with a doctor, came back, gave me a shot, laid me down on the wooden bench I had been sitting on, and went to cutting away at the flesh around my wound. Every so often, he would yell something at the doctor, the doctor would look over at me form across the room and yell something back, and the corpsman would resume his cutting.

I began to realize that this guy did not know any more than I did, but at this point, I just wanted to lie down and sleep. After the corpsman finished hacking, he put in a drain tube, gave me a massive dose of antibiotic, instructed me to return twice a day for more antibiotics, and I was finally out of there. It was late afternoon on February 2, I think. I had to hitch a ride to our company area at Quang Tri. I didn't even know how to get there by road since I had always gone in and out by chopper.

I was given a place to sleep when I got to the company area. There were few people around since the company was in the bush, just new guys waiting to head out to join the rest of the company, a couple of guys either going or coming for R&R, and us, the walking wounded. We were in a tent that was stretched over a frame, but it did have a wooden floor and a single light bulb hanging in the center. Pretty comfy accommodations compared to what I had been used to. There was even a shower tent with hot water. I took the first shower that I had taken for months and was issued a clean set of utilities. I had been wearing the same clothes since I got in country months earlier.

Things fell into a regular routine for the next couple of weeks: over to Delta Med in the morning and afternoon for a dressing change and a shot, then back to the area where I would read, eat, and sleep. A good bit of time was spent in a bunker during artillery barrages, but most of the time, it was just read, eat, and sleep.

After about two weeks, the drain tube was removed by the same corpsman that had put it in. Delta Med was still a mad house, as there was fighting going on in all areas and causalities were flooding in on chopper after chopper all day and night. I was once again in the hands of the corpsman that had treated me initially. Under the directions of a doctor, the corpsman removed the drain tube and cut the opening of the wound from circular in shape to where it was longer than it was wide. He said he did that so it would be easier to close. By the time he finished, a wound that had originally been about the size of a pencil was as big around as a fifty cent piece and about four inches long. I kept telling him the bullet was still in me, but no one seemed too concerned.

I spent about another week having to get the antibiotics and was then released to my unit on light duty. I was put in charge about a half a dozen new guys, given a 6' and cans of diesel fuel, and assigned the task of burning the body waste that had accumulated in the half barrels under the holes in the outhouses—better known as shitter detail.

As the noncommissioned officer in charge, NCOIC, all I had to do was drive them to the various toilets in the area, drop off a guy and a can of fuel at each toilet, and then pick them up a couple of hours later. They had to drag the half barrels out from under the hole, pour diesel fuel in the barrel, light the diesel, and stand there and stir the shit until nothing but ash was left. It took a long time to turn all this crap to ash, and the smell was horrendous. One of my least favorite memories of Vietnam was the smell of burning shit. That was one reason I preferred being in the bush to being in a more secure rear area. In the bush, you just dug a trench, did your business, and then covered it up.

Pretty easy duty until Pvt. Lacheski arrived and was assigned to me. I dropped him off at the officer's shitter, a real nice two-holer, gave him a can of diesel, and told him to burn the shitter. I did not bother to explain the process to him since it was so obvious any idiot could figure it out, or I guess I should say almost any idiot. Lacheski didn't.

As I made my rounds picking up all my work detail, everything went well until we got to Lacheski's outhouse. There was Ski lying on a sand-bagged wall, half-asleep, smoking a cigarette while the few remaining embers of the officer's shitter were dying. At about the same time that we arrived, a full bird colonel also arrived on the scene. He had a copy of *Stars and Stripes* folded under his arm, and the look on his face made it obvious that he had urgent business to take care of.

I guess it was a good thing that his business was so urgent because he started to chew on my ass when he found out I was the man in charge of the work detail but had to cut it short or mess his pants. As he headed out to find another outhouse, he yelled and told me that there had better be another outhouse here when he took his afternoon dump and that Pvt. Lacheski and I were to report to him as soon as I had a new outhouse.

Luckily, I had gotten on good terms with the Seabee's in the area. The Seabee's had the best club in Quang Tri Provence. We had no club at all, and anytime I knew we were going to be back in the rear area, I would gather up a pack full of war souvenirs. I would walk right into their club, right up to the bar, and with all eyes on me, I would start to pull things form the pack and lay them on the bar—gook helmets, belt buckles, knives, ChiCom grenades, etc. There was no end to the guys that wanted to buy me a drink.

I drove over to the Seabee area and looked up a senior chief that I had gotten to know. He had several outhouses already made setting there ready for use. He even had a crew haul it over and set it up for me. It was a real fancy four-holer with screen wire to keep the flies out. Lacheski and I reported to the Colonel, and after inspection, he was so pleased with the new outhouse that he was glad that we had burned the other one down.

I could probably have remained in the rear area indefinitely, but I preferred to be in the bush. There were entirely too many officers in the rear area, too many petty work details, and dumb regulations, so about the first week of March, I requested to be sent back to the bush.

When I returned to the company, almost everything had changed. We had the same company commander, Capt. Sams, and the same platoon commander, Lt. Carson, but that was about all. Not only had my squad gotten wiped out at Cam Lo, but nearly the whole company had gotten hit hard just west of Cam Lo a few days later by the remains of the unit that had hit us. It was on that hill with the abandoned perimeter that my squad had used when we were dropped by the convoy to look for muzzle flashes, except this time the gooks were on the inside of the barb wire perimeter, and the company had to recapture it.

This was where the company was when I rejoined it. We were assigned the task of trying to keep Route 9 open to Camp Carroll and the Rock Pile. It was closed from the Rock Pile to Khe Sanh and had been for a month or more. All supplies had to be flown into Khe Sanh; most were dropped by parachute, or the plane would just touch down but not stop, and the supplies were kicked out while the plane kept its power up and continued down the runway to take off again.

B-52 bombers bombed the area all around Khe Sanh almost continually, and the guns from Camp Carroll fired nonstop in their defense while we continued to work our way up the road to try to reach them. We saw action every day, and the signs of war were everywhere. The bodies of dead NVA were everywhere. We even had one sitting on an ammo box outside our front gate. We had him dressed up in a Marine Crops helmet and flak jacket. About all you could see of him was his skull with most of the meat rotted off and the bones of his hands. It was really a gruesome sight, but it sure got the attention of those that approached the perimeter.

The smell of death was everywhere from the thousands of decomposing corpses that lay unseen in the jungle and just out of sight along the road. Everywhere we went, we found bodies in various stages of decomposition. While on patrol in the valley just north of Route 9 and Camp Carroll, we came upon a mass burial site of over a hundred graves. Capt. Sams wanted us to dig them up so we could get an accurate body count and see if there were any weapons or valuable information buried with them. This was the only direct order that I was given that I could not carry out. We tried, but the smell was so bad that we could do nothing but wretch and puke. We got down to where we could see clothing in the first grave, but on the rest of the grave, we just dug deep enough to loosen the dirt in case the skipper checked on us. In the first grave, we did find a tin can that had been opened up and flattened out with holes punched in, giving the solder's name, rank, and no telling what else because there were a lot of words stamped into it.

My new squad leader was a corporal from Laurel, Mississippi by the name of Jerry. He had a college degree in forestry and had been working as a smoke jumper for the U. S. Forest Service out west somewhere. Really a great guy. We hit it off immediately, becoming good friends. We saw a lot of action and spent many days cold, wet, and hungry together over the next couple of months. He was killed by a sniper while we were on a routine patrol.

We were on patrol outside of the Rock Pile, which was an igneous intrusion of some kind, probably a volcanic neck or sill, when we got pinned down by automatic weapons fire. I was directly ahead of Jerry by a few feet but not quite close enough to touch. We were all firing in all directions, hoping to hit something when Jerry's M-16 jammed. I heard him cuss, so I looked in his direction to see what was wrong. At that instant, Jerry kind of rolled up on his elbow and reached back to retrieve his cleaning rod, which was in a pouch on his pack. I heard the shot that killed, but he never did as he was shot in the head and died instantly with just a slight quiver. I knew he had been killed instantly, but still I wanted to get to him. Every time I tried, the sniper would shoot at me, and I was not that well protected. We finally fired enough rounds that either we got him or he snuck off into the jungle.

Jerry was very close to his family, which I felt like I knew from our many conversations together, and I knew that they would take his death very hard. I decided that I would gather up the few personal belongings he had with him and send them to his family along with a note telling them what a good Marine he was and all that bullshit. What could I say that could possibly make any difference? But still I wanted to do something. Maybe it was just to let them know that there were others that would miss and remember him.

Jerry's mother wrote me several times trying to find out how Jerry died, but I could not make myself answer her. I would not lie to her, and she did not need to know that he had died because he got careless and made a mistake. One of the few regrets that I have in life is that I did not answer that poor woman, but I guess I am just too big of a coward about some things. There are a thousand things that when I hear them, I immediately think of Jerry and his mom.

I took over the squad after Jerry but made a vow that I would not get as close to any of them as I had gotten to Jerry, but I found this vow as hard to keep as my New Year's resolution to quit smoking has been. Under those conditions, it was impossible to keep from knowing everything about them.

Around the first of April, we were finally able to open the road to Khe Sanh and relieve the siege that they had been under for seventy-seven days. We settled in as security on several bridges just out of Khe Sanh. The company was split up into platoons, one at each bridge. Capt. Sams had been wounded again, so Lt. Carson was acting CO in his absence. While traveling between the company HQ and the bridge that Third Platoon was guarding, his Jeep was hit by a Claymore mine. When we heard the explosion and went to investigate, we found both Lt. Carson and his driver dead. He was the best officer I ever served under. As a matter of fact, after Mister Carson, we went through a half a dozen platoon commanders, and I can't even recall their names for we went through them so fast.

Shortly after Lt. Carson's death, we were pulled back to Camp Carroll for a few days' rest after about three months of continual combat, but our rest didn't last long. We had only been there standing lines for a couple of days when the word came to draw new ammo, saddle up in full combat gear, and assemble at the LZ in ten minutes. Third Platoon would be on the first wave in. Evidently, a Marine Corps recon team had gotten into an ambush on the hill just north of Camp Carroll, and we were going out to get them.

I don't think the hill had a name that I ever heard; it was just referred to by its elevation, Hill 357. Going up from the river on the south side, the hill was covered with dense jungle about two thirds of the way up. From there up almost to the top was elephant grass and then jungle again on the summit. The body we were going after was lying just inside the jungle on top of the hill.

The only place that choppers could land troops was in the elephant grass on the south side, and even that was not an easy task. The elephant grass was so deep that the pilots could not tell where the ground was. To make matters worse, the side of the hill was so steep that the choppers could not land; they had to let the rear of the chopper descend down through the elephant grass until the rear tailgate bumped the ground and then hover in that position until we were all able to exit out the rear of the chopper. During all of this, we were taking both small arms and mortar fire.

There was room to land two choppers at a time, and my squad and the CO, along with his HQ, was on one of the first two in. The men on the other chopper in our group were to establish a defensive perimeter for the other choppers coming in, and my squad was to start the assault on the summit to be joined by Second Platoon when they got on the ground. When we got to the top of the mountain and located the body, we were to retrieve it as quickly as possible but remembering that the body would be booby-trapped. That was the plan anyway, but like most well-laid plans, and this was not, things tend to get all screwed up. Or as the old saying goes, "It's hard to remember that your initial objective was to drain the swamp when you are up to your ass in alligators."

My point fire team was to be the first off our chopper followed by myself, my radio man, my M-79 grenadier, and then the rest of the squad. I told my point man, a guy by the name of Alvie, to get the hell off as fast as he could as soon as he felt the tailgate on the chopper touch the ground, for I was sure they would be expecting us since it is known worldwide that Marines never leave their dead. As we were making our final approach to the LZ, we started to take small arms fire. The green tracers were flying through the chopper like pissed-off hornets. The chopper pilot was bringing us in as cool as could be under the conditions and started to lower the tailgate. The tailgate or rear wheel touched the ground with a hard bump. Since we were all standing up, it caused us to lose our balance for a moment. Moring regained his balance and started down the tailgate at the same time a green tracer round crossed right in front of his face, at which point he started to back away from the rear of the chopper. I thought Alvie had just got a case of cold feet, so I had to go around two guys to give him some reassurance. When I got to him, I told him to get hold of himself and shoved him out of the chopper. I had not noticed that the chopper had moved a little to the side and lost contact with the ground. When I shoved Alvie out of the chopper, we must have been twenty feet off the ground.

I saw Alvie disappear into the elephant grass, hit the ground, and bounce up almost to the top of the grass before rolling down the hill to the edge of the jungle where he lay perfectly still. I just knew that I had killed him, for with the added weight of the full combat gear, a fall of twenty feet would be deadly. As it turned out, he was not killed, just busted up real bad and was sent back to the states and discharged. Forty years later at Christmastime, Alvie called me at home. We had a good visit, but all the while, I kept thinking about what I had done to him and thinking that he was probably going to come and get me now that he knew where I was. He finally got around to mentioning the incident and asked me if I saw who threw him out of the chopper. Being the fine, upstanding person that I am, I lied and said I had no idea who had done such a thing.

We finally got on ground after what seemed like forever with small arms fire zipping through the chopper continuously and mortar rounds falling like rain on the LZ. They knew we were coming to get him and knew that the only place to land an assault force was in this opening in the jungle. They had plenty of time to get the opening zeroed in. We started fighting our way up to the side of the hill through the elephant grass, but the going was slow. We had to wait on the rest of Third Platoon to get on the ground before we could continue up the hill. Things were starting to go to hell as usual. First Squad had already taken some casualties, so "dust offs" were already starting to come in to medevac them.

After we finally got our assault force assembled, we started up the hill again and got about two thirds of the way to the top when the order was passed up the line for us to pull back. I turned and looked back down the slope, and all I could see were bodies scattered down the entire way I had come. I had taken the point after Alvie's accident and had been pressing on so hard that I had no idea what was happening behind me. The gooks had the hill zeroed in so that they were walking the mortar rounds right up the hill as we climbed. Being on point, I was ahead of the impact from the mortars. We headed back down the hill, dragging our wounded after abandoning their gear on the slope.

The LZ was in the state of total confusion. Choppers were coming and going in all directions, mortar rounds were falling everywhere, and men were separated from their units, not knowing what to do. The XO, whose name I don't recall because he had only been with us a few days, attached what was left of my squad to another squad, put me on point since I knew the way, and sent us up the hill again. This time, I did not escape the mortar fire. We were getting hammered all the way. The going was faster since the grass was getting beaten down, but that also made us more visible.

As we approached the tree line, a mortar round hit directly behind me. The concussion was strong enough to knock me to the ground. I was not sure if I had been hit or not since I had been peppered with rocks, dirt, and other debris, which hurt as if you had been hit by shrapnel. Directly behind me, my radioman, Calvin, and my M-79 man had both been hit and were calling for a corpsman. I crawled back to see if I could help them when the word came to fall back again. So I helped get them back to the LZ.

After a few minutes, we regrouped with another squad and headed up again. I can't remember how many men were left in my squad by this time, but I think it was just George and me. That damn George never got hit, you talk about luck. This time we were under the command of the XO, whose name I have forgotten since he had only been in the outfit a week or so. I was at point again, and we made the tree line in good time. I could see the body about eight or ten feet in the jungle. I held up at the tree line looking for trip wires and booby traps. All the while, the XO was yelling for me to hurry up because we were getting hit hard, as if I didn't know this. After all, this was only my third trip up that damn hill. I had covered about half the distance to the body when the XO caught up to me, gave me a look of exasperation, and blundered on by me. I turned around and dove head first as far down the hill as I could when the jungle exploded. I could hear the XO moan, but it took me a couple of seconds to locate him underneath all the vegetation that had fallen on him. I was afraid to try and treat him there, so I drug him out of the jungle and treated his wounds as best I could.

Both of his legs were almost blown off above the knees. I took his web belt and made a tourniquet for the worst leg and put battle dressings on the other. There was no one to help me, and I could not stand him up where I could get him over my shoulder, so I just had to grab him by his flak jacket and drag him down to the LZ.

By this time, the LZ was a mad house—so many wounded waiting to be medevac'd, so many men not knowing what to do, gear strung from the LZ to the top of the mountain, and about one half of the company still circling around in choppers waiting to get on the ground. All I knew was that I did not want to go up that hill again. I didn't care if it was President Johnson himself that was lying there.

The decision was made by someone to pull us out finally but not before we had gotten our asses kicked, and I had not so much as seen the enemy. The fact that all this occurred directly across the valley from Camp Carroll made it worse. The entire base had been witness to our ass kicking, and a lot of the personnel at Carroll were Army personnel that we were always giving a hard time about being in the Army instead of the Corps. I have to give them credit for being kind enough that they never mentioned what they had seen. It was a pretty sorry-looking bunch that gathered back at Carroll that evening for chow. We had no one killed except an ARVN scout that I never saw, but we had taken around 60 percent casualties and had not been gone but about an hour and a half.

That evening while I was cleaning my weapon and combat gear, I found a place where a piece of shrapnel had hit my helmet and left a fairly sizeable dent in the helmet and a big hole in the cover. I guess it was just not my day to die. To a large degree, staying alive had as much to do with luck as it did with anything else. Oh sure, you could do something really stupid like the XO had, but for the most part, it was just pure dumb luck. Some of the best died hard while some of the dumbest never received a scratch.

After a few relatively quiet days standing lines at Camp Carroll, we were once again loaded onto choppers and flown into another hot LZ over around the Rock Pile somewhere. This time, things went about as well as things ever go in combat, few casualties, kill the enemy, mission accomplished, and back to Carroll in time for chow.

A few days later, it was back on the choppers and another hot LZ. This time, we were over near the coast and a village called Qua Viet. It was kind of hedgerow country, a real change from the jungle, flat and open with the sun beating down on you. The heat was terrible, well over one hundred degrees, with a surface temperature a lot higher than that. There were snipers everywhere, so we spent most of our time with our faces buried in the sand. We suffered heavy casualties that day but mainly from heat exhaustion and stroke. We lost a good number of our officers, mainly lieutenants, due to the snipers. As you can probably tell by now, we went through a lot of brown bar lieutenants.

I did lose a good man and friend at Qua Viet, a Mexican kid named Oscar. He had been with me a long time and was as tough as they come. I could always count on the Beaner to get the job done, no matter how bad it was, and he would never complain about or question an order. A sniper got him in the right ass cheek with what looked like a flesh wound. Entry and exit holes were about two inches apart, but Beaner was in a tremendous amount of pain for such a wound, and he was as white as a ghost. We loaded him on the dust off and expected to see him back in a few weeks, but we later learned that the bullet had gone up into his abdomen before exiting a few inches from where it entered. He never came back to us.

About forty years later, I was sitting at home with my family when the phone rang. It was Beaner calling from up North somewhere. He had been in contact with Willie in Oregon and had gotten my number from Willie. Beaner moved from place to place trying to find the right location to call home. He battled the typical issues most of us faced after the war.

I heard from Beaner every year for a couple of years after that. Then neither Willie nor I heard from him since. I guess it has probably been around five or six years since our last contact. Another causality of the war, just several years later; but the war killed him just the same. It might have been better if he had been killed over there. I think he would have suffered less. Hanging in my family room today is a picture of Willie, Beaner, and me taken at Camp Carroll in 1968. Rest easy, Beaner, wherever you are.

As dark approached, we dug in for the night in the middle of this swarm of enemies. Sporadic fighting continued for several hours but not in my area for once. Sometime during the night, Puff arrived and patrolled our perimeter for the rest of the night. Puff was an old converted bomber or cargo plane of some kind in which they had mounted Gatling guns of 7.62 mm small arms and 20 mm exploding projectiles. The pilot would bank the plane to the left, fix his left wing on a center point, and just circle around kicking out flares and firing at the enemy. They put out so many rounds that there was a ribbon of fire from the plane to the ground and what sounded like a continual growl from the weapons.

The morning dawned bright and clear with not a sign of the enemy anywhere, or at least one that was alive. It was as if nothing had ever happened. We spent most of the day mopping up, getting a body count of the enemy KIAs, and licking our wounds. While mopping up, we received mortar attack and were caught out in the open with no place to hide. There was a small shell crater just to my right, which was not big enough for me to get in, but I did stick my face down into it. A mortar round hit next to me and peppered me with rocks, dirt, and shrapnel. I knew I had been hit in the ass, but I didn't know how badly. It hurt like hell, and I could feel this warm liquid that I assumed was blood, running down my crack. I yelled for a corpsman and told him my ass had been blown off. I couldn't reach back and feel my ass because of my pack and cartridge belt. The corpsman came crawling over during the rain of mortar rounds to treat my wounds. I felt him pull a piece of shrapnel from my right butt cheek. The corpsman took my hand and laid a small piece of metal in it and said he would put a band aid on the wound later. The wound was very minor, but shrapnel had pierced my canteen and that was the liquid I felt running down my crack. I was too embarrassed to put in for a purple heart, and my mom had taken it pretty hard the last time I was wounded, so I did not want to worry her again.

We had suffered few casualties from enemy fire except for the brown bars, but the heat had nearly wiped us out. We had so few men that we were not rally functional as a combat unit, so they had us hump over to Qua Viet and set up a perimeter around the vill.

Qua Viet was a picturesque little village located on a river of the same name, just a short distance from the South China Sea. They were going to have elections of the village leaders and did not want the VC to be able to vote, so we were called in to set up a perimeter. Qua Viet was by far the best duty we had ever had since I had been in country. It was like in country R&R at our own private beach. During the day, we would leave just a skeleton crew to watch the perimeter while the rest of us swam, bathed, did our laundry, or slept. It felt rather strange to be swimming naked with all these Vietnamese. Mamma-sans and kids were doing their laundry and swimming, playing, and laughing butt naked with the rest of us. You would never have guessed that there was a war within a thousand miles.

One of my men had been negotiating with a papa san over the price of a chicken, had finally gotten exasperated with the negotiation, threw some money at the papa san, and wrung the neck of the chicken and carried it off. The papa san went crying to the skipper, who paid the papa san a case of C-rations for the chicken and then took the equivalent of a case of Cs from my ass with a good ass chewing. The only problem was that one chicken and a squad of hungry Marines merely served to arouse our appetite. We had been buying Tiger Beer and 45 cal. whiskey from the villagers all afternoon, so most of us were in no pain and up for anything.

My first fire team leader was a guy from Detroit by the name of Jim. Jim was one of those men that just invited trouble for himself and anyone around him. Jim had been the chaplain's driver until he got drunk one night, stole the chaplain's Jeep, and wrecked it in the vill. He had gotten busted back to a PFC and sent back to the bush. Jim and I hit it off immediately.

Jim and I dreamed up this plot to kill a water buffalo calf that was foolproof. At just about dark, we would radio the skipper that we had movement in front of our position. We knew the skipper would tell us to shoot if we got a shot. Another guy in my squad named Buckley, who fancied himself as a sniper, would take the shot. Everything went as planned; the skipper gave us permission to fire, and Buckley dropped it with one shot. We reported the kill back to the skipper, and he told us to go out and get the body. Johnson and I went out, cut its throat, and drug it back to our lines. When we radioed the skipper and told him we had mistaken enemy movement for that of a water buffalo calf, there was a long pause. When the skipper answered, all he said was, "God damn it, Grit," he always called me Grit, "I better have a steak up here in the morning." And wouldn't you know it, the same papa san whose chicken we had killed earlier in the day also owned that calf.

A few days later, the fun was all over; back to the war, we went. Choppers came in, picked us up, and flew us into a new base on Route 9 called LZ Stud originally, later changed to LZ Vandergrif or something like that. This place was in a small bowl-shaped valley with steep mountains all around. I don't know who picked this place, but it was a nightmare. The gooks could sit up on the mountains and throw rocks down at us. Just outside the wire at Stud, there was a smaller perimeter on top of a small but high mountain that was called Static Hill because of all the radio antenna and equipment up there.

Third Platoon was assigned the task of guarding the perimeter on Static Hill. It was pretty fair duty since we saw no action while we were there. When Stud would take incoming artillery, we would just sit up there and watch the show. Nights were pretty nerve-wracking though; there were a lot of rock apes in the area that were constantly tripping our flares in the middle of the night or just moving around, making noise all night, which made it difficult to sleep.

From LZ Stud, we move to the area between Khe Sanh and the Laotian border—beautiful country, mountainous rain forest, untouched by the bombing, but it was tough to patrol though. We hacked our way to the top of some mountain, blew all the trees from the top, and established an artillery base. The only purpose for this base would be to support an invasion of Laos, which according to the President was not even being considered.

From where we were, we could see vehicles moving down the Ho Chi Min Trail over in Laos. A few times on ambushes, we would venture across the border and knock out a convoy; however, one time, we lost a man over there, so the skipper put an end to it. This country was so wild and primitive. There were tigers, elephants, snakes and lizards of all kinds, and plant of all kinds. I just loved to go on patrol just to see what we would find, and there was something new every day.

We could also see all the way to the coast and ships out at sea. It was not at all unusual to be able to see a half a dozen or more engagements or air strikes going on in different places across the country at the same time. It was our entertainment. I guess we had gotten so callused to the sight of death that watching the enemy blown apart or incinerated with napalm was laughed at as if it were a cartoon.

Third Platoon had been detached from the company once again and sent on patrol to God knows where and for what reason. I'm sure no one knows. We hacked our way up to the top of another mountain and set in for the night. Just at dark, we thought we heard the gooks yelling at us, and it sounded like they were yelling, "F— you." As it turned out, it was a type of bird, but it sure fooled us for a while. Many guys even yelled back at them. It was always something new in the rainforest.

A couple of months earlier, a kid by the name of Perry joined my squad. He was real gung ho and wanted to go to scout sniper school. I tried and tried to convince him to just stay with the squad, but he was adamant; so I eventually recommended him. He was accepted, and he left the company. I didn't think we would ever see him again, but sure enough, here he came just one day later. That night, Perry and I shared a foxhole together, had a couple of cans of ham and eggs chopped, and coffee for breakfast the next morning, and then set off down the ridgeline. My squad was at point with Perry leading the way. I had been called forward to look at the trail ahead and decide which way to go at a junction. I told Perry which way to go and was still with the point fire team when I heard and felt the explosion. Perry had been hit by a Claymore-type mine but was still alive. We sat down by suppressing fire, but I could not get to Perry. Every time I tried, the small arms fire would drive me back. Every time Perry would move, they would shoot him again. We were finally able to get artillery on the position and overrun it. Perry was dead by the time we could get to him. Perry was nineteen years old, married, and had a new daughter that he had never met. He always carried a picture of them in his helmet. I made sure it was there when we loaded his body on the chopper, but I remember thinking how strange it was that I felt nothing, no anger, no remorse, just nothing. He was just another load of meat.

We moved on down the mountain to the valley below where we blundered upon a large bunker complex complete with a mess hall, armory, hospital, and supplies. I guess they knew we were coming after the encounter we had at the top of the mountain, for it looked like they had abandoned everything and fled. I got me a new SKS with a fold-out bayonet, put a tag on it with my name, and sent it out to our battalion armory where it was supposed to be stored until I picked it up on my way home. Of course, it had disappeared by the time I went to pick it up. There were all kinds of combat gear, from helmets to belts, Jesus boots, and canteens. One room just off the mess hall contained tons of rice and canned fish. I guess there was going to be a bunch of hungry gooks for a while. We set up a perimeter around the complex, a team of engineers was brought in, and we blew bunkers for a month.

While we were there at the bunker complex, we continued to run daily patrols and nightly ambushes. We didn't venture out too far on both because this was real bad Indian country, and we just operated with quad-sized patrols. One day while on patrol, we came to a pretty large creek that we needed to cross. We could get in the creek all right, but the bank on the other side was too steep and jungle covered for us to be able to get out. Jim called me up front to look the area over and decide on a course to take. Jim wanted us to get into the creek and wade downstream until we could find a place to get out easily. We could see a place about a hundred or so yards down the stream that looked as if it would. I didn't like the idea because of the possibility of getting ambushed in the creek. Jim and I scouted downstream to check the other sight and found that we could get out of the creek all right, but the bank was too steep and high to get into it.

We decided to go back to the first sight and do as Jim had suggested. I still didn't like it, but we had little choice unless we wanted to spend a lot more time scouting up and down the creek for a better crossing. I told the men to stay a long distance apart while in the creek. Jim and his fire team were all in the creek and moving to the right downstream when I entered the water, which was about up to our mid-thighs. All of a sudden, we were opened up on by automatic weapons from a hidden bunker on the far shore. I fell back into the jungle, and we opened up on the bunker with everything we had. While lying there against the bank, I saw the bullets kicking up the dirt to the left side of me and coming right at me. I just knew that this was it; there was no way the bullets could miss me. I closed my eyes and waited for the worst to happen, but nothing happened. When I opened my eyes, the bullets were kicking up dirt on my right. To this day, I cannot believe that they missed me. In my dreams, I have relived that moment a thousand times, and I am still just as scared and relieved as I was forty years ago. Every time it happens, I still expect to be wounded or killed.

I could see Jim's fire team out there in the creek acting like pearl divers and seeing how long they could stay under water, but not Jim; he was charging the bunker through knee-deep water with bullets kicking the water up all around him with every step. Jim had to travel nearly fifty yards through the hail of bullets until he got close enough to throw a grenade into the bunker. Somehow, not one of my men was injured, not even Jim, but then, Jim never got hit. He was bulletproof.

It was Jim's philosophy that if it was your time, it was your time. We had discussed this several times because Jim would never dig in like the rest of us. Me, I was like a mole and always dug in deeply if I was in an area for very long. I asked him point-blank one time that if a gook had him in his sights and the slack squeezed off his trigger that he wouldn't die. Jim said that's right. If it was not his time, either the gook would miss, his rifle would jam, or something else would save him. Who was I to argue? Jim never seemed to get hit.

What we had blundered into was an NVA paymaster and a security guard. The paymaster had thousands of dong in his possession, which we took and sent back to battalion HQ. Poor gooks—not only were they going to be hungry, but also they were broke.

HQ eventually sent the money back, which I split up among the rest of the company. I sent a few bills home since it had Uncle Ho's picture on it, but the rest of it we spent in the vill. Jim got a haircut and a shave in the vill and tipped the barber a five hundred dong bill, but of course, Jim had me hold my 45 cal. automatic on the barber all during his shave.

The Vietnamese would take anything that looked like money. There were thousands of guys returning from R&R from all parts of the world, and most still had a little of the currency from the R&R port, so they would just take it into the vill and spend it, no problem. There was one time that on one of our unauthorized recon missions into a vill, we even spent a lot of Monopoly money that we had taken out of a game. We spent it on beer, whiskey, and anything else that struck our fancy. It was real funny until the gooks started to take the money in for exchange. The next thing we knew, there was a big counterfeit investigation going on. Capt. Sams covered for us when he was questioned about the incident. I wasn't aware of it until later when he casually mentioned it and warned me to keep my squad under better control. I guess we were so deep in the bush by that time that even the Treasury Department didn't want to mess with us.

A few days after we had killed the paymaster, we were patrolling further down the valley when we discovered about twelve or fifteen miles of hard-surfaced road completely under canopy, not at all visible from the air. The Air Force started to spray Agent Orange over the entire area, including us. It was bad enough getting sprayed, but we never got to take a bath or change clothes, so we just wore the herbicide until it finally wore off. I am convinced that many of the repeated skin problems that I have had ever since are due to the Agent Orange, but the VA doesn't agree.

It was while we were in that area that I decided to put in for R&R. I wanted to go to Australia, and we got very few quotas for there, so I wanted to wait until my last month in country before putting in for it. That way, I should be senior on the list and have first choice of where I wanted to go. I also had another reason for waiting so long. In my company, they would usually pull you out of the bush a couple of weeks before your flight date home, so you could get cleaned up a little and unwind a little. Everyone tended to get very nervous and edgy that last couple of weeks in country, so you were not of much use anyway. I thought that by the time I got back from R&R, they might not send me back to the bush, particularly since the new company gunny was my old platoon Sgt. Wright.

The company only received one quota for Australia that month, and some officer with only a few months in country pulled rank on me and took the quota. I decided I would settle on Hawaii and had a good time anyway. The only problem was that when I got to Da Nang, they made me turn in my weapon. I felt so uncomfortable without it that I could not really relax; after all, I had been sleeping with it for twelve months.

While at the R&R center at Da Nang, I ran into a bunch of other guys I knew that were either coming from or going on R&R. We went into the vill, which was off limits to us, to this place that was notorious even for Da Nang. They advertised that they had fifty virgins. I have been in some wild places in my life, but this place topped them all. Anything you wanted was available, and I mean anything. I left pretty early in the evening because I had an early flight out in the morning. Sometime after midnight, this whole bunch of drunks came rolling in all fired up because a couple of them had been rolled at that club. They wanted to go back and try to get their money back or burn the place down. We went back, and the vill was still burning when I got back from R&R a week later.

Hawaii was beautiful, but I felt so uncomfortable. I had to sleep on the floor because I just could not go to sleep in the bed. I had an upset stomach and diarrhea from all the fresh fruit, vegetables, and rich food. There were people everywhere, just doing what people do on vacation, but I just could not relax and enjoy myself. In the back of my mind, I kept expecting incoming artillery, mortars, or small arms fire. R&R was neither restful nor relaxing for me. I did not feel safe until I got back to the bush with my weapon in my hand.

On my return to Da Nang from Hawaii, I ran into some more buddies, so I decided to take a few extra days at China Beach before returning to the unit, which would mean that I was AWOL. It was customary in my unit to take a few extra days, and nothing was said unless it got excessive. Every time the company gunny went to Da Nang to identify bodies, he would get all drunk up and stay there until the XO went and got him. It was strange; I had just left one of the most exotic beaches in the world but felt so out of place I really couldn't enjoy it. But at China Beach, which was primitive compared to Hawaii, I felt more at ease and was able to relax somewhat.

We were having a good time drinking cheap, cold beer; I mention the cold because we rarely had cold beer. Every night there would be a USO show, usually an oriental group singing Elvis, the Beach Boys, or even Johnnie Cash. There was usually a movie of some kind afterward. We would swim, sail, and lie on the beach all day.

One evening, however, we decided we would sneak into the vill. To do this, we had to sneak out of the perimeter at China Beach, which was surrounded by a tall fence and a triple strand of barbwire and guarded by Korean Marines. One of the guards shot a few rounds over our head as we were on the way out. We had a good time in the vill this time, no fights or problems of any kind until we were sneaking back into China Beach. A guard was sitting there waiting for us where we went out. One of the guys with us got into an argument with the guard; a fight ensued, and during the course of the fight, the guy with us drew his K-Bar and stabbed the Korean just under the heart, killing him instantly. We left him lying there and snuck back in.

At daylight, busloads of MPs rolled into China Beach and took the thousand or fifteen hundreds of us into custody. A few were interrogated, but most of us that were AWOL were taken to the airport and put aboard the first available aircraft back to our units. I couldn't help thinking about that Korean and how cheap life had gotten that we could just kill a man not in combat, but in an argument, and then just leave him lying there while we went on to bed. I began to think that maybe I had been here too long.

I had been considering extending my tour for another six months for a couple of reasons. First, I would still have about eighteen months of enlistment left at the end of this tour, and secondly, I preferred life in the bush to stateside duty. I didn't think I could get used to the spit and polish again.

Two things eventually convinced me to leave at the end of my tour. I was getting where I liked it all too much. I guess I had become an adrenalin junkie. I got a high every time we saw action, which was most every day. And the anticipation of what was going to happen next was almost unbearable, almost like the anticipation of Christmas when I was a little boy. Life was so simple. I had no personal belongings except my tooth brush, when I was lucky enough to have one. We also used a tooth brush to clean the chamber of our weapon, which would wear them out quickly, so if it came down to my weapon or my teeth, the weapon had first priority. The M-16 was a tough weapon to keep clean, especially the early models. Once they went to stainless steel chambers, they got much better.

Flying from Da Nang to Quang Tri gave me a good opportunity to look the country over again. It did not look like the same country I had flown over a year earlier. It no longer looked like a tropical paradise but more like the moon. Bomb and shell craters were everywhere. Few trees remained in many areas, and those had been defoliated with Agent Orange. Almost all the villages up north along the DMZ had been destroyed or relocated.

The company was in the same location it had been when I left for R&R; the monsoons were starting again; I was eating C-rations and sleeping on the ground with my weapons at hand again. Life was back to normal. I had been acting platoon sergeant, even though I was just a corporal when I went on R&R, but while I was gone, a new sergeant arrived in the company to take the position. And would you believe it? He was from Mulberry. David Partlow, who had graduated from high school in 1960 with my brother, was now the platoon sergeant. I became the supply sergeant for the few weeks I had remaining of my tour. David returned to Mulberry after getting out of the Corps, attended C of O at the same time as I did, and now has a business, Alma Farm Supply, in Alma. He and I have remained friends ever since that rainy monsoon day in 1968.

The new CO of Echo Company, whatever his name was, would not let me leave the bush until three days before my flight date out of country. A typhoon had set in, and nothing was flying when it came time for me to leave the bush, so I just sat there in the rain and mud for a couple of days until we had a slight break in the weather. We were in desperate need of rations by this time, and I was able to get on one of the supply choppers that braved the weather to get to us on top of whatever mountain we were sitting on. It was a wild ride from there to Quang Tri. I almost wished I would have waited for better weather, but that would have meant missing my flight date, and Willie and I would not have traveled home together.

I had a tough time getting everything done that I needed to in just part of a day. I had to go to payroll, supply, sick bay, and a half a dozen other places to pick up my records. Supply had me charged with three M-16 rifles, even after I had turned in the one I had been carrying for a while. They were going to charge at me four or five hundred dollars a piece for them unless I could get a statement from a superior officer that they had been combat lost. Luckily, Capt. Sams was now assigned to G-2 or G-3, and he was more than happy to help me out.

I had to get to sick bay for a couple of shots and to pick up my records. A corpsman buddy of mine said he would get my records for me and even forge my records so it showed that I had received my shots, which suited me just fine since I still needed to go by payroll for my pay and records. With the help of my corpsman buddy, I was able to get everything done in time for evening chow.

That night, Sgt. Wright, Willie, Dr. Chargin (the corpsman), and I threw one last drunk together before boarding a C-130 for Da Nang. We had more processing in Da Nang and went through the first of many searches. The last step before getting on the plane was getting our shot record checked. Willie had to get a couple of shots for which I gave him a lot of crap for not being smart like me and having it taken care of. After Willie had gotten his shots, I stepped up and confidently gave them my shot record. They studied it a second or two and said, "Sorry, Marine, you have to get them all." That's more than a dozen or fifteen shots all at one time. I'll bet Dr. Chargin and Sgt. Wright are still laughing. If it was not for the fact that it would cost me my flight date, I would have flown back to Da Nang and shot Chargin. Oh well, like they say in the Corps, "Never trust a sailor."

My arms were already starting to get sore by the time we boarded the plane, and that night, I ran a high temperature. As we headed down the runway, artillery rounds were landing just short of the runway we were on; a fitting good-bye, I guess. I looked out of the window for one last view and was amazed at the changes that had occurred in a little over one year. The military base at Da Nang had gotten huge, with the airport becoming the busiest in the world. The vill had also doubled, tripled, or quadrupled in size with most of it made of C-ration boxes, ammo boxes, or sheet iron, and, of course, it was burning. I don't know if it was still burning from when we had set fire to it or not, but I would not doubt it. The surrounding country was devastated from bombing, artillery, and Agent Orange. It no longer reminded me of the hills of home.

All of a sudden, I became so depressed and drained of energy that part of me wanted to stay with the company, for the rumor was flying that we were going to be going into Laos after the gooks. I guess I had been living on coffee and adrenaline for so long that when I realized the war was over for me, I just sort of crashed. The depression lasted for several years, though not as bad.

We first went to Okinawa, Japan, where we spent the night and were issued a uniform to wear home, since all our sea bags had been destroyed by artillery at Quang Tri. From there, we hit Guam or Wake Island; I can't remember which because we hit them both, one going and one coming. Whichever island it was had nothing but a runway and a liquor store. The runway ran from one end of the island to the other. As a matter of fact, I was not sure we were going to get stopped before we hit the beach. The liquor store was for big shot officers and politicians traveling to and from the Orient. We were able to buy five fifths of booze packaged in a box cheap because it had not tax on it.

This island was the main base for the B-52 bombers headed to Vietnam. It was interesting to see them close up and see how big they were. Their wings almost drug the ground as they taxied for takeoff. As they started to gain speed on takeoff, the wing tips started to rise. It was reassuring to see them take off for as big as they were. I knew we would have no trouble, but when we left the runway on takeoff, as soon as the wheels cleared, we were over water. There was nothing between the end of the runway and the ocean except a very narrow beach.

When we got back on the plane, some full bird colonel stood up in front and ordered us to put the boxes of booze under the seats and not touch it until we were off the plane stateside. A soldier sitting with Willie and me already had the lid off one bottle. He looked at the bottle, then the lid, and threw the lid to the front of the plane, bouncing it

off the bulkhead in front of the colonel. He took a big gulp, passed it
to me, and said, "What are they going to do? Send us back to Nam?"
That started things off, and it was a long, wild twelve- or fourteen- hour
trip home.

This guy we were seated by was really a strange guy. I don't know
if the war had done it to him or if he had been that way to start with,
but he had a sick sense of humor. He asked what unit I was with,
and I told him Echo 2/9. At hearing my unit, he said he knew a lot
of guys form 1/9 and 2/9 both. At first, I thought this guy must have
some connection to the 9th Marines, even though he was in the Army,
so I asked what unit he was with. In a very matter-of-factly manner,
he replied that he was with Graves Registration, which is the unit
responsible for handling the bodies of those killed in action. I thought
about hitting the guy, but I guess those guys develop a weird sense of
humor to keep from going insane.

It was just starting to get daylight as we approached the west coast
of the U. S. around San Francisco, which was where we were supposed
to land. It was just about one of the most emotional times of my life to
look out the window of the plane and just barely be able to distinguish
the land mostly masked in fog with the sun rising in the east. At the last
minute, we were diverted to El Toro, a Marine air base just south of L.
A. I overheard one of the officers telling another officer that we were
diverted because there were a large number of war protesters waiting for
us at San Francisco, and the military did not want an incident. Incident
hell, it would have been a slaughter. A large number of us were combat
Marines and soldiers who had become numb to injury and death, and
the officers on the flight had little control over us since we had not
served under them. We would have thought very little of spilling the
protesters' blood. I can't believe that whoever arranged the protest would
risk confronting us unless a blood bath was what they were wanting.

About twenty-four hours after leaving Vietnam, I was back in
Mulberry for a thirty-day leave. Mulberry had not changed, but I had,
which I guess is the reason I felt like a total stranger. I would run into
someone I had known my entire life, and they would greet me with,
"Hi, John. I haven't seen you in a long time. Where have you been?"
I would usually just say that I had been out of town working. For the
most part, most people did not care that there was a war going on,
unless they had a family member that was there.

I had only been gone a little over a year, but I felt as though I had been gone a decade. The world had changed tremendously in that time—politically, socially, and morally. Every value that had existed before was being challenged and replaced with things like "if it feels good, do it." This was my generation, but I wanted no part of their culture. I just wanted to be left alone.

I finished my tour with the Marine Corps stationed at Camp Pendleton, California, in HQ Company of the Fifth Marine Division, where I processed troops headed to Vietnam. There is not much to tell about this time except I drank too much whiskey and got into too many fights, but I did get promoted to sergeant just after the first of the year. Not too bad, going from PFC to Sgt. in about a year and a half.

Sgt. Wright had asked me to check in on his wife at their home in Ocean Side, which was just off base. I called and talked with her, and she was glad to hear from me. Her husband had told her he had asked me to check on her occasionally. I took her out to dinner one Friday night and told her all about her Tim and how he was when I had last seen him. It was a pleasant evening up until she tried to seduce me. I was not the same inexperienced boy I had once been, but there is no way I would ever consider betraying Tim's trust. I held her by the arms and talked to her of the bond between her husband and me and that it had nothing to do with her; she was a very attractive lady. She cried for a little while then apologized to me. It was a very uncomfortable situation and was never mentioned again when Tim came home and we would go out together or I would have dinner with them.

Willie had gotten married while home on leave and was stationed at Camp Pendleton but in a different area. I was at Main Side, which was where the HQ was, and Willie was stationed on the west side of the base at the rifle range. It was so typical for the military; I could hardly type, file, or do anything else that was done in our office. About all I did was make coffee for our office and march the troops to chow three times a day. Most of the time, I could be found at the handball courts getting my ass kicked in handball by the company gunny. Willie, on the other hand, could hardly shoot and was not very good mechanically, so they put him in the armory.

Willie and Connie, his wife, had an apartment just off base at San Clement, a real nice little coastal town, or at least it was until President Nixon decided to make it his home. I would spend a lot of time at either

Tim's place or Willie's. We did a lot of sightseeing around southern California, but mostly in the interior, not along the coast. People along the coast were totally different than those that lived just a few miles inland. The inland people were real people while the coastal crowd was very phony, weird, or drugged out.

This was the way most of the rest of my enlistment went until May when the gunny called me in for a conference. I was given my choice of three different options. I could get a ten-month, early discharge on the first of June, finish my regular enlistment with another stripe, and if I chose to reenlist at that time, I would receive another stripe, which would make me an E-7, a gunny, but of course I would be sent right back to Nam. It was a very tempting offer; to be an E-7 in three years was remarkable. Tim had seventeen years in the Corps and was still an E-6 and would go no higher because he did not have a high school diploma.

There were three main reasons to get out. The first was I did not think that I would survive another tour of combat, and I would probably end up as a company gunny in some grunt company. The second reason was that at that time, it was very unpopular to be associated with the military in any capacity. The draft dodgers that went to Canada were national heroes, and we were baby killers. The third reason had to do with something that happened to a good friend of mine, Rubin Scott. Scotty, as we called him, had joined the Corps during the Korean War and had worked his way up the rank structure to a rank of E-6. He was given the same options they were offering me, which he accepted, and he planned to make a career of the military. At the end of the war, he was not needed anymore, so the Corps just discharged him. He drove a truck in civilian life and joined the Corps again as a PFC when Nam broke out; he was assigned to the weapons Platoon I, my company, and we became good friends. He was still planning on making a career of it and eventually did, retiring just recently with about forty years. I still hear from him on occasions. I figured the Corps would do the same to me when the war ended, so I just decided it would be best if I took the early discharge, return home, and finish my education.

I had bought an old 1962 Nash Rambler four door sedan, gold in color with typewriter drive for $200. A running s.o.b. but was prone to go through an alternator about every one thousand miles. On June 1, immediately after my discharge, I had all my possessions loaded and was headed east toward the Arizona line. I was in no big hurry to get home, so I spent several days at the Grand Canyon hiking and riding the mules to the bottom.

I spent the summer working construction for Barber Bridge Builders out of Ft. Smith. We were working on I-40 between Mulberry and Ozark. It was hard work but paid well with a lot of hours. We typically worked at least sixty hours a week, and I was being paid $2.25 an hour. It was good to be with a crew of guys working together again. I love working with men much more than women. With guys, there is always some good-natured bullshit going on, and if someone does get mad, they have a fight, and when the fight is settled, they get up and go back to work. Working with women is totally different. You have to watch what you say or they get their feelings hurt and cry, and if they have a disagreement, they bear a grudge forever. They also can get upset at the most trivial things—things that a man would not even notice and wouldn't care if he did notice.

I reentered college at Westark in Ft. Smith, which had grown a lot in the nearly two years I had been away. It was still a commuter's school with no dorms, so most all of the students were local kids of good working class poor people who could not afford to send their kids to the U of A at Fayetteville. I enjoyed Westark and was treated no differently than any student, and the education was as good, if not better, than any other school I have attended.

The following summer, I again returned to bridge work, but this time, we were working on US 71 between Texarkana and Shreveport. We were staying in the little town of Faulke, Arkansas, near the Louisiana line. Faulke's one claim to fame is that they have a Big Foot Sasquatch in the area that has been encountered by several people. There has even been a "B" movie made about it. I tend to be skeptical of such things, but all I know is that you did not tease the locals about Big Foot; they would get instantly defensive and mad.

In the fall, I had to transfer to another college as I had taken all the hours that I could at Westark. My best friend from high school, Roger Benham, was going to The College of the Ozarks in Clarksville, so I decided to transfer there. C of O was a lot different than Westark. It was a private church school; most of the kids were from wealthy families from the northeastern part of the U. S., and there were a lot of foreign students, mainly from the Middle East, Saudi, Iran, and Iraq. There were even a few from Thailand. These made me nervous because they looked too much like the Vietnamese. It was a fine arts college, very liberal, anti-war, anti-veterans, and anti-everything as near as I could tell.

Most of the students were not openly hostile toward us veterans. On the contrary, I felt they were afraid of us, and we were several years older than the average students. A few of the instructors were very critical of the war, and veterans were often treated badly. I actually had one professor, Dr. Dawson, who gave me an "F" on a report I had been assigned on the musical *Hair*. The report was not good, but I had completed the project and turned it in on time. Several of the long-haired hippie types that never even bothered to come to class or do the project got much better grades than I did. I decided to put an end to the bullshit once and for all. I stormed into his office, past his secretary, and threw my report card on his desk. He jumped up from his desk with fear and anger on his face and wanted to know what I wanted. I went into my best crazed Vietnam Veteran act where I can let my eyes look as if I were a wild animal with all the white showing, and in my best drill instructor imitation, I told him I was not going to accept that grade and that he was going to change it. He said, "And what if I don't?" I did not even answer him but just stood and glared at him. He then said he would have me expelled, at which I just commented that I didn't really think he wanted to do that but that it didn't make me much difference. I would get my satisfaction one way or another. There was a long pause with us just looking at each other. I had been pushing troops long enough to know that I had him whipped. He finally sat down at his desk, picked up my card, and changed the grade. I told him to be sure it was changed on my transcript, thanked him, and left. After that, I had no problems with any of the faculty or students.

It was while I was at C of O that I met the Grober brothers, Vince and Wayne—a friendship that exists to this day. I had bought an old 1952 model Spartan trailer made by the Spartan aircraft of Wichita, Kansas. It looked like a B-29 bomber without wings or tail and was built just as well. When we would have a bad storm, all the other trailers in the park would be shaking and moving, but my little trailer would just set there as if nothing was going on. The Grober boys had a brand new fourteen wide behind me. We became acquainted very well.

My landlord, Jim Perett, was the head of the business department at C of O and lived in the trailer just in front of me. Jim was a great guy, a young bachelor and a good teacher. He would have a poker game every Friday night for faculty members, and the Grober boys and I were always invited. We really had some good times that year.

The day that I finished the spring semester, I received a letter form Yellowstone National Park informing me that I had been hired for seasonal employment and needed to report to work Monday morning at the Lake Ranger Station. It was already Friday, and I was instructed to wait until I had received my employment packet in the mail before leaving. The packet arrived in the Saturday morning mail about 1000. By noon, I had my truck loaded and was headed out on another adventure, which would have as much impact on me as the war had.

From my youngest days, I have always loved to go and see different places and experience new things. Mom would tell how I used to sit in her lap when we traveled and never sleep as long as we were moving. At the end of a trip, I would cry because it was over and ask when we were going again. Yellowstone would provide me with a lifetime full of adventures and new trails.

Yellowstone Years

I will never forget that first trip headed to Yellowstone. The weather in Arkansas was already hot and humid with the temperature in the mid-1990s. I headed up through Tulsa and Wichita to Salina, Kansas, where I picked up I-70 west to Denver. I drove through the night, and the sun was just beginning to rise when I was about an hour east of Denver.

Daylight has always been my favorite time of day. Everything looks best at this time of day, and on that day, the Rockies looked the most spectacular that I have ever seen them—and I have seen them hundreds of times. They were covered in snow for the most part, except for the lower elevations, which had already started to melt. A few storm clouds hung in several places near the peaks, but the morning was bright and sunny. Denver was even visible that morning since smog was not yet a real big problem there.

From Denver, I headed north toward Fort Collins and Laramie, Wyoming. I did take time to drive up to Rocky Mountain National Park to see a friend of mine on the way. I had been to RMNP several years earlier, but not this early in the season. The roads were still in the process of being plowed, so the park was not really open yet.

I was starting to get tired as I headed north from Fort Collins. I had been on the road for about sixteen hours or so, but the country was so impressive that I just could not wait to see what was around the next curve. The weather had turned cold with snow squalls blowing through occasionally in the higher elevations. I went up through the Snowy Range from Ft. Collins, through Virginia Dale, to Laramie on mostly snow-covered roads; the snow was several feet deep at Virginia Dale. It was hard to believe that it was late May from what I had been used to back home.

John at the Ranger Station, Yellowstone Lake

From Laramie, I picked up I-80 and headed west toward Rawlins. It was a hundred miles from Laramie to Rawlins up through the Medicine Bow Mountain, with nothing in between—not one gas station, house, or anything. The elevation of the road must have been around ten thousand feet or more. Over the years, I found this to be the worst stretch of road in the entire interstate system. I don't know how many times I got stranded in either Laramie or Rawlins because the interstate was closed due to bad weather.

I headed north out of Rawlins and went by the small town of Bair Oil. I remember Dad telling about working in Bair Oil during its boom day. There was no town there back then, just a tent city filled with oil field workers. As a matter of fact, Dad was working at Bair Oil up until just before I was born, so I came very near to having been born in Wyoming rather than Arkansas.

I ran parallel to the Wind River Mountain up to Lander and Dubois, then over Towgatee Pass to Moran Junction. The road over Towgatee Pass was completely snow covered and slick with "chains required" signs still posted. I had no chains but made myself a mental note to get a set. As it turned out, I had no problem anyway.

From Moran Junction, the Teton Mountains were staring you in the face at about maybe five miles distance, across Jackson Hole. The view of the Teton Mountains from Moran Junction is one of the most inspiring and uplifting I have ever seen during all of my travels, and no matter how many times I see them, I am always affected the same way. It is as if I am seeing them for the first time again. There was a beautiful sunset behind them, and the mountains were bathed with alpenglow, which is a phenomenon that occurs as the sun sets and the mountains take on a glowing pastel color.

I decided to go into the small town of Jackson, Wyoming, for the evening as it was starting to get dark, and I did not know exactly where I was to go when I got into Yellowstone. I thought it would be much easier to find my way around in the daylight hours, and besides that, I wanted to go to Jackson again anyway. I had been there just before going into the Corps and had fallen in love with the whole area. By the time I got there, though, I was so tired that all I did was grab a quick bite to eat and go to bed.

I was up early the next morning and headed back to Moran Junction. The Teton Mountains were just as impressive in the early morning light as they had been at sunset. There is just a special feel about this part of Wyoming. I don't exactly know how to describe it, but it's a little like stepping back in time to when buffalo and beaver filled the valleys and streams, and the mountain men and Indians roamed the area in search of both. And then there is the feeling that because places like this still exist, maybe the world is not as screwed up as it seemed in LA. Most big cities leave me with the feeling that surely God is going to wipe out this place.

I entered Yellowstone midmorning, found the District Office at Lake, and got checked in all right. I had no uniforms since my hiring had occurred so suddenly, but we were able to call the company and place a rush order, which only took a couple of days. It felt good to be back in uniform again, and the Park Service was very similar to the military in many ways. I felt right at home. My first duty assignment was to the East Entrance, twenty-eight miles away from Lake on a shoulder-less, narrow, winding road that went up over Sylvan Pass, one of the highest passes in the park. The road had been plowed out but was still barely wide enough for two vehicles to pass with snow banks on each side of the road that varied in depth from about four feet to twenty feet or more depending on the elevation. At the pass, the telephone poles were just sticking out of the snow by a few feet.

At the East Entrance, which is at a much lower elevation, most of the snow was already gone. The only other man at East was a seasonal like me by the name of Dave Phillips. Dave was from a family of dairy farmers in Vermont, which he returned to each fall. The full-time ranger at East was gone on vacation, so Dave had been left in charge in his absence. There was very little traffic through the gate being so early in the season, so I had plenty of time to learn the system before it got busy, and it did get busy. Within two weeks, every kiosk was open, and traffic was still backed up for a half a mile down the road. I don't know if I would have come back for a second season if all I had to look forward to was entrance duty, but as usual, my good luck came to my rescue, and I was transferred to an interior station after only two weeks. Most new employees spend at least one or two years on the entrance before getting an interior station.

I found out later that a seasonal ranger that was to report to Grant Village called at the last minute and turned in his resignation. Being unable to get another experienced seasonal to report to work early, Dale Nuss, the south district ranger, called Dave at East and asked if he thought I could handle duty at an interior station. I guess Dave gave me a good recommendation, for the next day, I was headed for Grant village about twenty-five miles north of the South Entrance.

Grant Village proved to be a great place to work for me. My boss, Marvin Miller, was about five years older than me, single, enjoyed a good drink of Scotch, good food, good times, and like me, he liked to travel. We became good friends almost instantly, but then Marv was friends with everyone except his boss, District Ranger Dale Nuss. Dale was such a grouchy old hard-ass and liked to intimidate anyone that was under his command. I had dealt with many gunnies in the Corps that were a lot like Dale. Their philosophy was "do your job, and do it right or I will rip your guts out and feed them to you." I had no problem with Dale; after all, I had been intimidated by the best, Sgt. O'Donnell, my DI in boot camp. The main difference between Nuss and O'Donnell was that I knew O'Donnell would do it.

Marv was easygoing, liked to get along with everyone, and was intimidated easily—a perfect target for Dale. Dale was always on his ass about something even though the sub-district ran smoothly. We had a very experienced sr. seasonal, Bob Gross, who had been coming back to the park for over twenty years and knew his job well. The senior seasonals actually were responsible for the daily operations of the seasonal rangers. How well a sub-district and district ran was determined by how good the sr. seasonal in that area was. The rest of the year, Bob was an English instructor at some little school in Nebraska. Bob's wife and young daughter would come with him each year and just vacation for the entire summer.

I got along well with Bob and enjoyed working for him until one early spring a few years later. Bob reported to work at Grant a few weeks earlier than usual, and instead of being accompanied by his wife and daughter, he had a girlfriend with him. The girlfriend stayed until the day before his wife and daughter showed up. I just never felt the same about Bob after that; I still liked him well enough and had no problem working for him, but I had lost respect for him as a man.

Grant Village was a new development on the south shore on a part of Yellowstone Lake known as West Thumb. There was not much at Grant Village except the ranger station and visitor center, a camp ground with several hundred sites, a gas station, and a marina. None of the other facilities that were supposed to be there had been started except there was a huge parking lot in the area where the lodge and general store were supposed to have been built. At this time, the old general store at West Thumb was serving the area. Grant Village was supposed to replace all the facilities at the area known as West Thumb.

The developed area known as West Thumb was just a couple of miles north of Grant Village. There was a small but very nice geyser basin at Thumb that was located on the shore of Yellowstone Lake. It was about the first stop after coming in the South Entrance, and the first thermal features to be seen, so it was a very popular attraction. West Thumb was one of the oldest developed areas in the park. All the facilities were old and worn out, which is why the Park Service decided to build Grant Village and obliterate West Thumb and turn the area back into wilderness. Grant Village was to be a real show place, much more environmentally friendly than West Thumb, which had been built long before the word environment even existed. Grant Village was to be completed before Yellowstone's centennial in 1972, but funding cutbacks, mainly due to the war in Vietnam, had delayed the project for years.

For training, I rode patrol one night with an experienced seasonal named Dan, who was originally from Rhode Island but was now living in Bozeman, Montana, and attending Montana State University as a pre-vet major. Dan was married to a short, slightly overweight, fiery, redhead named Donna. I loved to aggravate Donna just to get her stirred up, which was no problem. Dan was also short, but there the similarity ended. He was easygoing and cool-headed with little to say. When he did say something, it was worth hearing. The night I rode patrol with him, we got tied up on something in the campground and did not even get to cover the whole patrol area, which went about halfway to South Entrance, the west halfway to Old Faithful, and north half way to Lake. The next night, I was given a patrol car and assigned to the 5:00 p.m.–2:00 a.m. shift by myself. I really had no real problems since most of our duties involved assisting the visitors whenever possible. I have always been able to get along with most anyone.

I really had to spend a lot of time studying to learn enough about the plant, animals, and history of the park so that I did not sound like a total idiot. I also had to tour around the park every day and learn about the geyser basins and other features. The visitors expected you to be an expert on all aspects of the park and its surrounding area. I traveled as far east as Cody, Wyoming, and tried to learn about everything from there to the park. I also went south into The Teton Mountain, and Grand

Teton National Park, all the way to Jackson. I did the same thing every direction from the park.

It was a busy summer, and the fact that we got no television and very little news from the outside only made it better. None of the news from outside the park was good, anti-war protests and riots on most of the college campuses, returning Vietnam Veterans being portrayed in the news and in movies as drugged, burned-out psychotic killers, and the draft dodgers that went to Canada as true heroes was a little bit more than I wanted to hear. I just wanted to be left alone and not have any contact or reminders of the war.

There was another Vietnam veteran in our ranger station, Steve Clement, a smallish man from California. He had been a lieutenant in the Army, a line officer at that had served as a platoon commander under Capt. Tommy Franks, later to become General Franks, the commanding general of all Allied Forces in Iraq during its occupation. Steve was a ranger naturalist while I was a protective ranger. We wore the same uniform, but our duties were totally different. Naturalists were the ones that led the nature walks and gave the evening talks at the amphitheater in the campground each evening, while protection rangers were responsible for protecting the park from the visitors and the visitors from the park. We were mainly law enforcement but very low-key. At that time, we did not wear firearms, though we had them in the car, but I usually wore a concealed weapon while patrolling at night. We also functioned as the park paramedics, ambulance service, fire department, game wardens, health inspectors, and anything else that needed to be done in the park. We had all authority in the park except for the FBI that would come in on felony cases.

As you can tell from the description of our duties, we stayed extremely busy. I would work sixteen hours a day most days, not because it was needed in most cases, but because I loved it. I had found my true niche, and I was good at it. I rapidly acquired a reputation as someone you could count on to give you a fair deal, and I would get done whatever tasks were assigned to me. There were so many incidents that happened that summer that I could write an entire book on that summer alone.

I threw Marv into a real panic one day when I wrote a ticket to Melvin Belli, probably one of the three top criminal lawyers in the U.S. He had defended Angela Davis and the Chicago 7, and in later years, he would go on to help defend O.J. Simpson, but by that time, he was just second string. I had caught him with undersized fish at the marina fish cleaning station. I did not know who he was, but I knew he was someone or at least thought he was someone by the way he acted. It's not every day you see an old man with snow white hair wearing bright red double knit slacks, white shirt with a red tie and white shoes driving a red Rolls-Royce with personalized California tags "Belli." It was a $15 violation, but he was going to fight it in court. How dare we fine him! The parks service dismissed charges rather than go through the publicity. I never saw Marv show any kind of anxiety until Belli came rolling up to the station in that Rolls.

One of the funniest incidents concerned the removal of a roadside black bear with a new cub. Being a farm boy, I had a lot of experience handling animals, so Marv wanted me to help him get these bear from the side of the road. Dale had driven by and got hung up in a bear jam, so he immediately called Marv, chewed him out, and told him to get rid of them. Marv was a big city boy from Portland, Oregon, and knew nothing about animals any larger than a dog.

We made our plans, gathered our equipment, and prepared to do battle. Everything went according to plan at first. We walked right up close to the sow and shot her with a tranquilizer dart. The sow went down quickly but not quick enough to prevent her from sending the cub up the tallest lodgepole pine in Yellowstone. We got the sow into a culvert trap without a problem, but getting the cub was where things went to hell. The cub was too far up the tree to shoot it with the tranquilizer gun, and if we did manage to hit it, we were afraid it would climb still higher before the tranquilizer took effect and injure itself when it fell. So we waited, hoping it would come down close enough to give us a shot. As the hours went by, the crowd of visitors got larger, but the cub did nothing except every few minutes it would squall for its mother. At first, we kept the sow there, but we decided that the cub might be more inclined to come down if its mom was gone.

After several hours of this, we began to get impatient. I had a hot date that night with a cute little nurse from the Lake Hospital, and it had taken me all summer to get her to agree to go out with me, so I didn't want to stand her up. I had a big time planned; I was going to take her to Jackson, have a good dinner, drink and dance all night, close down the bars, have breakfast at the Elk Horn Café, and drive back to the park in time to see the sunrise on the Pitchstone Plateau.

We went plan B or whatever it was. I was to take a climbing rope, tie a noose in the end, and climb up the tree until I could get the noose over the cub and lower it to the ground. It sounded like a good plan at the time being that I was a good climber and had handled animals a lot larger and meaner than a fifteen-pound cub. This tree was huge; I could not reach halfway around it, and there was not a limb on it for the first fifty feet. I had learned to climb as a small boy to get away from my older sister, Mary, who would have killed me if she caught me, so I saw no problem with this tree. I took my flat hat off and dropped it at the base of the tree, slung the rope over my shoulder, and headed up the tree. There must have been a three hundred cameras clicking all at once, and a crowd of five hundred visitors, so the pressure was on.

Everything went according to plan at first. I made it to the first limb with no problem, got my noose ready, and headed on up the tree for the cub, which was only a couple of limbs above me. I got close enough to reach the cub with the noose, but as I tried to slip the noose up over him, he let out with a squall, pissed all over me, and climbed a little higher. A cheer went up in the crowd as if the cub had scored the winning touchdown in the Super Bowl. My buddies were falling all over themselves laughing and yelling encouragement while remaining a safe distance from the piss.

My sporting blood was on the rise, and I made up my mind that I was going to get that cub if it killed me. I wiped the piss from my eyes and headed for the cub again. The cub and I repeated the scene several times with the same results, and each time, the cheer would get louder. Finally, the cub began to run out of piss and tree. We must have been one hundred feet or more above the forest floor in the very top few feet of the tree. The cub was agitated by me trying to get the rope over him, the tree was swaying back and forth, and my buddies and the crowd of visitors were yelling encouragement to the cub, "Piss on him again." The cub finally made a run at me, sunk his claws into me, and climbed right over me until he was below me.

From this point on, things went better. I just kept pushing the cub down the tree until it got into the range of the tranquilizer gun. Bob Gross popped him with a dart, and the cub dropped from the tree onto the ground a few minutes later. We put the cub in the same trap with its mom, and everyone was happy, except the visitors. I guess they felt that the bears should be left on the side of the road so they could see, feed, and run over them as they wanted. As for me and my date, I could not get the smell of bear piss washed off enough to risk going on a date, so I called Sweet Sue and broke our date. I don't think she believed me when I told her what happened, for I was never able to get her to go out with me again.

I was a local legend for a short while. Many of the visitors at the scene of the bear capture brought their Bear Warning brochures up to me for an autograph. The story circulated throughout the park for years—for all I know, it may still be circulating. I was reminded of the incident every time it would rain and my hat would get wet. My hat that I had laid at the base of the tree got as wet as I did. The smell never came out of it, even after I sent it off to have it professionally cleaned. It smelled good enough until it got damp. I would catch visitors wrinkling up their noses after a few seconds when they would come up to me for help. I eventually had to buy a new hat for front country use and retire that one for backcountry use. Even then the flat hat cost over $100, being John B. Stetson XXX Beaver.

I was amazed at the stupidity of the general public that visited Yellowstone when it came to the wildlife. How well-educated, intelligent people could go so brain-dead at the sight of an elk, moose, buffalo, or bear on the side of the road was not only amazing but contagious. The bigger the traffic jam got, the dumber they got. The fact that there were not hundreds of people killed by the wildlife each year was due to the tremendous tolerance of the wildlife, not to the caution of the visitors. When I first arrived in Yellowstone and I would get caught in one of these traffic jams in my own vehicle and not in uniform, I would often get out and just listen to the conversations of the people. The women tended to have better sense than their husbands and would try to keep their family at a safe distance. The men, on the other hand, would say things like "if they were dangerous, the park rangers wouldn't leave them by the road," and off they would go right up to the animal.

On many occasions, I would have to go out to retrieve the body of some mutilated visitor. One such incident involved a bull buffalo that weighed well over a ton and was lying down in a meadow about three hundred yards off the side of the road in Hayden Valley. Most of the buffalo spend the middle of the season in the timber during the day to escape the insects, so seeing one just lying there drew a large crowd. Most of the people stayed at the edge of the road, but a dozen or so foolish souls walked the three hundred yards out to the buffalo and completely surrounded it from only a few feet away. The buffalo just lay there and appeared to ignore their presence. Well, I guess the picture of a buffalo lying down was not impressive enough for the fools, so one member of the group snuck up behind the buffalo and kicked it in the ass to get it up. The buffalo got up all right, and the race was on—three hundred yards across an open meadow. It was reported to me by an observer that the buffalo hit one of the men like a freight train and that the man must have been thrown twenty feet in the air. The buffalo then ambled on off across the meadow into the timber.

I recovered the victim's body and transported it to the hospital in Cody. He must have had almost every bone in his body broken because he was difficult to load and keep on the stretcher. The following day in red letter headlines, like war had been declared or something, on the front page of the *Billings Gazette* was the headline "KILLER BUFFALO STILL ROAMS YELLOWSTONE'S WILDERNESS." The entire article, though fairly accurate in content, was so slanted in its presentation that even I began to think that this buffalo was sneaking up on visitors like an Indian in the dark.

My roommate that first year was a totally worthless screwup named Miles. He was the most helpless person I had ever encountered. He was a congressional appointment, which means that his congressman had recommended him for the job. His family lived in Chevy Chase, and his father was some hotshot lawyer in D.C. Miles had been so sheltered and pampered that he could not do even the simplest tasks like laundry or cooking. I don't think he could even fix a sandwich right.

He was also the most nonassertive person I had ever dealt with, which is not a good trait in law enforcement. I hated to work with him because every violator that he encountered would just run over him, and he would call me for help. By the time I would get there, the violator would have the feeling that they would just run over me or Dan as they had the last ranger. Dan, who rarely said anything derogatory about anyone, would just say, "It should be an interesting night. I am working with Miles," and it usually was.

I remember one time when Dan was working the same evening shift that Miles was. Miles had found a horse running loose down the road leading to South Entrance. The horse would not let Miles lead him up to the patrol car where Miles could use the radio, so Miles asked a visitor to hold the horse for him. Miles walked a short distance to his patrol car and then heard the sound of yelling as the visitor ran the horse into the forest, ran back to his car, and took off. Things like that happened only to Miles and always happened to Miles.

One night while working alone on the 5:00 p.m.–2:00 a.m. shift, I received a call from the dispatcher that the manager of the Hamilton Store at West Thumb had reported that he had heard noises in the store after the store had been closed for a couple of hours. The manager lived up above the store and kept a pretty close eye on things, so I was pretty sure there was something to the report. This was during the back-to-nature, living-off-the land, hippie movement, which usually meant smoke all the dope you could, do no work, and beg or steal anything you could. I half-suspected that some stoned hippie was involved before I even got to the store.

I got the keys from the manager and entered through the back of the store, working my way behind the lunch counter. Just as I was easing by the ice machine, using all my stalking skills, the ice machine dumped a load of ice. In the quiet darkness, it sounded like a dump truck had dumped a load of rock. I almost shot that damn ice machine before even thinking about it. I just froze and waited until my eyes had adjusted to the darkness. Vietnam had taught me well about night operations, and out of the corner of my eye, which is what you use to detect motion in the dark, I saw a movement to my left in the back of the store. If you look directly at an object in the dark, it always seems to be moving. I eased along on a path that should put me ahead of the suspect on the far side of the store near the front door where I would have a better element of surprise. The suspect still did not act as if he was aware that I was in the store and was making no effort to conceal his movement or noise. The only thing that worried me was that I could tell that he was a lot bigger than my 5¢ 10² 145 pounds.

As he approached the front of the store, I yelled for him to freeze where he was and identified myself as a park ranger. I was in the shadows near the front door, so I was still sure that he did not know exactly where I was. The suspect made a run for the front door at the same instant that I stepped from the shadows to confront him. Seeing him come charging directly at me startled me for just a second. I managed to get hold of him, and using his own momentum, I kind of body-rolled him into the big heavy front doors hard enough to break the latch that was holding them closed. The suspect started trying to get up, but I strongly encouraged him to stay where he was. I had just finished cuffing him when the cavalry arrived from everywhere. Upon looking around the outside of the building, I found a grocery sack filled with about $30,000 worth of Indian jewelry. The suspect was a stoned hippie in his early twenties and had been hanging around in the park for a good part of the season.

At the end of the season, just before Labor Day, the park was already beginning to slow down. Camp grounds were not filling as they had been. Starting about the second week of June, the campgrounds were always full; as soon as one family pulled out, there was another waiting to pull in. Some of the concession facilities were beginning to cut back on open hours or were closing altogether. All the seasonal personnel were starting to pack their belongings, clean their apartments for final inspection, and make plans for their trip home.

The maintenance crew was also busy preparing the park for the winter season. Snow stakes about twelve to fifteen feet tall were put out, marking the edges of the roads. Apartments were being drained of water, winterized, and locked as they were vacated. It was always a sad time of year for me, having to say good-bye to friends, many of which you may never see again. A lot of the summer help were college students like me, and you knew that most of them would go to something else when they graduated and would not be back.

I was no different than the rest except I was in no hurry to leave, even though my contract ended in just a couple of days. I was in no big hurry to leave since I had about three weeks before my school started. I was going to stay with Marv a couple of weeks; he was going to take some vacation, and we were going to do some hiking into the backcountry of Yellowstone. Both of us were new in the park that year and had gotten to see very little of the backcountry during the busy summer season.

Once again, my good luck came through for me. Dale Nuss called me in for an end-of-season evaluation, or that is what I thought it was for, but when I got there, he offered me an extended contract through the first of November. He needed to fill two backcountry positions for the fall. One of them, the Thorofare Ranger job, had been occupied by

Dave and Mary Phillips. Dave and I had talked about the Thorofare area when I was working with him. I knew it was during the hunting season that Wyoming held in the wilderness area surrounding the park, and it was all done by horseback. The primary duty was to patrol the park boundary and prevent hunters from entering the park. The other job that I was offered was the Shoshone Lake Ranger position. Shoshone Lake is a backcountry lake that is very popular in the fall for lake trout fishing. The main duty there was to monitor and assist the fisherman. Canoeing was the main means of travel for this position, and I had a considerable amount of whitewater experience on the Mulberry River back home, but no lake canoeing experience.

I did not have to think about it but a second. I knew that the Thorofare Ranger position was considered to be the best duty assignment in the entire Park Service, not just in Yellowstone, and thanks to Dave Phillips, who recommended me again, it was mine for the taking. Shoshone Lake was also a very good position and not nearly so isolated, being only a few miles from the road to South Entrance. Thorofare, on the other hand, was in one of the most isolated positions in all the lower forty-eight states. It was thirty-two miles from the nearest road, and that was the East Entrance road going toward Cody, Wyoming. I would have to go in by myself for the entire two-month period, taking all the supplies and personal gear I would need on the backs of three pack mules. It was an adventure made in heaven. I would have to delay my schooling for another semester, and snow would be ass-deep before I came out, but I didn't worry about the small details. I jumped at the offer.

I would be working for another sub-district ranger, Gerald E. Mernin or Jerry as he was called. Jerry was a ranger's ranger and a legend in the Park Service even at his young age. Jerry was about thirty years old at this time, a bachelor, a graduate of Harvard Business School, and one of the most interesting characters I have been privileged to know. I have worked for a variety of fanatics, eccentrics, and demanding people, but Mernin was the toughest. The standard of performance that he demanded of his employees was nowhere nearly as tough as those standards he set for himself. He analyzed every incident, no matter how insignificant it might seem to the rest of us. When we first met, I could tell that he was analyzing my every behavior and what I was saying. It made me uncomfortable at first, but I soon learned this was the way he approached everyone and everything. Jerry didn't miss much that went on around him because he paid attention to every detail. I learned a lot in the years I worked for him and was constantly amazed by him.

He helped me gather what supplies I would need and make a list of things I needed to buy in town, mainly cold weather gear. I took a couple of days and went into Bozeman, Montana, for supplies. Bozeman was a real nice college town, a little larger than the other towns around, so they had a much better selection of goods.

When I got back to the park, Jerry spent about an hour instructing me in the fine art of packing a mule. He showed me how to throw a box hitch and a diamond hitch. These were the main hitches I would use for most of my packing. I spent about a half a day practicing until I had them down pat. The next day, Jerry and I took saddle horses and five pack mules into the backcountry to bring one of our fire lookouts out for the season.

We went up onto Pelican Cone, an old extinct volcanic mountain that overlooked the entire central part of the park. It was snowing hard when we left the trailhead headed up the valley. It was a wet heavy snow much like we have at home, the kind that will soak you in a matter of minutes. It was a long, wet, miserable day, but I loved it just the same. While we were up on the Cone, the weather cleared just a little, well enough that I had a good view of the entire area.

By sunup the next morning, I was already at the trailhead with my horses and mules saddled and packed. Mernin gave me a handful of fifteen-minute topographic maps, a compass, and pointed me down the trail with instructions that my main objective was for me and my stock to survive, and my secondary objective was to keep hunters out of the park. At first, I thought he was just joking, but after a while in the backcountry, I began to realize just how much of my effort was involved with just taking care of me and the stock.

It was a bright, clear, beautiful morning. There had been a heavy frost early, but it began to burn off quickly after sunrise. I had twenty miles to cover that day, due south along the east side of Yellowstone Lake. For the most part, the trail stayed out of sight of the lake in the timber, so it was not one of the more scenic routes; but to me, it was enough to be off on a great adventure on such a beautiful day. The horse I was riding, Brownie, was the best horse I could have had for this type of work. For one thing, we were about the same age, both of us in our twenties; luckily, Brownie had more sense than I did and had been used by the Thorofare Ranger for a couple of decades. He knew where every camp, trail, shortcut, and hazard was. He was slow but as sure-footed as a mountain goat and could maintain his two miles an hour pace, no matter how steep the trail got. He would just keep plodding along, even in whiteout conditions. Just give him his head and hang on; he would get you through. He was the last of the fouls out of the big percheron stud that Yellowstone had for many years. They bred their own mountain horses like Brownie, for they were the best suited for hard use in mountainous country.

The trip along the east side of the lake was uneventful, and after a while, it got pretty monotonous just riding through the timber hour after hour. There were only a couple of short stretches that you could see the lake at all, just south of the Park Point Patrol Cabin and just north of Beaver Dam Creek. It was after sundown when I finally arrived at the Cabin Creek Patrol Cabin, twenty miles from where I had started that morning. I had pushed Brownie hard all day, not that it did any good to push Brownie, but it still took from can to can't to cover the twenty miles. Not being used to setting a saddle all day, I was so stiff and sore I could hardly straighten up or walk when I finally dismounted. After unsaddling and feeding the horses, I went into the cabin to see what I could find for supper.

Cabin Creek Cabin, like most of the patrol cabins in the park, was built by the Army in the early years of the park history when the army had control of the park. The National Park Service did not come into existence until around 1920 or so. The cabin was very typical of all the cabins in the park. It was about 10¢ ′ 12¢, made of log, with an overhanging roof on the front of the cabin. There were a small window and a door on the front of the cabin and a larger window at the rear. The windows were covered with strongly built shutters to prevent bear from breaking into the cabin.

The interior of the cabin was dark and smelled strongly of smoke and horse feed. There was a wood cookstove in the front corner and a wood heater setting beside it. Mounted on the wall were a food pantry and a cabinet containing a set of China dishes that contained the QMD label (Quarter Master Department), a remnant of the Army days. This pantry was made of heavy material and covered with sheet metal to keep out rodents and such. Only dry goods were kept in this cabinet;

anything that could freeze was kept in a food cache under the floor. There were four folding Army cots against the wall with the mattresses and bedding folded neatly over a pole that hung from the center log at the peak of the roof. It was the same in every cabin in the district. The flannel sheet blankets folded lengthways twice went over the pole first, nice and neatly, then the wool Army blankets folded like the sheet blankets went neatly over the sheet blankets. The ends of the bedding had to form a nice neat V where the bottoms of the blankets all met. The mattress would go over the top of the bedding with a pillow on top of the mattress. The mattress and bedding for each cot was folded separately so if you were by yourself, you only had to get down one set of bedding.

The conditions of the stoves were even more important to Mernin than anything else. Both stoves had to be cleaned of ashes and coals before leaving the cabin, and the makings for another fire had to be left in the fire box with three matches lying on top of the stove. The makings had to be left in such a manner that the fire would start with only one match. The extra two matches were just in case you dropped one or one broke. It became a matter of pride to be able to leave a fire laid that could be started with just one match.

Before the end of that first season, I had figured out what Mernin expected, or more appropriately, what he demanded regarding the condition of the cabins. I had not encountered any superior in the Corps that was more demanding than Mernin, but damn, I loved to work for him, and I could tell if things were up to standards as soon as he opened the door of the cabin, he would kind of "hmm" softly and say, "You're not all bad." If the cabin was not up to standards, he would swear softly under his breath but say nothing at the time. Later, usually during dinner, he would point out the infraction and relate a story that happened to some rangers on a winter ski trip.

According to Mernin, three rangers had left the cabin one morning on their way to another cabin where they were going to spend the night. They had gone but a short distance when they had to cross over the river on the ice. While crossing, the ice gave way and one ranger fell into the water. A second ranger tried to rescue him, but he too fell through. The third ranger lay down on the ice and tried to rescue his companions and got soaked in the process. The first two rangers died in only a few minutes, so the one remaining ranger skied back to the cabin that they had just left earlier. The weather was typical Yellowstone winter weather with the temperature well below zero. By the time the ranger got to the cabin, he was suffering from severe hypothermia. He struggled but was finally able to get the door open and light the fire. He survived to tell the story and said that if the fire had not lit with the first, he did not think he would have been able to have struck the second match. I don't know if the story is true or not, but it makes a good story anyway, and I never knew Mernin to lie; but then he was just repeating what had been told to him.

Cabin Creek Cabin was located at the junction of the Thorofare Trail with the trail that headed west toward Heart Lake. The cabin was set up in the trees a short distance on a bench above the surrounding marsh area. I always loved to walk down to the marshy area at dusk with a cup of coffee and my pipe and listen to and watch the wildlife that abounded in the area. The bull elk would be bugling all over the valley, Sand Hill Cranes squawking with their unusual sound, and ducks and geese quacking and honking by the thousands. There is no place like Yellowstone at dusk. I never got tired of listening to the evening as the light faded in the west. I would check my stock that was on a picket line a short distance away, or at least Brownie would be on picket and Punkin would be running loose with just a bell on him.

I was up before daylight the next morning because Punkin, as I was to find out, always would come up to the cabin before daylight ringing that damn bell continually until I got up and lit the lantern. I got a fire going, put water on to boil for coffee, and headed out to feed the stock. It was always a little unnerving to go get the stock at this time of morning, never knowing when you would run into a Grizzly or black bear. By the time I returned to the cabin, the water would be hot enough to brew a pot of coffee and make breakfast, usually pancakes and bacon. Very seldom did I have eggs since I had to ration what eggs I brought with me so they would last two months.

After breakfast was finished and the dishes were done, I would clean out the stoves and scatter the ashes where they could not be seen and let the stoves cool down. Next, I would saddle my horse, then saddle and pack the mules. The last thing was always to fill the lantern, lay a new fire, double-check everything about the cabin, close the shutters, and lock up. By early sunup, I was headed down the trail toward Thorofare.

From Cabin Creek, I was headed up the Yellowstone River valley. The Yellowstone above the lake was much smaller than it was below the lake. It runs through a broad flat valley of meadows broken by patches of timber and marshy areas. In the early spring and summer, the valley would be flooded from side to side, and a haven for mosquitoes, buffalo gnats, and black flies. It was almost impossible to go into that area until late summer and fall. The first year I was in the area was an average year. The valley was mostly dry, so you could ride most anywhere, and Brownie knew where you should not go. I really learned to listen to his good sense. He was not one of those horses that resisted just because he did not want to do; if he did not want to go, there was a good reason.

That first trip up the Yellowstone was inspirational. I felt as though I had stepped back in time. The country I was riding through was as untouched by man as it had been since the beginning of time, and I was living as a part of that history. The valley was nestled between high mountains and plateaus on both sides. In places, the valley was at least two or three miles across, and mile after mile of the twelve mile trip up the valley, I rode through several herds of elk, so undisturbed by my presence that they just casually watched as I rode by. There were eagle and osprey flying most anywhere I looked and nests in almost every large dead tree. Moose were in almost every marshy area. I was truly riding through paradise.

As it began to get on to late afternoon, I got my first view of Thorofare Ranger Station setting in a small meadow at the base of a towering cliff that was bathed in the light of a sun that had already set on the valley floor, causing the sheer cliff to radiate with alpenglow. A perfect end to a perfect day.

The Ranger Station was larger than the patrol cabins. It was a two-room cabin with a larger covered front porch that was enclosed on three sides. Thorofare also had a log barn and corral back in the trees just out of sight. The inside logs of the cabin were covered with tongue and groove planks painted white, making the cabin much lighter than the patrol cabins. I eventually found out that the reason for the planks covering the walls was to cover the signs of a fire that had nearly destroyed the cabin many years earlier. The Ranger Station also had more windows, which let in more light. There was a real nice wood cookstove in the kitchen and a big wood heater in the back room, which served as sleeping quarters.

The barn was also made of logs and had a small loft in it. I never really used the barn for housing the stock but mainly to store their grain, and I did have a few bales of hay dropped to me from a slurry plane that I kept in the loft. Mostly, it served as a place to store tools and such. I did not even keep my saddles in the barn because of a terrible mouse and chipmunk problem. I was afraid that they would chew up the cinch or straps on a saddle. I chose instead to keep all my tack on the front porch where there was a pole mounted that you could sling several saddles over. Panniers, mannies, and lash ropes I just stacked up or hung from a nail.

There was a small spring-fed stream a short distance from the cabin where I got my water and an outdoor toilet just out of sight in the tree. The cabin was well stocked with food, firewood, and Coleman fuel for the lanterns. There was also a well-stocked library that contained about every western novel and Playboy magazine ever written. There were also old-time and *Look* magazines from back in the 1930s and 1940s. It was great to read about WWII as if it was happening today.

I got settled in pretty quickly after taking care of the stock and supper. Afterward, I poured myself a cup of coffee, lit my pipe, and went outside, where I leaned on the hitching rail in front of the cabin to enjoy the wilderness as dusk faded to dark. After finishing my pipe, I would walk out to where my stock was picketed to check on them and then go to bed with one of the many westerns and read for a while. I would not usually read too long before I got sleepy, even though it was still early. I had to get up so early every day, long before daylight, on most mornings since it took so long to get everything taken care of before I even started to patrol the boundary.

That first morning of patrol, I did not get on the trail early since I had no idea where to go. I spent a good bit of the morning studying my maps of the area so I could become familiar with the location of the outfitter camps. The area surrounding the park was all designated wilderness, as was Yellowstone, which meant that no motorized vehicles or equipment was allowed. You either had to hike or ride a horse into the area. No chain saws or generators were allowed in any of the hunt camps. The Forest Service had control of the area surrounding the park, which was designated as the Bridger Teton Wilderness Area. All of this area covered an area many times larger than Yellowstone and was referred to as the Yellowstone ecosystem, which included most everything from Jackson, Wyoming, in the south, nearly to Livingston, Montana, in the south and from Cody, Wyoming, in the east, to West Yellowstone, Montana, on the west side of the park.

While studying the map that morning, I noticed a small lake just outside the south boundary of the park with trails that converged from all directions.

The name Thorofare, I assume, came from this situation. There was the trail that I had traveled on coming from the north that continued on south for another thirty-plus miles. There was also a trail coming in from the east, in the direction of Cody, more than forty miles away. From the west were two different trails coming in, both of them ran parallel to the south boundary of the park, one just a short distance inside the park, and one a short distance outside the park, but in different drainages. All these trails converged around Bridger Lake; it truly was the Thorofare for that whole part of Wyoming.

I headed south from the station and crossed Thorofare Creek, which was as large as the Yellowstone River at this point. The ford on the Thorofare was fairly shallow at this time of year, but earlier in the season, I am sure it was very difficult. Shortly after crossing the creek, I located the south boundary of the park extending east and west in a straight line across the valley. In less than a quarter of a mile, I came to the west end of the lake. I was right out in the middle of the valley by now and could get a good view of the entire area. It was spectacular; I could see for twenty miles or more back up into the park from the direction I had been traveling for three days. I could see Coulter Peak, near Cabin Creek, and even though it had to be more than fifteen miles away, it looked as if it was just barely out of my reach. I got my first good look of the Trident Plateau, which was where my Ranger Station was located. As its name implies, the Trident had three very prominent arms that stuck out into the valley. Thorofare Ranger Station was located at the base of the middle arm. All three arms were sheer rock cliffs from the valley floor to the flat treeless plateau on top.

Looking to the east on up Thorofare Creek, I could see about another ten to fifteen miles to mountains making up the Absorka Mountains, where the trail went out over Dear Creek Pass, or out over Fish Hawk Pass. I had the feeling a man could ride these trails forever and not see it all. I made myself a vow that I would somehow ride all of it that I could, even though it was far outside the park and my patrol area, and as my luck would have it, I did eventually get to ride most of it.

Looking toward the southeast up the Yellowstone, the mountains continued to rim rock the area at about ten or fifteen miles. Separating the two drainages, the Thorofare and the Yellowstone, was this high mountain that extended all the way from the mountains to the east nearly all the way to Bridger Lake, ending with a prominent mountain of sheer cliffs that extended far out into the valley. This peak was known as Hawks Rest, and located at its base was a cabin belonging to the U.S. Forest Service that was unoccupied most of the time. The Forest Service seemed to monitor the backcountry operation very little. Hawks Rest Patrol Cabin was in a beautiful location and a good location to monitor all the movement around the lake and up and down the valley.

Looking on around to the south and west, the mountains were near at hand, a distance of just a couple of miles. The entire ridgeline was made up of Two Ocean Plateau, a high plateau about one hundred feet above the valley floor. It was not a treeless plateau like the Trident but was a mixture of trees and meadow. Its name comes from the fact that up on the top of the plateau, directly on the continental divide, there is a small stream running off the plateau from the north and another one from the south into a marshy basin and spreads out. Eventually, the water flows out of this basin in two different directions; the part that flows to the east is called Atlantic Creek because its water eventually runs into the Yellowstone, which runs into the Missouri River, then into the Mississippi, and then to the Gulf of Mexico. The water that flows from the west side of the basin is called Pacific Creek, and it eventually ends up in the Snake River, which is a tributary of the Colombia River that flows into the Pacific Ocean.

There were several steep valleys coming down off the plateau; so with established trails and others with just game trails. My description of the valley is not very good and probably confusing, but just take my word for it; the Thorofare Valley is one of the most beautiful places on Earth. What would be better is if you could go see it for yourself.

That first morning of patrol, I located a camp of resident hunters at the west end of Bridger Lake that had come into the valley from the Atlantic Creek trailhead, which was about thirty-two miles to the south. One of them had a moose permit, but the rest were after elk. Most of the hunters with moose permits liked to come to Bridger Lake, which was prime moose habitat. Most of the hunters managed to kill a moose without leaving camp; they would just wake up about daylight, look toward the lake, and find their moose. Not much sport if you ask me, but to each his own.

I visited with these hunters for a short while and inquired about any other camps they might have seen. They had only seen one other camp a mile or so up the Thorofare, right at the ford. I rode on around the south side of the lake just checking everything out and then headed on up the Thorofare looking for this other camp.

I rode by Hawks Rest on my way and stopped to see if there was anyone at the cabin. There was no sign of any recent activity around the cabin. There was no stock in the coral, and judging from the lack of horse manure, I doubt if there had been anyone there that season. It was a good location for a cabin but didn't have the shine of my cabin.

I located the camp at the upper ford on the Thorofare easy enough but visited for just a few minutes as they were in a process of breaking camp. They had been fishing for a couple of weeks but were on their way out since hunting season had started and none of them held hunting licenses. They acted pretty nervous while talking to me, even though I had no direct jurisdiction in the forest outside of Yellowstone. In fact, being a federal officer, I did have jurisdiction on any federal land, but it was one of those things that lawyers would make such a big issue of in court that we rarely used our authority outside of Yellowstone.

Only one of the fishermen was a resident; the others were all nonresidents from different places. I checked all of their fishing permits, and everything seemed in order, but I knew they were acting suspicious. I recorded their names and permit numbers so I could check with Wyoming Game & Fish concerning them. I got to thinking later that the one resident was probably acting as their outfitter and guide without an outfitter and guide license. When I radioed in that night, I relayed the information to Mernin, who checked with Game & Fish. They agreed with my conclusion, but without any evidence of an exchange of money, nothing could be proven.

It was beginning to get late in the afternoon when I left the fishermen, so I decided to start working my way back toward home. I took a left fork in the trail, which according to my map would take me back toward the cabin. Shortly after the fork, I came across a cabin belonging to Wyoming Game & Fish setting just a few feet outside the boundary of the park. Again, there was no sign that the cabin had been occupied that season. I saw fresh horse tracks coming down the trail that cut off into the timber near the cabin. After following the tracks a short distance, I located a guide with two hunters that were just starting to set in for their evening hunt. They were going to be watching a narrow finger meadow that came running out of the park. They were hunting so close to the boundary that if the animal fell the wrong way, it would be back inside the park. The guide was from a hunt camp about three or four miles up the Yellowstone around the far side of Hawks Rest. I made a mental note to follow this meadow up into the park as soon as I could to check for any sign of horse activity in the park. I also planned to locate their camp tomorrow just to let them know I was in the area and be neighborly. I did not want to interfere with their hunting, so I continued on the trail for a short distance before I picked up the boundary and worked my way back to the cabin.

The next morning, I worked my way along the boundary west of the ranger station, to the confluence of the Yellowstone River and Thorofare Creek. There was a deep hole of water at the confluence, just teaming with large trout; I knew where I was going to come to supplement my food ration. I rode west to the far side of the valley where I located the trail coming down Lynx Creek from Two Ocean Plateau. I followed the trail to Bridger Lake and on up the Yellowstone around Hawks Rest until I located the outfitter camp.

It was an impressive sight. There must have been fifty to sixty head of horses and mules grazing in and around the immediate area of the camp. The camp was located where a spring ran from the base of Hawks Rest onto the valley floor and continued on to the Yellowstone River. There were about a dozen or so large wall tents pitched back in the timber and a large cook tent composed of two large wall tents lashed together end to end, pitched in front of them. On back in the timber, I could see a corral and a tent used to store tack. I didn't see any sign of human activity except for smoke from the chimney of the cook tent, but I could smell fresh baked cookies. I helloed the camp but stayed in the saddle until a man came out of the cook tent and invited me to get down and have a cup of coffee. As I learned much later from another outfitter, it was considered rude if you dismounted before being asked to by the camp. It just seemed to be the right thing to do at the time.

The camp belonged to a L. D. and Ted Frome, from Afton, Wyoming. As it turned out, I had started with the best. The camp was run by a no-nonsense Mormon named Monte Harmon. The cook was his younger sister, Ilene, and her husband, Bruce, was one of the guides. They employed several other guides, assistant cooks, wranglers, and camp jacks, but Monte, Ilene, and Bruce were the ones that set the tone for the camp and kept everything running smoothly. There was no booze in this camp, unless the hunter kept it in his tent, and none of the usual loafing that went on in a lot of the camps. The dudes were hunted, leaving camp around 5:30 a.m. or so, depending on how far they had to ride to get to where they were going to make their morning hunt, laying out all day until the evening hunt, and returning to camp an hour or more after dark. By the time they got cleaned up and ate dinner, they did not feel like doing anything but going to bed because they knew that they would be up by 4:30 in the morning.

Frome always brought their dudes in via Atlantic Creek, thirty-two miles from the trailhead to their Hawks Rest Camp, and they traveled it in one day. Several times, I met them coming in with dudes; the dudes were pleading with them to let them get off and walk, but Monte would just tell them to stay in the saddle. "We're almost there." I guess eight or ten miles is almost there when you have already covered twenty or more.

Frome had another camp thirty miles on up country on a side fork of the Thorofare. I have forgotten the exact location as I was only at this camp one time. This camp was too far from the boundary for them to hunt it, so I had no reason to visit this camp other than curiosity. The poor hunters that were going to this camp would spend the night at the Hawks Rest Camp, and then ride the twenty-eight or thirty miles to their Upper Camp the next day.

On any given day, Frome would have at least one hundred head of stock in the mountains. Every day, they would have ten hunters in each camp and a guide for two hunters. They would have a string of pack animals going from each camp headed to the trailhead loaded with meat and another pack string going from the trailhead to the two camps with supplies.

Over the years, I developed a lot of respect for the Frome camps, even though I had never met the man that owned the operation. The only problem I had with them was that they would shoot the elk as soon as they stepped out of the park, and unless it was an animal that died instantly, it would get back into the park. Bruce would come by the cabin if I was in the area, and I would go with them to trail it down. If there was a good blood trail showing, it had been shot outside the park. I finally had to make them leave a couple of elk lie to get them to back up from the boundary a little.

I would usually visit their camp once during each ten-day hunt, and I had an uncanny knack for always showing up on cookie baking day, or at least that is what Ilene always said. Ilene was by far the best cook in the mountains since most of the other camps had a cook that had been a guide for many years but was too old to do anything else. They sure could tell some great stories though.

To the Frome camp, all of this country was their personal hunting domain, and all of the other outfitter camps and resident hunt camps were encroaching on their territory. They kept me posted on everything the other camps did along that fifteen-mile stretch of boundary that they hunted. Of course, they never did anything wrong and hunted strictly by the books. They were either very good or very honest; I don't know which, but I never was able to find any indication of any violations where the park was concerned. The only violation that I was aware that they were making had to do with the number of livestock they were allowed to have in the mountains at any one time. Forest Service regulations limited them to maximum of fifty head, and when the forest rangers would check their camp during the day, they were easily within the legal limit, but at night when all the guides, hunters, and pack strings were in camp, they would have more than double what they were allowed. I don't know if the Forest Service just turned their head or what, but they were never charged.

The next day, I rode the boundary east from the station to the southeast corner of the park, or at least what little of it I could ride since most of it ran along the sheer slope on the south side of the Trident. I did locate another outfitter camp on the Thorofare, just south of the corner of the park. As I rode up, it was evident that this was a different kind of camp than Frome's.

This camp was owned by an old outlaw named Speigleberg. One look and you could tell that this was an outfit to watch. As I rode into camp that first time, I rode really slowly, which was fine with Brownie and Punkin, who were traveling along behind just free reining along. The setup was about the same, except everything was poorly kept and was shabby. Every horse I saw was in rather poor condition, and all of them had saddle and cinch sores. A tale was told on Speedy, as he was called, that a hunter once asked him what he put on the sores on the horses' backs, and Speedy replied, "Saddles, man, saddles." To catch his horses, his wranglers had to drive them up this box canyon at the base of the Trident, where he had a brush coral constructed.

Speedy's camp was a lot smaller than Frome's with not as many hunters, but they usually were very successful and usually got some really nice heads, which made me pretty suspicious of them since most of the big bulls tended to stay just inside the park until the weather really got bad. One of the big contrasts that really emphasized the difference was the cook tent. Both were similar in that there was a big long table down the middle of the tent. In the Frome camp, in the middle of the table for its entire length, it was covered with food stuff, breads, jelly, butter, peanut butter, cookies, you name it, and it was there. In Speedy's camp, the table was the same except there was no food; it was covered with every kind of booze imaginable. I was never in that camp when it did not seem that they were at least half-drunk. If it was a good time I was after, and I was not as concerned with killing an elk, I would choose Speedy. There was always some kind of bullshit going.

One of Speedy's guides, R.B. Wallace, was one of the funniest characters I have ever had the fortune to meet. R.B. was a part-time painter, a part-time guide, and a full-time drunk and outlaw. He was from Cody, Wyoming, as were Speedy and the rest of the outfit. I always enjoyed visiting with R.B., but I knew he was taking animals out of the park; I was never able to catch him at it. I got close a couple of times, but that was all. I stumbled onto a gut pile that was still steaming in a small meadow near the Game and Fish cabin one morning and followed the horse tracks until they picked up the trail and I could no longer distinguish the tracks, but it was headed in the direction of Speedy's camp, which was the only camp in the immediate area. I rode into their camp, but there was no meat hanging on the rack. R.B. was in camp and had blood on his hands, even though Speedy had said that they had not killed anything yet. I went back to the gut pile and searched around for additional sign but found nothing. I had not heard a shot that morning, so I was surprised when I found the gut pile. A couple of years later, one of Frome's guides found a 30-06 with a scope and silencer behind a log at the edge of that meadow. It was just the first of many encounters that I would have with that camp over the next ten years.

After three or four days' patrolling in the Thorofare area, I packed up a few supplies and headed across the valley to Lynx Creek where the South Boundary trail headed to Fox Creek patrol cabin on Two Ocean Plateau. The trail up Lynx Creek was steep and narrow, much different than the trails down around the lake, but then it got much less horse traffic. It was about fourteen miles to Fox Creek, with about a 1,500 foot gain in elevation in the first four or five miles. After you got up on the plateau, it was just kind of rolling topography of open alpine tundra in the exposed areas and trees in the sheltered areas. Two Ocean Plateau was a beautiful area but was very fragile and very hard to patrol. The likelihood of ever stumbling across a poacher was much less than being mauled by a Grizzly. This was some of the best Grizzly habitat in the park, and most of our problem bear were sent to Two Ocean because of it and the fact that it was one of the most isolated areas in the park.

There was an outfitter just a few miles south of the park that I feel was just as dishonest as Speedy, but there the comparison ended. The Turners had a dude ranch in Grand Teton National Park, Triangle X. The matriarch, Burche, I never met, but I heard she was a tough old hide. There were three brothers; John was a state senator and a very polished, smooth-talking politician. I can't recall the names of the other two brothers, but one of them was fairly cordial to me, and the other one was downright rude. I don't think it was me personally that they resented but the fact that I was Park Service. A part of their ranch had been taken by eminent domain when Grand Teton National Park was created, and they had an intense dislike of anyone or anything Park Service. The fact that the remaining part of the ranch was a virtual gold mine after the creation of the park was overlooked by them.

I would usually ride by their camp each hunt, just to let them know I was around, but I seldom dismounted for a visit. I was always polite and professional but never friendly. The Turners were very well connected politically and impressed with their status, so I always had to be careful when dealing with them.

The plateau was such a large area and hard to monitor because of being comprised of grassy areas surrounded by trees. The conditions on the plateau were much harsher than down below, so a good bit of the area was alpine tundra or sub-alpine tundra at the best. Any damage to the turf would take many decades to repair, which meant that any horse tracks in the area would take decades to recover. It was hard to tell which tracks were old and which were new. I tried to stay out of the area as much as possible because of its fragile nature, but because of the proximity of the Triangle-X camp on Mink Creek and the high incidence of horse tracks in the park, I spent a lot more time there than any other area.

Sorry, I lost the trail for a while and wandered around on the plateau. The trail continued west across the plateau and by a beautiful little alpine lake, Meriposa Lake, which was just loaded with trout. I don't really know how because the lake was so small you could ride a horse most of the way across it. As harsh as the winters were, I would think it would almost freeze solid.

Another mile or so past Mariposa Lake, the trail coming up onto the plateau from the southeast arm of Yellowstone Lake joined the South Boundary Trail from the north. Fox Creek Patrol Cabin was just another mile or so past that junction. Located on the far west side of a small, high mountain meadow, which are called parks, Fox Creek Cabin was almost identical to Cabin Creek, except the front door and window were reversed for each cabin. Fox Creek Cabin also had a small corral located behind it, which Cabin Creek did not have. I only spent about half of the nights on the plateau in the cabin, the rest of the time I tried to pick an area of plateau that I wanted to patrol and pitch a tent for a couple nights. It would normally have been great camping, but to lessen the environmental impact, and to try to stay hidden, I would usually make a cold camp off in the timber somewhere.

Farther to the west of Cabin Creek, the trail went up over Big Game Ridge on its way to Harebell Patrol Cabin, fourteen miles away. Harebell was not part of my patrol area, but Big Game Ridge was. Big Game Ridge went on up above Two Ocean Plateau at least another one thousand feet or more. It was above tree line, true alpine tundra, and wind-blown, cold, and miserable. I would have hated to have ridden up there but for one thing—the view was spectacular. Off to the southwest, The Teton Mountains, which are the most impressive mountains in the lower forty-eight states, are eye to eye with you at about a distance of twenty miles. To the south, the Wind River Mountains are clearly visible. To the east lie the Absorka Mountains. I could see mountain ranges in all directions, many of which had to be over one hundred miles in distance. I would stay up on top as long as I could just looking around. Then just before I froze to death, I would head back down.

There was one hunt camp located on Wolverine Creek at the base of Big Game Ridge on its southwest side. To get to this camp by trail, I had to ride south from Fox Park and all the way around Big Game Ridge, a distance of at least five or six miles. I could cut that distance in half by going over the ridge, but it was a horse killer. I would usually go over the ridge on my way to the camp but take the trail back.

The camp was owned by Ted Adams, an older man who had been riding the mountains as a packer, hunter, guide, and outfitter for decades. During the summer months, he bases his operation out of Flagg Ranch, just a few miles south of the South Entrance of Yellowstone. From there, he gave trail rides, packed fishing trips into the backcountry, and chuck wagon trips that included an authentic cowboy meal prepared over a campfire in Dutch ovens.

The first time I met Ted, my reception was not much warmer than it was with the Turner brothers at the Triangle X camp, but as we talked, he began to become more cordial. He eventually asked me to get down and have a cup of coffee. I quickly learned that in Ted's camp, a cup of coffee was only half coffee, the other half was Ancient Age whiskey. I have been in his camp on real warm days when Ted did not even bother with the half that was coffee, and he used those metal coffee cups that hold about a half pint of liquid.

On one occasion several years later, I was in Ted's camp with one of my bosses that had just transferred into Yellowstone, named Oakley Blair. Mernin had sent him in to ride with me for week or so to help him with his horsemanship, packing, and backcountry skills, as by this time, I was a good packer and horseman. It was an unusually warm day, hunting was poor, and everyone was just lying around the camp when we entered. Ted invited us to get down and have a cup, except this time, it was straight whiskey, and I don't mean just a shot. Like I said, each cup would hold about a half a pint. We were there for about an hour, so I kind of nursed mine along, but Oak, who was not much of a drinker anyway, drank his as quickly as Ted drank his. He and Ted had a second cup, but I had to finish a good bit of Oak's for him. I decided we had better leave while Oak was still able to get into the saddle, but I had to keep a close eye on him all the way back to Fox Creek for fear that he would fall from the saddle. I had taken time to tie his reins around his saddle horn so he did not have to keep up with them; all he had to do was hang on. It was on this trip that Oak stuck me with the nickname "Mad Dog," a name that stayed with me for the remainder of my years in the park. On a couple of occasions, I would have a visitor ask me if I was "The Mad Dog Ranger."

I guess I lost the trail again. Anyway, Ted and I got along well, and I never found any indication that he encroached on the park. Quite often in the summer, I would stop and see him while on my way to or from Jackson, and as usual, I would have to have a drink with him, and it had to be Ancient Age. He had a theory that Ancient Age could be drunk without any ill effects. It seemed to work for Ted because you could never tell he had a drink, but I'll bet Oak Blair would argue the point with him though.

On one of my patrols on the plateau, I came through a patch of timber and was on the edge of a small meadow when I saw a Grizzly, weighing about 250 pounds. It was a blustery day with the wind blowing from the bear toward me, so it did not wind me. The bear was busy hunting mice or some small rodent of some kind. The bear would pounce on the mouse like a cat with both of its front feet. The ground was so soft that the bear was just pushing the mouse into the dirt. The bear would get its nose right down next to its feet, open its feet to catch the mouse with its mouth, but the mouse would take off running between the bear's legs before the bear could grasp it with its mouth. The bear would spin around in an instant and trap the mouse again. I watched this bear and mouse routine for several minutes before the mouse finally escaped from the bear, and at that instant, the bear just went totally insane. It slashed around at the air with its front feet and claws, bit its rear leg, and then attacked a small pine tree about head high. By the time the bear got through with this poor little tree, the tree was little more than a pile of kindling. As soon as the bear had finished taking out its anger on the tree, it turned and walked away as calmly as if nothing had happened.

I had another bear encounter while camped up on the plateau, but this time, it was with a young black bear. It was almost dark, and I was just finishing supper that I had prepared on a small backpack stove that ran on white gas. I don't know if it was the smell of the gas or the food that attracted the bear, but I saw him coming from a pretty good distance. He was moving toward my camp at the edge of the timber sniffing his way along. Brownie was on picket close by, but Punkin was running free, and I do mean running because as soon as Punkin became aware of the bear, he came charging back to Brownie at a dead run. He stood behind Brownie peering in the direction of the bear and would flare his nostrils and snort like only a mule can snort. Punkin's antics were what made me notice the bear in the first place. I learned that this was always Punkin's reaction to the presence of an unwanted animal, be it bear, moose, or a strange horse.

I don't think the young bear had ever encountered a human before because it appeared to be more curious than anything. It would stand up on its hind leg to get a better look, and then drop down on all fours, and move a little closer. Punkin would snort loudly, and the bear would retreat. This went on for over an hour or more, but the bear never got much closer. Punkin finally settled down some time after dark; I assumed the bear was gone, so I crawled into my two-man backpack tent for the night. I slept poorly that night because of recurring bear dreams. Shortly before first light, I was awakened by a weight bearing down on me. My first thought was that the damn bear was lying on me, but when I rolled over in my sleeping bag, the weight slid off. By this time, I was awake enough to realize that the weight I was feeling was snow that had fallen during the night that had mashed the tent down on me. My movement had caused the snow to slide off the side of the tent.

We had received about ten inches of snow during the night, which made the world look like a post card wonderland. The elk and deer were everywhere, moving down from the higher elevation toward the lower valleys. At times like this, I did not worry about poaching problems as much because there were elk everywhere outside the park.

After a few days of patrol out of Fox Creek, I would usually return to Thorofare via the Mink Creek Trail, which passed by the Forest Ranger cabin at Fox Park. On only one occasion did I ever encounter a ranger at Fox Park. Just east of Fox Park, the trail went through an old fire scar of several thousand acres that had burned in the 50s, I believe. Farther east, the trail climbed to Phelps Pass and continued down Falcon Creek on the far side. Just before dropping all the way to the valley floor, I would have a good view of the entire valley below. It was always a great sight and a great feeling sort of like returning home after an extended absence. I would usually swing around the Bridger Lake on my way to the cabin just to see if any resident camps had moved in while I was gone.

The next day, I would usually spend along the boundary in the area around the Game & Fish cabin, trying to keep an eye on Speedy and R.B., and then on the following day, I would pack up Punkin again and head to Eagle Pass. To get to Eagle Pass, I had to travel back down the Yellowstone, up into the Park about six miles, and then go up Mountain Creek for six or eight more.

We did not have a cabin in this area during my first four or five seasons, so I had to camp again. We had an outfitter-type wall tent that I would take with me on the first hunt, September 10 to September 20. I would find a secluded meadow a mile or so below the pass away from the trail and pitch camp. I would leave the camp pitched most of the season but would pull it before the snow got too deep, which was usually around the second week of October.

This trail was the only trail that hunters were allowed to travel on through the park. There was a trailhead on the East Entrance road, about five miles from the East Entrance toward Cody, Wyoming. If I remember correctly, it was about fifteen miles up Eagle Creek to the Eagle Pass, where the trail entered the park. Once the hunters entered the park, they must travel straight through, without stopping to camp until they had left the park at Thorofare. Their guns must be unloaded at all times while in the park, and they were required to check through the Ranger Station, going and coming. If I was not there, they were to register on a form posted by the front door.

The entire trip from the trailhead to Bridger Lake was well over thirty-six miles, with an elevation gain of about four thousand feet. There was a small meadow about ten miles in from the trailhead called Eagle Creek Meadows, where most resident hunters would camp for the night rather than attempt to cover it all in one day. There was an old abandoned gold mine at Eagle Creek Meadows that still contained a lot of heavy machines, which made me wonder how they got all that stuff up to the mine. The trail from the trailhead to the Meadows was steep and narrow all the way; there had never been a road into the area, and many of the pieces of equipment would weigh nearly a ton or more. I guess the mine had been abandoned early in the 1900s. Those old-timers could always find a way.

From the Meadows to the Pass, the trail really got steep, winding, and narrow. In many places, the trail was all but obscured from view because it would travel over bare, steeply-sloping rock for a good distance. Thank goodness Brownie knew the way, and where other horses would be nervous and skittish, old Brownie would be just the same as if he were walking on a flat trail down in the valley. God, I would have loved to have ridden Brownie when he was in his prime.

Once you cleared the pass on the Yellowstone side, the country was not nearly as rough. For one thing, the entire Yellowstone Plateau was a much higher elevation at the trailhead, so you did not have to go down nearly as far as what you had come up. It was just a gradual descent down Howell Creek to Mountain Creek and down to the Yellowstone River.

There was only one outfitter in the area, all the way up to the head of Mountain Creek, about a mile east of the eastern boundary of the park. The camp belonged to the Crossed Saber Lodge, located on the East Entrance road toward Cody. Dode Hershey was the owner at that time, but the Lodge changed several times over the years. Crossed Sabers was the only commercial outfitter that traveled through the park on a regular basis, but quite often, some of them would take a moose hunter to Bridger Lake. Dode actually was only in the park for a couple of miles. Not far below the pass, they would cut off from the main trail, on a trail that that headed east up a steep side hill into a small, high valley that covered not much more than a few thousand acres. It was a beautiful area, surrounded on three sides by high mountains with the west side opening into Yellowstone down Mountain Creek. This was the best Grizzly hunting camp anywhere around. They were always having bear trouble in their camp. The largest Grizzly I saw during all my years in the park had been killed by one of their hunters. It was a big bear that weighed 650 pounds. I was headed to their camp one morning when I noticed a bunch of magpies and ravens fighting over something at the edge of the small meadow I was riding through. I rode over to see what they were fighting over, and at first sight, I thought it was the body of a very fat man but quickly realized it was the carcass of a bear. When I arrived at the camp, they had the hide stretched out on the ground fleshing it out; it looked as big as a quilt for a king-size bed.

The old cook in Dode's camp had been in the mountains for decades and was a great storyteller, so I always enjoyed my trips to the Crossed Saber Camp. I have forgotten the old man's name, but not his face or tales. His face was what you would expect to find on an old mountain man, wrinkled, scarred, tanned like leather, unshaven, but eyes that sparkled when he talked of the old days. I could just listen to him for hours.

He told of the time he was sleeping in the cook tent when a large Grizzly stuck its head through the tent flap right by his head. Jake, which was his name, said he gently raised the flap of his sleeping bag and peered eye to eye with the bear that was only a foot or so away. I asked him what he did, and Jake replied that he just gently closed the flap of the sleeping bag right back over his head. Luckily, one of the dogs in camp chased the bear from camp before there was any damage.

One of the later owners of the Crossed Sabers showed me an old article from *Outdoor Life* that told the story of a bear mauling a hunting guide just outside of Yellowstone; the guide was Jake. I don't remember the entire three or four page article, but the bear had been wounded by the hunter, and Jake was trailing him out when the bear ambushed him. The repeated mauling and struggle went on for a long time until the bear was finally killed by the hunter. It was one of the worst mauling tales I had ever heard, and I had worked several mauling incidents and heard of many more, but by far, Jake's mauling was the worst I had heard. This was one tale that he never told me.

The location of the Crossed Sabers Camp was one of my favorites. They were always the only camp in that entire area, the scenery was spectacular, the hunting and fishing were good. What else could a man want?

From their camp, I would usually ride on down Mountain Creek to the boundary, patrol along it until it got too rugged and steep, and then return to camp. Of the three areas I patrolled, I would usually spend less time here than the other two areas. There were several reasons. One was that there was no cabin to use as a base, which meant that I had to pack everything that I needed for me and the stock, and more time and effort was required to take care of day-to-day housekeeping matters such as cooking and cleaning up afterward. Another reason was that the area did not have nearly as much hunting pressure, and I never found any indication that the outfitter encroached into the park.

On one occasion, I was riding along the boundary through the timber when I heard what sounded like a helicopter hovering as if to land. It was a blustery day with wind coming from different directions, so I could not get a fix on its location, and being in thick timber, I could not see anything. In a few minutes, the chopper took off and was gone without me ever seeing or locating it. I checked the entire area for hours but never found a thing. When I radioed in that night, I asked if the park chopper had been in that area, but at that time of year, the park does not even have a chopper under contract. Later that year, a special agent with the Bureau of Sport Fisheries and Wildlife announced that they had arrested a guide and hunter for poaching elk from an Indian reservation in Montana and bighorn sheep from Yellowstone National Park. Not many details were given except that they used helicopters to locate the animals, then either dropped off the hunter and guide or shot the animal from the chopper, drop off the guide, who would take just the head, and get picked up a few minutes later. I guess it was a big business for the outfitter, who would take pictures of the animals and then send out brochures to wealthy clients. That area of Eagle Pass would have been ideal for such an operation, very isolated and a good-sized population of bighorn sheep.

The hunter, an heir to the Procter& Gamble estate, was fined $90,000 and given a nine-year jail sentence because it was his second offense, while the guide was fined $40,000 and sentenced to four years. The outfitter, I think the name was Standish, lost his outfitter's license, but I have forgotten the other punishment. Fish and Wildlife had been working the case for several years and finally got an agent on the inside.

This was the way most of my fall was spent; I would ride hard for ten days while the hunt was on then take one day to rest my stock, get a bath and a change of clothes, do my laundry, bake bread and cinnamon rolls, and rest up before the next hunt started. Of course, if there were resident hunters in the area, I still had to keep an eye on them.

Usually once during each season, I would have to go up to the lake for grain for my stock. I usually tried to take care of this before the first hunt when I still had all my pack animals, but sometimes, I did not get it done before, so I would be forced to do it between hunts. That first year was such a year. I would ride down the Yellowstone River almost to Cabin Creek Cabin, where I would take the trail around the south end of the southeast arm of the lake to Trail Creek Patrol Cabin. Trail Creek Cabin was located on the lakeshore, so it was accessible by boat. Even though it was located in that portion of the lake that was designated as a hand-propelled zone, the Park Service would send a boat in loaded with grain. Trail Creek also had a barn and small corral for stock. The cabin had been built much later than the others and was quite a bit larger. Besides being in a beautiful location overlooking the lake with a great view of Coulter Peak, Trail Creek Cabin was well known for its mouse infestation.

Being accessible by boat made Trail Creek one of the most popular cabins among park employees during the summer months. Supplies needed in the entire Thorofare sub-district were always brought to Trail Creek for distribution to the different cabins. I spent a lot of time packing supplies out of Trail Creek.

Over the years, I packed wood shingles the seventeen miles to Thorofare Ranger Station to re-roof the barn. The bundles of shingles were so large that I could not pack them in panniers; I had to wrap four bundles together in mannies (a type of canvas tarp) and lash one of these large bundles on each side of a pack animal with a barrel hitch. These loads were much heavier and bulkier than what the animals were used to carrying that for the first few miles. They skinned the bark from any tree that was close to the trail. But before we got to the ford across the Yellowstone, they had figured things out, and from there on, we made good time.

On another occasion, I had to pack a wood cookstove seventeen miles from Trail Creek to Fox Creek. The fire box on the old stove was burned out from burning coal at some time in the past. During that summer, I had been assigned the task of finding new cookstoves to replace three stoves that were burned. At that time, no one was making new wood cookstoves, so I had to drive around outside the park to all the antique shops. I finally located three in a shop over in Idaho. The one that was taken to Thorofare Ranger Station was real fancy with a lot of chrome, two warming ovens above the stove top, and a water reservoir on the end of the oven. The old stove at Thorofare was a good stove, so it was taken to another cabin by chopper when the new stove was flown in.

To get to Fox Creek from Trail Creek, I would take the trail toward Heart Lake, but before I even got to the south arm of Yellowstone Lake, the Two Ocean Plateau Trail diverged and headed south up Chipmunk Creek. The trail went through an old burn of several thousand acres just before it started to make its climb up the north side of the plateau. The view from the north side of the plateau was great. Yellowstone Lake stretched out in front of you in its entirety, and the Lake Hotel was easily visible along its north shore. I could never pass on that trail without stopping to admire the view from the plateau. Even Brownie would not try to graze while we were at the overlook but would just look out across the landscape as if he were taking in the scenery. The trail up Chipmunk Creek continued on south across the plateau until it joined the South Boundary Trail between Mariposa Lake and Fox Creek cabin. It passed by a couple of small alpine lakes not as big as Mariposa, near which I camped on several occasions while patrolling the plateau.

Most of that first fall was spent just learning the country and the people running the camps. I averaged riding between fifteen and twenty miles a day, rain or shine, except it was usually snow or shine. By the middle of October, the weather was getting to where it was cold and snowy most of the time. The slopes and side hills were so hard frozen that I had to quit riding a lot of the areas I had been riding; even Brownie couldn't keep his feet under him. He would go down with me a half a dozen times a day, so I had to be ready at any instant to get my feet clear of my stirrups.

Most of the hunt camps had already been pulled or were in the process of being pulled, mainly because they all had high passes that they had to scale, and enough of the elk had left the park that hunting was good down in the lower country. I was about the only human left in the mountains for about forty miles in any direction. When I would think about it, I would get kind of lonely. The snow was starting to get deep in the high country like Fox Creek and Eagle Pass. Some years, it was stirrup deep, and one year, I could not even get to Fox Creek after the middle of October.

One of my last duties of the year was to pack winter rations into all the cabins in the sub-district so they would be available for the winter ski trips that the rangers had to take each month. The rations would be brought across the lake by boat and stored in the Trail Creek cabin. Most years, Mernin would ride in to Trail Creek with extra stock, and he and I would spend the last ten days or so going to each cabin with supplies and give the cabin a good cleaning, making sure that the snowmelt pans were clean and that there was a good supply of wood. We would load everything on three or four mules and ride to one of the cabins the first day, spend the next day cleaning the cabin, and on the third day, we would return to Trail Creek.

We would repeat this until all the cabins had been stocked. Thorofare Ranger Station often required two trips with supplies and two days to clean. The last cabin to usually get supplied was Cabin Creek Cabin, which we would usually stock on our way out of the backcountry going from Trail Creek Cabin to the trailhead at Ten Mile Post, a distance of twenty miles. That first year, Mernin stayed at Cabin Creek for the night so he could clean the cabin and get supplies put away, while I just headed on to Ten Mile Post.

The snow along the lake was only about a foot or so deep, but the temperature was in the lower 20s, too damn cold to be riding a horse. I would have to get off and walk occasionally to get the circulation back into my feet. Old Brownie seemed to be particularly slow that day, which put us to the trailhead just before dark. The stock truck was waiting for us, and I had no trouble getting Brownie to load, but Punkin was being a typical mule; there was no way he was going to let me lead him up that ramp. After about ten minutes of cussing, kicking, and threatening to kill him, Punkin decided he was ready to load and just took off up the ramp, leaving me standing on the ground.

The park had been officially closed for over a week, but the roads were still passable, though snow-packed. The next day, I turned in all my gear and checked out with Dale Nuss at the district office, which was in the process of being moved to Mammoth Hot Springs (Park HQ) for the winter. Marv had invited me to have dinner with him and spend the night.

It was a typical dinner with Marv; we had drinks until about 10 p. m., when Marv would take a couple of frozen steaks out of the freezer and put them on the grill on the back deck. The outside temperature was about 0°, snow about sixteen inches deep and snowing moderately, and here we were, standing outside having a drink and protecting the steaks from the pine martens that had already stolen the first two steaks from the grill. Six months earlier, if you would have told me I would be standing outside in that kind of weather having a drink and visiting as if it was a spring day, I would have told you that you were crazy. It was the same in Vietnam during the monsoons; we would be setting in a downpour, soaking wet, as if it was a fine sunny day. It has always amazed me what you could get used to, if you want to.

The next day, Marv and I went into Jackson for a night of civilization, dinner, and partying. Jackson was a great town for such activities, and being off-season, it was just the locals, so Jackson took on a different feel. The summer tourists and hippies were gone; ski season had not opened yet, so it was just the cowboys from the local ranches and the hunters in town. The next morning, I was headed to the southland and college with a pocketful of cash and a world of new stories.

I got home during the first week in November, just in time to go to deer camp with all my buddies. Somewhere along the way, I had lost all interest in hunting. I don't know if it was because of Nam or what, but hunting something that cannot hunt back was not exciting any more. I still love going to deer camp, except now I do my hunting with a skillet instead of a gun.

I went to work with Barber Bridge Builders again but just until school started in January. The winter semester went well; my grades were good, and I had enough money that I didn't have to scrimp and save. The Grober brothers and I went out to eat most evenings, with one night at Weidekehr's restaurant at their winery on top of St. Mary's mountain at Altus. Mostly though, I was just waiting to return to Yellowstone.

I was to report to the park near the end of May, and I had gotten out of school in early May, so I decided to take me a little vacation on the way to Yellowstone. I drove straight through to New Mexico, then up into southern Colorado, turned west over Wolf Creek Pass, through Pagossa Springs, and on to Mesa Verde National Monument. I camped there for the night, looked at all the cliff dwellings the next day, and headed for Moab, Utah, and Arches National Monument. After spending the night in Moab, I saw most of the archers that were in a short walking distance.

After spending another night, I was off for the Four Corners, through Monument Valley, by Glenn Canyon, to the north rim of the Grand Canyon. I had been to the south rim when I was returning to Arkansas after having been discharged from the Corps, but the north rim was a lot different, higher, more timbered, colder, and not nearly as crowded. I spent a few days there hiking and camping before heading on. I really like that Four Corners, Moab, and canyon country, and had hoped to get to spend more time there at a later date.

My next stop was Bryce Canyon National Park, which really I just drove through, then on to Zion National Park. I stayed a couple of days there hiking before heading out again.

After leaving Zion, I took to the back roads headed in the general direction of Salt Lake City. An old man in a bar at Zion had told me about the road, which sounded better to me than the interstate, and it was a spectacular trip through unbelievably beautiful country, mountains, and canyons. How Utah can be so beautiful and desolate at the same time has always amazed me, and little did I know that before many years passed, Utah would figure very prominently in my future.

I traveled on up to Provo, Salt Lake City, and Logan, a nice college town located in a high mountain valley. From there, I went up into Wyoming, through Afton, where I stopped to see Monte Harmon, then on into Jackson for the night. Around midmorning, I checked in with Dale Nuss at the District Office. I had been assigned to Grant Village again for the summer, which was fine with me, as Grant was a lot quieter than the Lake Fishing Bridge area.

That summer, I was housed in the Campground Ranger Station with Steve Clement, a ranger naturalist, who in the winter was a graduate student at UC Davis. He was working on his masters in Entomology, working with solitary bees, and doing his fieldwork in Yellowstone during the summer. He was also a Vietnam Veteran army officer, a platoon commander under Tommy Franks I believe.

The Campground Ranger Station was not the best place in the park to live; visitors came to the door at all times of the day and night. They did not know that the station was not manned at all and that it was just a residence. The only good thing about it was that we could entertain friends of the opposite sex without causing any comments. The Park Service was still pretty strict about what went on in government housing, or at least Dale was pretty strict.

We pretty well had the same crew as the year before except for Miles McGrail. He was not recommended for rehire. Marv was his usual easygoing self, so the summer went smoothly and quickly. It seemed as if one day, you would be asking each other how their winter went, and then the next day, you would be asking them what their last day would be and what their plans were for the coming winter. I worked with such a great bunch of people that it was always sad to see the end of the summer season, as I would be about the only seasonal ranger left in the park.

On the first of September, I headed for Thorofare, anxious for the first hunt that always started on the 10th. A fire guard, Bob Jackson, went in with me to help haul grain to all my cabins and make needed repairs to the pasture fence at Thorofare. Bob Jackson was from Fort

Dodge, Iowa, and had led a sheltered life until he entered college, discovered sex, and was trying to make up for lost time. I nicknamed him Action Jackson because of his many exploits with the ladies or exploits that he wanted to have, which he talked about continually. I liked to get him started, and all I would have to do was bring up some woman's name, any woman's name, and he would spend hours discussing their various attributes and then relate various fantasies about them. It helped pass the long hours on the trail.

We left the trailhead just after sunrise on a beautiful, frosty, and sunny morning headed all the way to Thorofare that day. I was riding a different horse that year; Brownie had wintered poorly, so he was just turned out into the pasture and used only lightly after that. My new horse was actually bought for the district ranger, Dale Nuss, but Dale never went into the backcountry except by boat. The horse, Apple, was a green broke Appaloosa and was very skittish and had poor night vision. I could see better at night than he could, and on bright sunny days, when the ground was covered with snow, he would get so snow-blind that he would trip and stumble. I used to take soot from the stove and darken around his eyes, like a ball player to help his snow blindness.

Action Jackson had stayed out all night with one of his lady friends and had not slept a wink. I had taken Peggy Henning, one of the secretaries from our Ranger Station, to Jackson for the evening. She was leaving the next day for school in California. Peggy and I had become good friends over the course of the summer. She was not planning on returning to the park the next summer, so we knew that we would probably never meet again. We had a nice dinner, danced until the Cowboy Bar closed at 2:00 a.m., had breakfast at The Elk Horn Café, and drove back to the park in time for me to load my gear and stock.

Bob and I made it all right until the sun came out and it warmed up. The next thing I knew, I woke up with a jerk, just before I fell from the saddle. I looked around, and Bob was asleep also, leaning precariously to one side. Both of our horses had their heads down grazing, and our five pack mules were scattered and grazing all around us. We decided that we had better trot a while to make up time and keep us awake. It was a long, painful thirty-two miles to Thorofare, but neither of us seemed to learn a damn thing as we repeated the same thing the next year.

Bob and I rode hard, hauling grain to all my cabins, repaired the pasture fence, and bailed the water out of the food cache beneath the floor in the Ranger Station. There had been heavy snow the past winter, so the whole valley was flooded most of the summer. All the fords were higher than usual, and the ground was so wet and boggy that you had to be careful where you rode. While Bob and I were coming in that first day, Punkin swung off the trail to avoid a puddle. Punkin didn't like to get his feet wet, but the ground was so boggy that he started to sink down into the mud, and the harder he fought, the deeper he went down. Finally, Punkin was all the way down on his belly in the mud, and he stopped fighting. I had to cut my lash rope and unpack him to get him out. I was afraid I was not going to be able to get him out and that I would have to shoot him. I would have hated to shoot Punkin, even though I had threatened it many times. I was finally able to get enough brush under him, and with both Bob and I using our horses to pull, we were finally able to free him from the mud.

By the first hunt, Bob had taken all the extra pack animals and had returned to his duties at Lake. I kept Apple and Punkin with me for the remainder of the season. Punkin was taking up with Apple pretty well, but they never formed the tight bond that he and Brownie had.

Apple and I were beginning to understand each other a little more, but every lesson he learned was the hard way. I learned that he had to be handled calmly and gently, for if you started to be impatient and rough with him, he would be skittish of it always. I learned this the hard way. On the way into Thorofare that first day, Apple shied at a rock formation by the side of the trail. He and I fought over it, and I made him walk up to the formation after a small rodeo. Six years later, Apple would shy at that same formation every time we went by it. Had I not made a big deal about making him go up to it, he would have stopped paying any attention to it after a few trips.

One of the worst times we had was the first time I had to put on my slicker. With Brownie, I would not even get off to put on my slicker. I would reach behind my saddle and untie it, unroll it, and pull it on while moving on down the trail. Apple was a little different though; I had to be very careful if I even moved in the saddle, or it would startle him. If I even tried to reach into my saddle bags, he would spook, and since I kept my pipe and tobacco in my saddle bags, I was constantly getting into them.

The first time I had to put my slicker on, I already knew that I had better dismount to do it. I untied the slicker from the saddle, shook it out, put it on, and turned to get mounted. I guess I should mention that the slicker was bright yellow and long enough to drag the ground. It was just a typical riding slicker that was split in half below the butt. When I started toward Apple, you would have thought that I was the devil himself. I was afraid he was going to break his reins, trying to get away from me. It was a good thing I was very agile in those days because the only way I was able to get on was by grabbing hold of the horn and slinging a leg over, but this really set him off. We bucked, jumped, farted, and rodeoed all over the meadow for what seemed like forever. He lost his footing and fell a couple of times, but I was able to get my legs free each time and stay on him as he jumped back up. Eventually he began to settle down a little, mainly because he had fought so hard he was wringing wet with sweat and worn out. Every time after that, it got a little better, and over the years, it got to where I could put it on without dismounting. But I could tell that he was ready to explode at any instance.

In spite of his decencies, Apple turned out to be a good horse, but I guess when you put nearly twenty miles a day on a horse, it tends to make them better. He was sure-footed as a cat, and it was a good thing since many of the foot bridges that we had to cross were made of logs with the topside flattened. Four logs were laid side by side to make the bridge, but most were so old that at least one or more of the logs had rotted away in several places. When I would head across one of these bridges, Apple would not even slow down or hesitate.

He was also very good at following game trails through the timber. I would just give him his head and be ready to duck. There were many days that we were never on the established trail but working along a steep side hill through the timber. He was so quick that when he would slip down, he would catch himself and jump back up before I was even able to get my feet clear. He was also able to follow the same path coming out that he had taken going in. In real steep sections of the boundary, I would ride as far as I could, dismount, and continue on foot. I would just leave him grazing there until I returned; sometimes, I would be gone for several hours.

One of his best attributes was that he was a people horse, and I was his person. I did not have to worry about him leaving me stranded in the mountains. When I would get to the cabin at night, I would just unsaddle, feed him, and turn him loose. Before daylight the next morning, he would be standing at the cabin door waiting to be fed. It was a lot better than having to picket him at night because he could graze in the timber where the grass stayed green longer. Unlike Brownie, he was a fast walker, and if pushed, he could walk seven miles an hour, but four miles an hour was his normal gait.

One year, I was running low on grain, and the ice at the lower end of the southeast arm of the lake where Trail Creek was located was already iced in so they could not get the supply in to Trail Creek. Instead I was to meet the boat at Beaver Dam Creek, on the west side of the arm. I left Thorofare at first light with all the stock, headed for Beaver Dam Creek, which is four miles north of Cabin Creek, making it sixteen miles from Thorofare. I pushed hard all morning, making good time until I arrived at Beaver Dam Creek. The wind had come up, and the boat was unable to beach. There was a sheltered cove several miles further north that the boat should be able to put in at. The only problem was that the trail was a long way from the shore up the side of a hill. I could not get my stock down to the shore, so I had to carry the sacks of grain up the hill to the trail. By the time I got my animals packed and headed back to Thorofare, it was well after noon. I pulled into Thorofare before sundown after having covered a little over forty miles. The mules were worn out, but Apple was good for another forty if needed.

I had become concerned that Speigleberg might be hunting the Trident Plateau after one of his hunters took an elk with seven points on each side, and that is as large as they normally come. About the only place you found bulls that large was inside the park, and they didn't normally come out of the park until very late in the season, if at all. I could see no obvious way to get on top of the Trident, but while reading one of the log books at the Ranger Station, I read an entry by the Thorofare ranger from the 1940s telling of how he was able to get to the top of the Trident by going up Cliff Creek. Cliff Creek was the stream that separated the northern tooth from the middle tooth; trident means three teeth.

I waited for what looked like it was going to be a nice day in terms of the weather and headed up Cliff Creek on a game trail. I just gave Apple his head and hung on as he picked his way through the standing timber, downed logs, and boulders. It took up about three hours from the time we left the cabin to reach the last steep pitch before the top. I had to dismount from the horse at this point and walk the rest of the way. I wrapped my reins around the saddle horn, and Apple and Punkin just followed me up the slope. The slope was a treacherous talus slope of small rock that slid down slope as you tried to climb. I had to traverse across the slope, steadily climbing all the while. Apple would wait until I had gotten a distance ahead of him then come charging to catch up.

It took another hour to get up to where the land started to flatten enough to remount. A cold, invigorating wind was blowing about 25 or 30 mph on top. I rode up the little rill that was Cliff Creek at this elevation and headed for the broad flat top. The broad flat top that I expected to find was narrow at this point and not very flat but more of a gentle roll. As I rode the short distance to the north side of the plateau where I could look off into the Mountain Creek drainage, I startled three large bighorn rams that were lying just beneath the crest on the edge of a sheer cliff that dropped a couple of thousand feet. The rams just baled over the side of the cliff without looking or hesitation. I thought I had killed them all, but as I watched them free-fall down the cliff, occasionally they would hit a ledge, but always landing on their feet before falling on down to the next outcrop of rock. It took only a few seconds before all three of the rams reached the bottom and ran into the timber. I believe it was one of the most impressive displays I have ever witnessed in all my years of dealing with wildlife.

I rode on southeast down to the main part of the plateau looking for any sign of the east boundary of the park but found none. I was riding along looking at my topo map of the area and the ground features when I noticed a couple of riders coming toward me from the east side of the plateau. The two riders stopped when they saw me and had a brief conversation before continuing toward me. Would you believe it? It was my old buddy R.B. from Speedy's camp. It was the only time I had ever found R.B. with little to say. All he said was, "We are not in the park, are we?" I think he knew he was, but I didn't and had no way to tell where the boundary was. All I could say was, "Hell if I know, but I am sure we are close." We visited briefly before parting ways; they headed east from the direction they had come while I continued on down the plateau looking for any evidence of the boundary.

I had already decided that the next time I met someone up here, I would know where the boundary was located. I eventually found a rock kern with a log sticking out of it that had a rusty, weathered boundary sign attached, but that one sign was all that was evident. I did see a couple of other stacks of rocks that could have been stacked by someone, but they could just as easily be naturally occurring. I was only able to stay on the plateau for a couple of hours before having to head back to the cabin.

When I checked in that night, I told Mernin what I had found or hadn't found. We laid plans for marking the boundary that included Action Jackson and another fireguard, Terry Small, coming in with a staff compass. The three of us would have to camp just below the summit in a small meadow that had a little grass and water for the stock.

If I was going to get it marked that year, it would need to be done in the immediate future, for the weather would not hold forever. I had already located the southeast corner of the park on the south slope of the Trident almost due north of Speedy's camp. Bob and Terry came in a day or two later, and we got right to it, but after only one day of work, most of which involved getting up on the plateau, the weather made a turn for the worse. The snow eventually made us break camp and return to Thorofare before we had even gotten a good start at marking, but at least, I had something for reference when I did get to return to the plateau. For several years after that, every time I would ride the plateau, I would put up a few markers. I eventually was able to find my way off the east side of the plateau, but it was a hard day's ride from the Ranger Station up Cliff Creek, across the plateau, down that drainage on the east side (I have forgotten its name), and then ride all the way around the south side of the plateau to the Ranger Station again.

One of the main problems with doing what needed to be done in Thorofare was safety, not only my safety but the safety of my stock also. I depended on my stock so much that we were truly a team, and anything that affected them affected me. Punkin was not shod, so every time I had to ride down a creek bed for an extended distance, he would get sore-footed and be lame for a few days. When this happened, I would not be able to cover as much area as I needed to. Much of the off-trail patrolling was in steep, hazardous terrain that was hard frozen most of the fall; then there were streams to ford of varying depths, widths, and swiftness. Many fords would be covered with ice so thick that a horse could get out on it without breaking, but when Punkin was dragged out on the ice, and I do mean dragged, the ice would break through.

I was most always alone with no communication to the outside world except a park radio at the cabin. In those days, a radio that had any range at all was too large to carry on your person, so the radio stayed in the cabin. There were only two stations in the park, Lake Ranger Station and Park HQ at Mammoth Hot Springs, that could monitor me even weakly. My radio was not powerful enough to trigger the repeater on Mt. Washburn, so my signal was very weak.

I had to check in with Mernin at Lake each evening at 7:00 to report anything important and to let him know where I would be riding the next day. If I did not check in of an evening, they would try to contact me at 7:00 the next morning, and if there was still no contact with me, they would start a search based on my last report. For years, Mernin was always there when I checked in each night, but after about six or seven years, Mernin was forced to transfer to another area of the park and a new sub-district ranger took over at Lake. I was constantly having trouble getting through to anyone, so I decided one evening after trying unsuccessfully to check in that I would see how long it would take before anyone missed me. Three days later, Terry Small had come back from his days off and was catching up on reading the log entries at Lake, which we were required to do each day, when he noticed that there were no entries for me having radioed in. After checking with the new sub-district ranger, he started trying to contact me. I had already left the cabin for the day, so it was that evening before we made contact. I knew after that, I was on my own and that if I were injured, I would probably die before I could be rescued. I tended to be much more cautious than I used to be.

The second season I stocked all the cabins by myself with Fox Creek being the last one taken care of. I decided that instead of having to ride the seventeen miles back to Trail Creek and spend the night there before riding the twenty-five miles to Ten Mile Post, I would just head west on the South Boundary Trail. It was only about fourteen miles over the top of Big Game Ridge to Harebell Cabin, which I had never seen. I could spend the night there and then ride only twelve miles to the Snake River Ranger Station at the South Entrance.

It was an exceptionally clear, calm, sunny day when I headed out that morning, but by the time I reached the top of the Ridge, there was a ground blizzard going on. Everything was indistinguishable in the whiteout, and I had no idea where the trail went. There was a strong wind blowing of at least 40–50 mph, which made it impossible to unfold my topo map, not that I didn't try but it was ripped to pieces instantly. Apple was impatient and wanting to go so, I just gave him his head, figuring at least he would get us down somewhere out of the storm, which he did, and we were right on the trail. That damn horse had followed that trail for a couple of miles across that ridge without ever having been there. As soon as we got down from the top, it was just as beautiful a day as it had been when I left that morning. I turned around in the saddle and looked back at the peak over which I had just come and saw that the blizzard was just at the top of the mountain. I learned a valuable lesson that day about the high country and how dangerous it can be on even a seemingly beautiful day. Apple's worth also went up greatly in my eyes on that day.

When I opened the front door at Harebell Cabin, I began to see what Mernin meant about cabin aesthetics and the need for neatness and order. Harebell was on the same design as Cabin and Fox Creek cabins, but everything seemed so chaotic and untidy. The cabin was stocked the same as the ones in Mernin's sub-district, but there was no apparent arrangement for anything. One major thing that I remember was that the snow-melting pans were not hanging behind the stove as in Mernin's cabins. The snow-melting pans were to be used for snow melting only, since that was where they got their drinking water on ski trips in the winter. At Harebell, the snow-melting pans were hung with the horse tack, where they had been used to feed the stock out of. Mernin would have passed a squealing worm, as my dear sweet mom was fond of saying. After that, I became as finicky as Mernin about the cabins.

The trail from Harebell out was a nice, pleasant ride along the Snake River most of the way. I could not help comparing the size of it there to its size up on Two Ocean Plateau. I forded the Snake at South Entrance in the middle of the afternoon, loaded my stock, hauled them back to lake, took care of their feeding, and checked out at the district office before dark. A couple of hours later, Marv and I were headed to Jackson with a pocketful of money and a gleam in our eyes. It reminds me of a poster I saw one time that showed an old cowboy at the bar with a mug of beer. The caption was "Ninety percent of the money I have made I spent on whiskey and women and the rest I just wasted."

Early the next day, I was headed east from Jackson Hole over Togwotee Pass toward Arkansas. The trip home was pretty uneventful since I pretty well drove straight through except for a few hours I slept in a rest area not far out of Denver. I pulled into the rest area planning on spending the night sleeping in my camper. I brushed my teeth in the restroom then went over to the urinal to relieve myself before crawling into the shell camper on my truck. As I started to relieve myself, I looked down at the partition on my left that separated the toilets from my urinal stall. It had a hole ripped in it that looked as if it had been done with an ax, and staring at my Johnson was this eyeball from the toilet stall. If I had not been so startled, I would have pissed all over him, but as it was, I just zipped up and got out of the restroom. I started to drive on, but I knew it was a long way to anywhere, so I decided to stay anyway. But I did take my pistol out of its holster and hung it on the outside door handle of my camper. I figured that even an idiot on seeing an empty holster hanging on the door would figure out where the pistol was.

Yellowstone had just started opening up for a winter season a year or two earlier, and Marv had been telling me what a different place the park was in the dead of winter, so I decided I would see what it was like. Marv had invited me to come spend a few weeks with him so I could experience the park at its best, as Marv called it.

I flew into Jackson Hole in the middle of a snowstorm on a little twin engine turbo prop operated by Frontier Airlines, a good little airline that went bankrupt sometime in the 1970s, just a few years after I had bought some stock in it. Flying into Jackson Hole was always exciting even on good days, but in bad weather, it was enough to cause you to recite the Lord's Prayer under your breath. There was not even a control tower at the airport; the pilots navigated off an electronic beacon, so I was a bit uneasy as we began to make our final approach. Even though I could see nothing but white as I looked out of the windows, I could tell by the way the pilot was cutting back on power and leveling it out that we were about to land. I looked out and saw a flash of Sage Brush as the pilot set the plane down on the end of the runway as if it had been clear day.

It was about ten to fifteen degrees below zero when Marv picked me up at the airport. We went into Jackson for the night before heading up to the park the next day. Marv had several errands to take care of in town, and being a night person, he was impossible to get out of bed before noon. So it was dark before we got to the parking lot at Flag Ranch, where all the people who were wintered in the park left their vehicles. From this point on, it was snowmobile or skis only. Marv's snowmobile was right where he had left it, but because of the cold, it took a lot of jerking on the rope before it started. We loaded all our gear onto the dogsled behind the snowmobile, and I stood on its rear. Marv and I had a good stiff shot of Blackberry Brandy before heading up the groomed road into the park.

The road was freshly groomed, making it as smooth as glass, so we flew up the Lewis River Canyon at top speed until we had to stop and warm up a little at Lewis River Falls. We had another good shot of brandy before heading out again, and it's a good thing we did. A few miles farther up, we were flying along the east shore of Lewis Lake when it happened. I'm not exactly sure what happened, but the next thing I knew Bill Brumand, a maintenance employee that had been following Marve and me, was asking me if I could move my arm. It was as if he was far away, but as I began to regain my senses, I realized that I was face down in the snow, but trying to get up onto my hands and knee, and my head was throbbing, and my neck was so stiff I could hardly move it.

Bill Brumand had seen the accident, and according to him, the sled had come loose from the snowmobile, letting the tongue drop down into the snow. We were traveling about 50 mph when it happened, and according to Bill, the rear end of the dogsled flew up and began to tumble end over end, sending me sailing through the air a considerable distance before landing on my head. Marv did not even know anything had happened and continued several miles up the road when he realized that Bill's headlights were no longer behind him. At some point, Marve did realize that the dogsled and I were no longer behind him, so he turned around and came looking for us.

By the time Marv returned, I was on my feet, still groggy and stunned, but still in one piece. Bill was checking out the sled that had come to rest in its upright position as if nothing had happened. Everything on the sled had been tarped and bungied down well, so nothing on the sled had been damaged, except me. It was just a good thing that I had a helmet on, or I would most likely have broken my neck; as it was, I suffered with a dull headache for over a month.

I had a great time seeing the park in winter, and I do think it is at its best during this season. There was about six to eight feet of packed snow at South Entrance, about twenty feet in Lewis River canyon, and about four to six feet in the rest of the park, except for Mammoth

Hot Springs, which had about six inches because of its lower elevation and being down below the north slope of the park. The storms come in from the south and west and drop tremendous amounts of snow in these areas. By the time the storms head down the north side, they have given up most of their moisture.

The view from Lake was very impressive, looking across the frozen lake at the snow covered Absorka Mountains, and down the southeast arm toward the Thorofare. Steam rising from the hot springs at Mary Bay with Bison drifting in and out added a surreal impression to the scene. Few snowmobiles reached the east side of the park, preferring to stay on the south loop from Old Faithful, where most of them spend the night, then through West Thumb, Lake, Canyon Village, Norris Junction, Madison Junction, and back into Old Faithful. Most snowmobiles came in through West Yellowstone, but a fair number came in the South Entrance from Flag Ranch. There were also commercial snow coaches carrying passengers, which ran on a daily basis from Flag Ranch to Old Faithful and back, and others that made the loop on a daily basis.

The wildlife that remained in the park during the winter tended to stay around the geyser basins and hot springs for the warmth and to graze on exposed grasses. Bison tended to form large herds in the valleys like Hayden valley. Many of the animals would use the packed, groomed roads to walk on, causing problem with snowmobiles that were also using the road. One winter that I was working in the park, I was headed out on the East Entrance road to Sylvan Pass on a cold, clear morning to shoot down avalanches at the pass, when I came upon a herd of buffalo on the road. I tried to ease around them, but they would just walk a little faster in front of me. Each time I would speed up, they would speed up also. I eventually decided to stop and let them go on when we got up to about 20 or 25 mph. As the herd thundered on up the road, I lost sight of them around a curve in the road. I continued on around the curve and found two people, the chief ranger and the park superintendent, crouching behind their snowmobiles and peeking down the road at me. They stood as I approached and asked I had seen that big herd of buffalo that had come stampeding over the top of them. I lied and said no but that I had seen their tracks in the road.

The Fire Hole and Madison Rivers on the west side of the park remained ice-free all winter due to runoff water from the geyser basins.

Waterfowl of all types wintered in the warm water; geese, Trumpeter Swans, and ducks of all types could always be seen up and down their length. Many elk could also be found grazing on algae mats in the rivers.

Old Faithful was the Mecca for snowmobiles; thousands of them would come through Old Faithful each day. Many would spend the night at the only lodging available in the park during the winter season, the Snow Lodge. The lodge also had a restaurant and bar, which was a good place to spend a winter's evening having drinks and playing cards. It was at the Snow Lodge a few years later that I was to meet the woman that would eventually become my wife and put an end to my Mad Dog Days, but not yet.

Marv and I spent a lot of time at the Snow Lodge or in West Yellowstone at a friend's house. Scotty, Ernest Othello Scott, was another of the real characters I have gotten to know in my life. Originally from the Cookson Hills of Oklahoma, Scotty had been out west working for the Park Service for a long time. He was about twelve to fifteen years older than I was and at least twice as wild. He was one of those intense guys that when he walked into a room, pictures would start to fall from the walls. Everything he did was at full speed and intensity. Damn the torpedoes, full speed ahead! He was as true and loyal a friend as a man could ever have, and we had some great times over the next few years and have remained in contact all these years. He has retired from the Park Service and now has a cabin on the Salmon River in Idaho. We usually visit by phone a couple of times a year, and I hope to go visit him in the near future, but I don't know if my liver can hold up to it anymore.

I guess I stayed with Marv for nearly a month before returning to school in Arkansas again. I had another good school year with the Grober boys but was more than ready for the term to end so I could return to the park.

I returned to the park as usual by some out-of-the-way course that I had not traveled before just to see new country and reported to Nuss at the district office. Dale actually seemed pleased to have me back for another year, and I guess I was glad to see that old fart too. Mernin was still at Lake as sub- district ranger, and Marv was still sub-district ranger at Grant Village. Dale wanted me to work at Lake that summer instead of Grant Village, and he was not someone that you said no to, so I moved into the front quarters of the Lake Ranger Station adjoining the rear quarters where Mernin stayed.

Lake Ranger Station was located on the shore of the Lake and had a great view down southeast arm toward Thorofare. In less than two minutes, I could be trout fishing on Yellowstone Lake or walk to the Hamilton store for coffee. In less than five minutes, I could walk to the Lake Hotel for a drink. I missed Marv and the rest of the guys at Grant, but there was a lot more action at Lake because of the large amount of concession facilities and employees. Most of the concession employees were females between eighteen and twenty-two years of age, and out for a good time. In the Marine Corps, a situation like this was known as a target-rich environment. Single male rangers were in great demand among the concession employees; God, it was great.

I went to working the 5:00 p.m.–2:00 a.m. shift with a Mormon named Jewel R. "Bud" Ross, a music teacher from Salt Lake City. Bud was married with nine kids and had been working at Lake for many years. He was the shift supervisor and tended to be pretty heavy into law enforcement, whereas most rangers preferred to be fairly low-key when it came to writing tickets. Most of us focused on visitor assistance with the least amount of law enforcement as possible. Bud liked confrontations, particularly with hippies, and anyone with long hair was a hippie to him. It was a good thing that Bud was a big guy, 6¢4² or 6¢5² and about 220 pounds, because he was always pushing someone to their limit. In spite of our different philosophies, we worked well together. We used the old "good cop, bad cop" routine real well. Bud would usually make the initial contact with a subject and push him to his limit, and then I would step in and calm them down, always with the threat that I would leave them with Bud.

The Lake area actually consisted of three different areas, Bridge Bay with its marina and large campground; Lake with its small hospital, general store, hotel, lodge, and cabins; and Fish Bridge with a general store, station, visitor center, and two large campgrounds. Add to this the large amount of wild life in the area and things got pretty exciting at times. Lake had the widest variety of things available to do in the entire park. Fishing, boating, and canoeing on the lake were among the most popular.

I used to enjoy going out onto the lake with our boat patrol ranger, Woody Jones, that I had worked with at Grant, and have him drop me and my canoe off in a sheltered bay somewhere. I would fish all day, and he would pick me up in time for me to get to work by 5:00.

There was a considerable amount of bear problems in the area, so I gained a lot of experience over the years of working with Mernin, becoming the bear specialist in the area after Mernin transferred. On one of the first bear hunts I went on with Mernin, we were in the Canyon Village Campground. Canyon had been having bear problems every night, and the sub-district ranger in the area did not feel confident enough in his abilities to handle the problem, so Mernin was volunteered by Nuss, and I was volunteered by Mernin.

Canyon Campground was restricted to hard-sided vehicles only, no tents allowed because of the grizzly problem. The problem stemmed from the Park Service having closed the trash dump just south of Canyon a few miles in Hayden Valley. For decades, the bear had fed on garbage in the trash dumps, so when they were closed, the bear started to forage for something to replace it with. The campground was basically the same type of food that they were used to, and it was handy.

The closing of the trash dumps had caused a big controversy between the Park Service and a team of biologist, John and Frank Craighead, two brothers that taught at the University of Montana in Missoula. The Craigheads had been working under contract with the Park Service in the park for ten years or more doing research on grizzly. Most of the modern techniques for trapping, tranquilizing, and transplanting grizzly had been developed by the Craigheads while working in the park, but they did not keep the Park Service supplied with demographic data that was needed to make management decisions.

The Park Service was growing impatient with them, and egos began to get in the way when the issue of the dumps came up. The Craigheads wanted the dumps to be closed gradually over several years to wean the bear away gradually from their dependence on garbage. To me, it made a certain amount of sense, as many of the bear had known nothing else but the dumps, being that their mothers brought them there as cubs.

The Park Service wanted to close the dumps all at once, forcing the bear to return to their natural diet, but many of these bear had known nothing else but the dumps and garbage. I have seen pictures from the early days of the Park Service where the garbage was dumped into big troughs and the bear would come in to feed. There would be a ranger naturalist on horseback giving an interpretive talk to a grand stand full of watching visitors. I think this is where the egos got in the way, and because the Craigheads wanted to close them gradually, the Park Service was going to show them just who ran the park, and since most of the Craigheads' work was done in the dumps, they would be losing their easy access to large numbers of bear. Just a year or two after I started working in the park, the controversy got so out of hand that the Craigheads were thrown out of the park, and we were instructed to give them no information concerning wildlife in general and bear specifically.

The first night that we went to Canyon, we trapped and tranquilized four grizzlies and saw four others. We went back for several nights with the bear getting more skittish each night. The last night we went, Mernin and I were stalking this grizzly through the trees in the campground about 2:30 in the morning. Jerry had the tranquilizer gun and a 44 Mag. pistol, and I had a 12-gage shotgun loaded with 00 Buck alternated with slugs, and I had a .357 Magnum on my hip. I was to be Jerry's backup in case the bear charged. I guess I should describe the scene a little so maybe you can get the feel of what one of these hunts was like. It's most usually in the early morning, between midnight and 4:00 a. m., total darkness, wooded, and most of the time, you just catch glimpses of the bear now and then. The bear can charge at any time, from any direction, and be on you in the amount of time it takes to blink your eye. When a grizzly charges, its mouth is open with teeth bared, lips curled back, and it emits a growl that's as much of a roar as it is a growl. Its eyes are fixed on you with a look that tells you that he intends to kill you or at least do bodily harm to you. Altogether, it is one of the most terrifying, life-threatening-scared-to-death-piss-your-pants situations I have ever experienced. Not since Nam had I felt such a rush of adrenaline, and in some ways, it may have even been more intense.

On this night, we were stalking this young grizzly, about 125–150 pounds, through the campground when it came charging through the trees toward us from about one hundred feet away. My first thought was, "One hundred fifty pounds, my ass." He was at least three hundred pounds if he weighed an ounce. I learned that how big a bear looks depends on two things, whether it is daylight or dark, and whether it is coming at you or going away from you.

This bear stopped at a distance of between fifty and seventy-five feet from us and stood up to get a better look at us. It then dropped back down on all fours and started to move parallel to us with its head dropped down lower than the hump on its back, all the time, it was sort of bobbing its head up and down. I was on Mernin's left at this time when he took the tranquilizer gun in his left hand and handed it to me. I transferred the shotgun to my left hand and took the tranquilizer gun in my right hand, which rendered me useless in the event that something happened. At that very instant, the grizzly charged at us, covering half of the distance between us before I even realized that he had charged. Mernin drew his sidearm and fired, the first bullet caught the grizzly in the left eye socket, but the bear kept on coming, and Mernin fired again, causing the bear to tumble, coming to rest at our feet. All the while, I was standing there with a gun in each hand, with piss running down my leg. This entire situation lasted no more than a couple of seconds but seemed to take an hour to play out. I did survive and learn a valuable lesson—never again would I take my hands from my weapon. I told Mernin after that incident, "If you do not want the tranquilizer gun, lay it down. Don't try to hand it to me because I was keeping both of my hands on my shotgun and both eyes on the bear."

Black bear were easier to deal with than grizzly but could be just as dangerous, mainly because they did not have that aggressive nature that all grizzly had all the time. Only on occasion would they be just as aggressive. Black bear tended to be more daytime bear and like to beg on the side of the road. They could be as gentle as the family dog and put up with a tremendous amount of stupidity and abuse from visitors, and only occasionally would one of them injure anyone. Unlike the old days when the roadside bear were just tolerated on the roads, we tried to remove them as quickly as possible to prevent them from being hit by a vehicle or from injuring someone, at which point we would have to destroy them.

Bowtie, her name coming from the white patch of hair on her chest, was an exception. She had worked the road around Pumice Point between Lake and West Thumb for over a decade. She was an ideal roadside bear and had raised many a litter of cubs on the roadside. She never got on the road but would just lie on the shoulder of the road with her cubs by her side and wait for the people to come to her and throw food. If she could not reach the food they had thrown, she would just leave it where it was. Her cubs would do likewise. I never saw or heard of her walking from car to car as most bear did. I have seen people put their young babies and kids beside Bowtie and her cubs so they could get a picture of them, and in some instances that I heard from other rangers, they would even put a child on Bowtie's back. In her entire life, she never injured or ever even acted aggressive toward anyone.

One year, there was a black bear on the East Entrance road that I had to remove every couple of weeks. It was a narrow, winding, and steep section of road with no shoulder to get off on. Every time the bear showed up, we would have several automobile accidents because of people slowing and stopping in the middle of the road to see and feed the bear. He would walk up and down the road, stopping at each car for a handout. He would stand up and lean on the car, looking at the people through the windshield. When the car would try to drive off, the bear would usually tear the radio antennae off. Often this was the first indication that the bear was back; I would start to see radio antennae on the road.

I had removed this bear so many times that I guess I got careless. Always before, I would just pull up to the bear jam with a ranger pickup pulling a culvert-type bear trap. I would open the door of the trap, borrow a loaf of bread from a visitor, and start dropping slices of bread, leading the bear to the door of the trap. At the door of the trap, I would throw the rest of the bread into the trap. The bear had always just gone on into the trap, and I would drop the door and drive off with him. On this one occasion, I handled the bear, though everything went as usual until it came time for the bear to go into the trap. I don't know if I was standing too close to the trap or what, but that time, the bear charged at me, and I had to dive into the trap and drop the door to escape the bear. The bear ran into the trees, but I was stuck inside the trap with bear shit all over me from where I had slid across the bottom of the trap. The trap locks from the outside automatically when the door drops, so I was only able to get out with assistance from some visitors; but only after they had taken several pictures of me incarcerated in the trap. The next day, I returned to get the bear and was ready for any situation, but the bear went into the trap as it had on every other occasion. I survived and learned another valuable lesson.

Transplanting black bear was also much easier than it was with grizzly. To transplant a black, I would drive to an isolated area in another sub-district on a service road and just open the door of the trap. The bear would usually stick its head out, look around, and then amble off into the woods. Most grizzly were transplanted by chopper, but on a few occasions, I did transplant some by truck, and like everything dealing with a grizzly, you took your life into your own hands when you did.

On one such occasion, Jerry Paro and I took a young grizzly over into the Gallatin for transplant. We drove out into the middle of this big meadow. I crawled on top of the trap to open the door, and Jerry got behind the wheel of the truck with the truck moving ahead slowly just in case. It's a good thing he was. I opened the door for the griz and was expecting it to come charging out headed for the far side of the meadow. It charged out all right and then turned to challenge us. It came charging and slapping at me on top of the trap. Jerry started to speed up to get away from the bear, but it kept pace with the truck and would slam into the side of the trap and fall. The damn thing would jump up and chase us again until it caught up and would slam into the side of the trap again. I was holding on for dear life as we flew across the uneven ground of the meadow. Jerry said he had to get up to 45 mph to outrun the bear, but it seemed more like 100 mph to me. In the panic of the moment, I do remember hearing Jerry laughing and yelling, "Ride 'im, Mad Dog, ride 'im!" With buddies like I have always had, it's a wonder I lived long enough to get out of diapers.

On another transplant of a big old bear griz to the top of Saddle Mountain on the east boundary of the park by chopper, I had another encounter. It was a hot day, for Yellowstone and the park is at such a high elevation that a chopper cannot lift very much weight. The weight of the bear would prevent me from being able to take someone with me for security, but the chopper pilot agreed to be my security, so no problem, right? I tranquilized the bear in the trap with M99, a drug designed to keep him out for up to twelve hours or until given the antidote, and as soon as the bear was down, we put him in the cargo net and attached it to the chopper with cable slings and headed across the lake for Saddle Mountain.

We set the bear down on a fairly level place in the saddle of the mountain, released the sling, and set the chopper down a short distance away. At this point, if I had a man for security, he would go with me as I approached the bear and the chopper pilot would stay with the chopper and keep his rpms up in case we had to make a quick getaway. Since it was just me and the pilot, he had to leave the chopper idling and accompany me, carrying a shotgun for my protection. I did not know the pilot and had learned a long time ago not to put any faith in people I did not know, especially when my ass was the one on the line, but I was not too concerned since the bear should still be out for hours. I loosened the net from the sling and dumped the bear out on the ground. The bear set up on its ass, raised its huge front paws with claws that looked as long as switchblades, and roared in my face. I could smell his hot, rancid breath as I turned to run, drawing my sidearm as I ran. I saw the shotgun was lying in my path where my security had dropped it as he headed for the chopper, leaving me at the mercy of a 450–500 pound grizzly. Knowing I could not outrun the griz to the chopper and feeling a lot more confident with a shotgun than a pistol, I snatched up the shotgun and turned to face the charging animal, only to find him fast asleep on the ground where he had been dropped. As I trotted back to the chopper, the pilot yelled for me to go back and get his net and sling. As I climbed into the chopper, I looked at him, hoping for an argument, and told him that if he wanted the damn things, he could go get them himself. Most of the way back across the lake, about a ten-minute flight, I told him what I thought of his sorry ass. The next day, he was unemployed and out of the park. As far as I know, the net and sling are still there.

Living in the park required a special set of skills, not unlike those that people living in a big city learn to survive. You never just barged out of your cabin without seeing what was outside. One night, I had just finished my 5:00 p.m.–2:00 a.m. shift, made my log entries, and finished my paper work. I stepped out of the back door of the Ranger Station, letting it close and lock behind me. As I turned toward the entrance to my quarters that joined the Ranger Station about thirty feet away, I saw a grizzly at the bear-proof trash cans by my door. The griz saw me at about the same time that I saw it, and for an instant, neither of us moved. I turned back to the door of the Ranger Station and stabbed one of the twenty keys that I had to carry at the lock, and luckily it was the right one. I stood leaning against the inside of the door until my heartbeat returned to normal and then peeked out to where I had last seen the griz. It was peeking back at me from around the corner of Mernin's quarters, which also adjoined mine. It then disappeared around the corner, and I made a run for my quarters.

I went to bed thinking no more about the incident since it was a fairly frequent occurrence until I was awakened by the sound of boards being ripped from the front porch. There was a small enclosed porch that separated my front door from Mernin's front door. The door that opened from the porch to the outside did not latch, so all you had to do to get onto the porch was push the door open. My bathroom window look directly onto the porch as did Mernin's. I went into the bathroom and could see that same grizzly tearing the wall out just to the left of the door. Mernin was looking out from his window also with a big grin on his face. I went to my kitchen and made sure the door from my kitchen onto the porch was secure and started to bang some pans together that scared the bear away—for a while. Twice more during the night, we had to get up to run the bear away. The next day, I set a trap and caught the young griz around 1:00 a.m.

In the backcountry, you had to be particularly careful when going out at night, which I had to do a lot of since I had to check my stock if they were picketed to make sure that their rope was not tangled up in something. I also had to go to the privy on occasion during the night.

One night at Thorofare, I had just gone to sleep when I heard something at the front door. I listened for a little while and decided that it was most likely just a black bear, so I reached down and got one of my boots and threw it into the kitchen to scare it away. A few minutes later, the bear was back, so I got up, lit the lantern, and started into the kitchen. As I entered the kitchen, the window on the east side of the cabin was shattered, sending glass flying all over me and the kitchen. I guess the bear had run around the corner in time to see me coming into the kitchen with the lantern and had slapped out at me before running on off. The next morning, I found the tracks of a medium-sized grizzly in the snow outside the cabin.

Another bear incident involved an extremely large grizzly that I am proud to say I never saw. The incident occurred in October just before hibernation with a report from some backpackers that Cabin Creek Patrol Cabin had been damaged by a bear. I notified Mernin, and he wanted me to ride up to Cabin Creek the next day to see what needed to be done to it to have it ready for the winter season, as it was one of the cabins used on ski trips.

I headed out early and rode the twelve miles to Cabin Creek, arriving before noon. There was a light covering of snow on the ground, and the closer I got to Cabin Creek, the more grizzly sign I was seeing. By the time I was approaching the cabin, I could see the tracks of an extremely large grizzly and those of a grizzly sow with two or three cubs. I rode up to the hitching pole in front of the cabin and just sat there, looking at all of the bear sign for a minute or two. There were bear tracks everywhere and piles of scat that contained nothing but oats. The front door of the cabin was open about six inches. I dismounted cautiously not knowing if the bear were still in the area or not or maybe even still in the cabin. With difficulty, I pushed the door open enough to stick my head inside, and the destruction I saw was unbelievable; but the first thing I noticed was that it was light in the cabin as if there was no roof on it. I looked up and noticed that the entire roof on the south side, except the log rafters, was totally missing. The roof on the south side was fairly low, about seven feet I guess, for I could just barely touch the overhang. I suspect this was where that large bear made its entry. There were fresh claw marks on the top log where the bear pulled itself up enough to start chewing on the overhang of the roof. Once the overhang was gone, the bear just kept chewing and chewing until the entire roof was gone. I don't know why the bear did not just chew a hole big enough to get in and then stop, but knowing grizzly like I do, I suspect that there was something about the roof that pissed him off.

I could not get the door open enough to get into the cabin, so I had to crawl through the roof. Splinters of wooden shingles and planks were everywhere mixed in with everything that had been cabin furnishings. Another mystery was that almost all the mattresses, blankets, and pillows had been thrown out of the cabin through the opening in the rear wall that had been a window. Shutters, window, and all the bedding were in a pile just outside.

Here again, I have a theory concerning this mystery also. It always aggravated me that you could hardly move around in the cabins without banging into all of the bedding stuff hanging from the pole, and if you took it down, you would have to straighten it all back up again before you vacated the cabin. I could just see this grizzly as he tried to move around in the cabin bang into this stuff. The grizzly went berserk, slashing the mattresses with its claws and then charging at the hanging stacks with such force that its momentum carried the bear to the rear window that it hit with such force that shutters and all were broken off.

Everything in the cabin was destroyed—stoves, lanterns, dishes, and even pots and pans. Cabin Creek had a complete set of china from the Army days in the park with the Quarter Master Dept. on the bottom of the set; one cup was unbroken, which I still have. The entire cabinet that hung from the front wall had been ripped from the wall and was lying face down on the floor with its back ripped off. The heavy cabinet had hit the floor with such a force that it broke the floor joists, causing the floor in the middle of the cabin to drop to the ground beneath, giving the floor a bowl shape.

In the cabin were two fifty-five gallon barrels, which held oats for the stock and were covered with lids held in place by heavy metal bands. These lids fit so securely that it was difficult to get into them even if you unhooked the bands. It was impossible to get into them with the bands in place, unless you happen to be a grizzly. The bear hooked its claws under the lid and jerked it from the barrel with the bands still in place and had proceeded to eat most of the five or six hundred pounds of oats that was in the barrels. There was a pile of scat in the back corner of the cabin that was nearly a foot tall and eight or ten inches in diameter, a really impressive pile of shit, which was composed of nothing but oats.

After surveying the situation, I radioed in to Lake Ranger Station and informed Mernin as to the extent of the destruction. I simply told him that the walls of the cabin were intact but everything else had been destroyed. Mernin, in that slow methodical voice of his, suggested that I plan on spending the night at the cabin and see what I could do to clean it up in the morning. I still don't think it had registered with him how bad the destruction was. I took a long pause, looked around at the door standing half-open, no roof on half the cabin, the rear shutters and window gone, and grizzly tracks everywhere, and not from just one bear either. Knowing that the bears would be back as they had been doing for several nights, I suggested to Mernin that he come spend the night at Cabin Creek, if he had a death wish, but I was going over to Trail Creek to spend the night.

I spent the afternoon sorting and sifting through things in the cabin, and luckily, I found the log books intact and none the worse for wear. The log books are the real history of the park as recorded by the rangers that spent the night in the cabins. Whoever spends a night in the cabins was required to make a daily log entry detailing whatever they wanted to relay, from why they were there, trail conditions, ford levels, wildlife sightings, or just whatever. There were poems, art work, and most anything else you could think of in the log books. The thing that always struck me as ironic was that from year to year, decade to decade, the entries were the same; without looking at the date of the entry, you could not tell if it was from the twenties or seventies. Life in the backcountry stayed the same decade after decade.

One of my favorite pastimes on snowy days when I didn't ride was to read the old log books. Some people had a real knack for making good entries; they could take just day-to-day occurrences and make them entertaining. My entries were always dull and unimaginative, no matter how interesting the day.

I headed for Trail Creek Cabin late that afternoon on a trail that was covered with grizzly tracks and oat-filled scat. The bear had been using the trail so much that it looked like one of those bear trails you see in Alaska. I became concerned that Trail Creek Cabin might have suffered the same fate as Cabin Creek Cabin but was relieved to find it intact, though slightly damaged. Trail Creek Cabin was higher above the ground than Cabin Creek, so the bear could not use the same technique to gain entry. The shutters and door showed signs that the bear had tried to rip them open but were unsuccessful. The barn also showed sign of damage more severe than the cabin, but still intact.

I put my animals in the barn for the night, had a good dinner, and turned in early. I slept poorly that night, as I had to fight off charging grizzly all night in my dreams. The grizzly of my dream was as large as the giant bear that became extinct at the end of the last ice age. As he would come charging at me with teeth bared and ears laid back, I would grab my trusty lever action 30–30 and fire, but all the time thinking I need a bigger gun. Every time I see the movie *Jaws* and they are on the boat when the shark attacks the boat and that actor says, "We need a bigger boat," I remember my dream.

I returned to Cabin Creek midmorning the next day to continue cleanup. I could see no evidence that the bear had returned during the night, but since most of the snow had melted, I could not distinguish any new tracks. I built a fire in front of the cabin and started feeding it with whatever would burn. I found the coffee pot and coffee, so I had a pot going by the time Mernin arrived, having ridden in from Ten Mile Post that morning with Action Jackson and Terry Small. Before the day was over, we got everything burned that was not salvageable and packed up the non-burnable stuff to be sent out for disposal. There was very little left to salvage.

I headed back to Thorofare as soon as the mess at Cabin Creek was cleaned up only to find that the bear that had destroyed Cabin Creek had struck the Thorofare Cabin but was unable to gain entry into the cabin. The bear tried the same technique to get in; it chewed about ten feet of the overhanging roof from the east side of the cabin but was not tall enough to hook its claws over the top log and pull itself up so it could continue chewing the roof.

The bear was able to get into the barn by breaking the hasp off the door. Again, he ate vast amounts of feed and shit everywhere. The damage to the barn was much less severe than the damage at Cabin Creek, but then there was much less to destroy. That night when I radioed in to Lake and notified Mernin of the problem, he consulted with the Biologist Office at HQ as to what I needed to do about the bear. The biologists came up with a game plan that seemed improbable at the time and ridiculous today. I was to ride back to Trail Creek the next day to pick up a bag of lithium chloride salts and then return to Thorofare the same day, thirty-four miles round trip. That evening, I was to cook up a double handful of oats until it would make a ball. I would then put a prescribed dose of the lithium chloride in the center of the ball and leave it in the barn where the bear could get it. The bear would get sick if he ate it and make the association that eating the oats made him sick, so he would go away and never eat oats again; right. Now, a griz can eat shit that would make a buzzard puke, but this little bit of salt was going to make him so sick that he would swear off oats forever? Let's say I was more than a little skeptical. I just hoped it didn't just give him a stomachache that pissed him off and decided to take it out on me. I decided to sleep with the shutters closed that night and keep the stock close by the cabin.

The next morning, there was a fresh skiff of snow, and I found sign that the griz had come as close as the spring where I got my water and realized that I was at the cabin and came no closer. I was at Thorofare for three or for more days and would always see his tracks, but he never came any closer. I went on about my business and headed to Fox Creek for a few days, but I left plenty of the lithium chloride balls lying about in the barn. Upon returning to Thorofare a few days later, I found that the bear had eaten all the balls and torn into the feed bin again. This game went on all fall until the weather turned bad enough for the bear to go into hibernation for the winter. For all the problems and extra work that the bear had caused, I never did get a look at the bear, and I would have really liked to have seen him from a distance, judging from his track. I judged him to be a lot larger than that big one I saw up Mountain Creek.

Sometime during the course of the winter, the decision was made to burn the remains of the old cabin and build a new, more modern A-Frame cabin the next summer. I hated to see the old cabin go for historical reasons, and it would have not taken much to put it back in shape, but Dale Nuss had never liked Cabin Creek because it sat back in the timber without a view, and it was old and dark. The new cabin would be built a short distance from the old one on the edge of a large marshy meadow near the ford across the Yellowstone River. It was aesthetically a much better location and was more removed from the trail, so it was not as seen by visitors.

Dale not only designed and prefabbed most of the cabin during the winter, he got permission to build a cabin at Eagle Pass of the same design. They were pretty neat little A-Frame cabins with a sleeping loft and a front porch. They worked well enough in the summer but were poorly designed for winter use. Even late fall could be difficult since they were heated by a Franklin stove that let most of the heat go up the chimney. They were also elevated several feet above the ground, so the cold came up through the floor. The steep-peaked roof let most of the heat rise so high that it did you no good. I spent one night at Cabin Creek on a winter ski trip and nearly froze to death; I have slept warmer in snow caves. I spent a lot of time the next summer packing material into the two cabin sites.

The cabin at Eagle Pass was actually a mile or so below the pass in a beautiful location on Howell Creek, right where the trail to Dod Hershey's camp diverged from the main trail. It sure made my patrolling of that area a lot easier than having to set up and break camp each time. The snow usually started to get deep in that area shortly after the first part of October, forcing Dod to pull his camp while he could still get out over the pass. One year, he lost a couple of horses just before he pulled camp, so he had to leave them. I found their bones the next year up near the pass.

The Thorofare was empty of buffalo except for one fall when a large solitary bull came wandering up the valley. It was an exceptionally large bull, which showed strong characteristics of the mountain bison, having an extremely large hump. The Yellowstone herd was one of the three small remaining herds of buffalo that had not been killed off while the U.S. Government was trying to starve the Indians so they would go to the reservations. The other two herds were plains variety bison, but the Yellowstone herd was the mountain variety. In the early 1900s, the herd had gotten so small that there was fear that it might become extinct, so the army that controlled the park during that time decided to start killing the large predators in the park, such as the wolf and mountain lion. The buffalo was saved, but the wolf was forced into extinction. Sort of save one species at the expense of another. The army also imported some plains bison to add to the buffalo population of the park, but it changed the genetics of the herd, so not many bison still retain the characteristics of the mountain bison. I had been seeing the buffalo's dung on the trails for several days before I actually located him, or more correctly he located me. He was standing in the meadow in front of Thorofare Ranger Station when I returned from boundary patrol one afternoon. I radioed Mernin at Lake, and he consulted with the biologist office at HQ, who wanted me to try and herd him back up into the park. I mounted Apple and galloped at the bull whooping, hollering, and doing all those things I had seen cowboys do in movies. The closer I got to the bull, the bigger he got and the smaller Apple was. The bull showed no reaction until I started to get pretty close to him; he then lowered his head and made a charge at us. Real quickly, Apple lost his enthusiasm for the project as the bull chased us to the far side of the meadow before breaking off the chase. The last I saw of the bull, he was ambling his way in the direction of the park boundary, but I got inquiries from hunters all fall as to his protected status. I had already checked with Dave Bragonier, a game warden with Wyoming Game and Fish, about his status. Dave told me that there was no mention of bison in any state regulations, so he could be shot by anyone the instant he left the park; but I was able to get the Forest Service to issue a protection order on this bull, so we were able to keep him alive through the fall.

Speedy's camp had been bought out that year by a young fellow about my age named Gary Fales. Gary's dad was also an outfitter out of the Cody area but did not hunt near the park, so I had never met him. Gary was a real nice guy and had a beautiful young wife from a wealthy family back east somewhere around Boston. As I rode into his camp that first time, I noticed that the camp looked as if it had been nearly destroyed. Some of the tents were down and looked as if they had been drug around. The corral and meat racks were all busted up, and the entire camp was in disarray and a beehive of activity. After introductions, I got down to give them a hand in straightening up camp. Gary said that he had several of his better horses picketed in the meadow in front of camp near the trail when this monstrous buffalo came ambling down the trail.

My horses paid almost no attention to buffalo, moose, grizzly, or any other kind of animals because they were around them all the time, except dogs. They were just never exposed to dogs, so on the occasions when I would ride in the Lake area where there were visitors with loose dogs that ran at them barking, there would be a rodeo. All the years I was at Thorofare, we had a cow moose that would come into the corral to lick the salt block that I kept out for my stock, and she did not care if the stock and I were in the corral or not.

The outfitter stock was not used to all of the wildlife that park stock were used to, particularly bison, so when this large bull came through in the middle of the morning and Gary's high-strung, high-dollar roping horse saw him, the horse went into a full-blown panic and took off running for the camp. When the horse hit the end of its picket rope, it pulled the picket pin that had been driven into the ground and continued toward camp, scaring all the other horses that were also picketed in the meadow. It was sort of like a row of dominoes; the buffalo scared this horse, which scared these horses, which all charged into camp and scared the rest of the herd that was in the corral. The horses in the corral became so panicked that they destroyed the corral and camp as they escaped from the horse devil that was after all of them.

No one was killed in the stampede, but two horses were either killed or had to be put down. Gary's high-dollar roping horse was killed as it tried to jump a log when the picket rope that was attached to its halter hung on something, breaking the horse's neck. High-strung, expensive horses just had no place in the mountains; they would most likely kill themselves and maybe the rider in the process.

The bull raised hell everywhere he went without doing anything; just showing up was enough. The bull was never seen again after that fall, but one of the guides for Triangle X found a buffalo skull on Two Ocean Plateau a few years later that was a Boone and Crocket record. Those big old bulls leave the herd when they are whipped by a younger bull. They just go off by themselves to die, which is not a bad life philosophy; when you have outlived your usefulness, just lie down and die, and that is just what my dad did.

I believe that was the same year that we had so much early deep snow, and by the first of October, I was already riding in stirrup-deep snow up on Two Ocean. All the outfitter camps pulled out early, and the ones that went out over Dear Creek Pass had real problems. Dear Creek Pass was extremely narrow, steep, and dangerous and had claimed the life of more stock than the rest of the passes put together. There were a dozen or more pack animals that had gone over the ledge to their death in the years I worked Thorofare. When it snowed hard, the wind would cause the snow to drift in at the pass so deep that the outfitters would have to shovel the trail for a hundred feet or more. That was the main reason that they would pull out pretty quickly when the snow started to set in. That year, I had the mountains pretty much to myself after the first week of October.

When it came time to stock cabins for the winter, the snow was well over a foot deep down in the Yellowstone Valley. Mernin and I met at Trail Creek as usual and sorted the rations into piles for different cabins. The amount of rations that each cabin received depended on the amount of use that each cabin would get, so Thorofare would get four or five times the rations that any of the others got. The other four cabins would get about equal amounts. Mernin would usually add his own personal rations to each cabin; a case of beer, a couple of cans of tomato juice, and beer nuts. After all, there is no need to rough it on ski trips.

I kept telling Mernin that I did not think we would be able to get to Fox Creek Cabin up on Two Ocean that year; the snow was just too deep. He would just say, "It may be a long day, and we might get cold and miserable, but I think we can make it." I can still hear that damn slow methodical articulate voice of his.

The next morning, we had all four pack animals loaded, packed, and were on the trail before daylight. The first couple of miles went okay, but as soon as we started to gain elevation, the snow started to deepen quickly. Mernin was leading the way but had to pull over and let me lead after a short while so he could rest his saddle horse, Dusty, since he was wringing wet and lathered. We continued to swap the lead every fifteen to twenty minutes, but we were not covering much country. By midafternoon, we had not even gotten halfway and had only a couple of hours of daylight left, and the worst of the trail was still ahead of us. Mernin came up with plan B; we would return to Trail Creek for the night and head out again for Fox Creek in the morning. Since we had already broken half of the trail, we should be able to go on in to Fox Creek. I knew Mernin well enough to not try to change his mind, but I would usually ask Punkin what he thought about the plan and then answer as if he had told me something. I would usually say something like, "So you think Mernin is a dumb shit and that plan will never work." Mernin would not even turn around; he would just shake his head and mumble under his breath about how bad I was and wondered how such a degenerate ever got to be a ranger. I was always quick to point it out when Punkin was right though.

We headed out from Trail Creek again the next morning, but the broke trail was mostly gone since the wind had come up during the night and had drifted it in. Only in the timber was the trail somewhat broken, but most of the first half of the trail was through meadows. Grudgingly, Mernin finally admitted that Punkin was right, and we returned to Trail Creek again with no plans to try for Fox Creek again. Oh well, there would be no red beer at Fox Creek that winter.

We headed to Thorofare the next day with a monstrous load of rations and spent the night there. The next day, I was to head to Cabin Creek to put away the rations that Mernin had dropped there on his way in to Trail Creek. Mernin was going to stay at Thorofare another night to give the cabin a good cleaning and then meet me at Cabin Creek the next night. I would give Cabin Creek a good cleaning and wait for Mernin to arrive from Thorofare.

I headed out from Thorofare in route to Cabin Creek in a virtual blizzard. It was snowing hard and a strong wind was blowing up the valley from the north, but the temperature was still pretty warm, upper teens or lower twenties. I had my collar pulled up and my flat hat pulled down over my face as low as I could get it to try to block the wind. I just gave Apple his head and hung on, but I would peek out to the side to watch the elk pass by. It was as if I were riding through a herd of cattle. The elk were all headed south in the direction of the elk refuge at Jackson Hole, and I was headed north toward the Lake. I rode through this herd all day, estimating its number to be in the thousands. Mernin rode in the next evening and said that he had also ridden through elk the entire way. The trip along the lake to Ten Mile Post the next day was slow and cold; the snow was stirrup-deep, and a lot of trees had come down across the trail during storm. The park had been closed to visitors for a couple of weeks due to the snow, so the roads were no longer being plowed. We thought we would have to ride down the road to the barn at Lake, another ten miles on top of the twenty miles we had already covered. Good ole Bill Brumand plowed out one lane all the way to Ten Mile Post and met up with the stock truck, and it was a good thing since we did not get to Ten Mile Post until dark. If we would have had to ridden an extra ten miles, it would have been around 9:00 p.m. before we arrived at the barn.

That last week or so was most always difficult, and I can hardly remember a trip out that the weather was not bad. On one trip, Mernin and I were going to stock Cabin Creek on the way out to Ten Mile Post. We would go from Trail Creek to Cabin Creek, which is five miles, and I would put away the rations while Jerry did the final cleaning. We hoped to accomplish our tasks in about an hour and then be on the trail again headed the twenty miles to Ten Mile Post. This was another of Mernin's plans that Punkin and I discussed thoroughly.

There was about a foot of snow on the ground with fresh snow falling lightly. The temperature was bitterly cold for October, lower teens or single digits. When we got to the ford across the Yellowstone River, the first half of the ford was covered with thick ice. Mernin, after much coaxing, finally got Dusty out onto the ice, but Irwin's mule would have no part of it. Irwin nearly pulled Dusty down a couple of times on the slick ice. I brought Apple up behind Irwin and used Apple to force Irwin onto the ice. Irwin tried to jump out onto the ice at the last instant but only managed to fall down on his belly, breaking the ice and sending Dusty into a panic. Dusty reared up and fell back, plunging Mernin to the waist in the cold water. We finally got into the cabin and built a fire to warm up and try to dry Mernin's clothes a little. If it were up to me, I would have altered my plans and have spent the night at Cabin Creek so we could have gotten all Mernin's clothes dry, but as soon as we got our chores done, we were on the trail again. We rode the last twenty miles with Mernin wearing more than damp clothing, but you would never have known it from Mernin's actions.

After the cabin was built on Howell Creek near Eagle Pass, it added to the problem of getting the cabins stocked. For one thing, it added an extra cabin and was hard to get to in bad weather. I made the mistake of leaving it until last one year. I planned to stock it and then go out over the pass to the trailhead on Eagle Creek, about ten miles or so out of the park from East Entrance. There were about six or eight inches of snow at the lake, so I did not expect it to be too deep at the pass. It snowed on me hard all day on my way up to Howell Creek and continued snowing throughout the night. I was going to lay over that day and put the cabin in order but decided I had better get over the pass while I could, if I could.

By morning, it had just about quit snowing, but I had a couple of feet of snow at the cabin with a strong wind blowing and dropping temperatures. I headed for the pass half-expecting that I would have to turn back and go to Cabin Creek for a night and then on out to Ten Mile Post. I had ridden that trail so many times, and it was such an uninteresting trail most of the way that I tried to avoid it if necessary. As I approached the pass, I could tell that the wind had caused the snow to drift in on the north side of the pass. Right at the throat of the pass, the trail crosses from the right side of the pass to the left side of the pass on a narrow ridge of rock that is just wide enough for an animal to walk; this is where I knew that I would have a problem, if I even got that far. I made it to that ridgeline with much difficulty and was about to give up when I started to notice elk tracks starting to converge from both sides of the valley, all heading for the pass. I struggled on across the ridgeline to where the trail started to break over the pass, and all these elk tracks had come together for a well-broke trail across the most treacherous part of the trail. Just as quickly as the tracks had come together, they started to diverge as soon as the pass opened up a little, and I was back to breaking my own trail. It was a tough trip all the way from the pass down to Eagle Creek Meadows, but from the meadows on down, the amount of snow decreased until by the time I arrived at the trailhead just before dark, there was only six or eight inches of snow.

The ranger from East Entrance, John Scott, was tied up at Sylvan Pass with stranded visitors and was going to be unable to bring the stock truck to the trailhead; so his wife, Dianne, drove the truck and was waiting for me when I arrived. John ended up closing the pass before I could get over, so I ended up having to spend the night with him and his wife at East Entrance. Dianne just couldn't say enough about the experience of picking me up. She said it was something right out of a movie; the sight of me riding out of the mountains in a snowstorm with a string of pack animals was something she would never forget.

During one of the fall hunts after I had a cabin at Howell Creek, I came back to the cabin after patrolling the boundary all day to find an outfitter starting to set up camp in the meadow where the cabin was located. I can't remember the outfitter's name, but he was from the Cody area. He wanted me to let him camp there for the night as it was getting toward late afternoon and they still had another twelve to fourteen miles before reaching the park boundary. Park regulations require that if they are going to use that trail, they must travel through in one day. When I pointed this out to the outfitter, he became indignant about it and wanted to know how much the fine would be if he camped anyway. I told him that was up to the judge, but that I would have to confiscate his entire camp, stock included, until his trial date, but not wanting to be an asshole, I would let them ride as far as Ten Mile Post. He decided to ride on.

While the outfitter and I were having our discussion, Dave Bragonier, the Game Warden out of Cody, came riding into camp with two pack animals heading for his cabin on the Thorofare. Dave was mounted on a sorrel gelding, a Missouri Fox Trotter that had to stand seventeen hands high. He was packing his old horse, Moon Shine, which I had thought was tall, but not compared to his new one. I invited Dave to stay the night with me at Howell Creek so we could catch up on things. I could fill Dave in on where camps were located and save him a lot of extra riding. He had come in to check on the outfitter that I had just encountered because the outfitter was packing in a prince from Iran, an heir of the Shaw, who was hunting moose on a Governor's complementary permit. Dave hated it when the Governor issued permits to all those rich, arrogant foreigners, so he always kept a real close eye on them, knowing that they all think they are above the law anyway.

We had a good dinner, drinks, and visit before heading to Thorofare the next morning. I let Dave lead the trip down since I did not know if Apple could keep up with that monster Dave was riding, but little ole Apple kept pace with him step for step and still was not at his top speed. Before we split up at Thorofare, Dave and I agreed to meet at his cabin in the morning and make our rounds of the valley together since I knew where all the camps were located.

I guess I should tell you a little about Dave Bragonier. He was short, not much over 5¢5² or 5¢6², with that little man's attitude that made him so tough. That was one reason that Dave rode such big horses; he wanted to look down on whomever he was encountering. Dave's reputation was larger than the horses he rode. He was one of the most suspicious-minded, tenacious, intuitive people I have ever met. I believe he would ride fifty miles through a blizzard and crawl another five to catch his own grandmother in violation of a game law. To prove a point, I heard him say on more than one occasion that he thought the post master of Wapiti, Wyoming, had mafia connections. Wapiti is located between Cody and the park and is so small that the only thing there is the post office and a bar. Cody had the bad reputation of being a haven for poachers. Unemployment was so high that many of the cowboys supplemented their unemployment checks by poaching. I have forgotten the exact number, but Dave had about sixteen poaching convictions in his first month in Cody. Everyone cussed about him, but they would all add that he was a damn good game warden. Just what Cody needed.

We located the camp with the prince on the south side of Bridger Lake and stopped in for a visit. I had no jurisdiction, so I was just along for the ride. After Dave had checked their permits, we were having a cup of coffee and having casual conversation, but Dave's eyes were scanning the entire camp and everyone in it. After Dave finished his coffee, he stood and poured the dregs from his cup onto the ground and set the cup on a log. When he turned around, he looked at the outfitter and asked who had killed the grouse. The silence was so thick that you could taste it. The outfitter started to deny that anyone had killed a grouse, but Dave walked over to a poncho draped across a log on the far side of the camp and picked a small, and I mean small, feather off the poncho and held it in the outfitter's face. The tone of Dave's voice had completely changed when he asked again who had killed the grouse. His tone left no doubt that this was no guy to mess with. One of the guides admitted to the violation and was issued a citation along with a citation to the outfitter. After that, the outfitter was not so hospitable toward us. He started to gripe about that ranger up at Eagle Pass that had made them ride all the way through the park the same day they had already ridden nearly thirty miles. He just went on and on about how unreasonable and inconsiderate that ranger had been. I just kept quiet and let him rant and rave; I guess he didn't recognize me. He finally worked himself up into almost a rage when he asked me who that ranger was and if he worked for me. I just casually replied that the ranger at Eagle Pass was me. Dave, who had headed for his horse so they would not see him laugh, could hardly get on his horse. All the outfitter said was, "Oh," and then mumbled something else about me being unreasonable. I went over to Dave's cabin that night for dinner, and every few minutes Dave would chuckle and say, "Who was that ranger anyway?" After that, every time we met, I was always greeted with the same question, "Who was that ranger anyway?"

On another occasion, I was lucky enough to observe Dave at work at his cabin. There was a long, narrow meadow that ran from the base of the Trident up behind my cabin all the way to Dave's cabin, the distance of a mile or more, and it was prime elk habitat. I tried to keep a close eye on this meadow as I knew it was one of RB Wallace's favorites. It was midday when I approached Dave's cabin. The back of his cabin was butted up next to the park boundary, and the meadow came out of the park on the east side. I saw that there were four men sitting around a small campfire in front of the cabin. They were outside of the park and my jurisdiction, but I knew that Dave would not appreciate them having built a fire right out in front of his cabin. I thought I would stop and get their names and suggest that they obliterate any sign of the fire when they left.

It turned out to be R.B. from Fales camp and three hunters, a father and his two sons. While I was talking with them, Dave came riding in from the trailhead. I could tell by the look on his face that he was not happy to see them with a fire and their horses eating down all the grass near the cabin. I had already checked their hunting permits and saw nothing that seemed unusual. As soon as Dave dismounted, he asked to see their permits. He took all three permits at the same time, and without the hunters knowing it, he mixed them up. Talking all the while, he would take a permit, read the description on it and walk up to the person, look him over as if he was a horse he was going to buy, and then hand his permit back. He did this with two of the permits, but one of them, Dave would read the description, look at the guy, and keep the permit. Dave would put the permit in his shirt pocket, talking casually all the while. Every once in a while, Dave would take the permit out, look at it, and ask the guy a question like, "Damn! You sure look older than twenty-six." Dave would put the permit back in his shirt and go on talking. In a few minutes, Dave would drag it out again and say, "You sure have put on a lot of weight since you applied for this permit." Dave would put the permit back in his shirt and continue casual conversation with the four. I had looked at the permits, and everything seemed reasonable to me. I thought Dave was just giving them a hard time because of the fire. The tension was mounting until at last the one guy blurted, "Okay, you got me. I am hunting on someone else's permit." Later, Dave said that he knew they were dirty as soon as he rode up; he did not know what it was, but by their actions, he knew something was not right.

If we came across a glove or a shell casing on the trail while riding along, Dave would dismount, pick it up, and bag it as evidence. He had made several cases on just such evidence: one, a grizzly poaching case that I had assisted him with. I had identified the cubs in question as having come from the park.

Another time, he called me in Arkansas while I was home waiting to go back for the winter season. I was married by then, and Dee had gone into Thorofare with me that fall. Dave wanted to know if I had visited the Fales camp on the third hunt and if so, could I remember what any of the hunters looked like? I knew I had been in the camp, but I could not remember any of the hunters, so I asked Dee. She said, "Don't you remember the one guy asked you if your horse was part mule, and you replied, 'Hell no, he's all mule'?" I was riding my mule that day. And she remembered that one of the hunters had a black eye, where he had crowded his scope too close, and it blacked his eye. I just gave the phone to her and let them talk. I can't remember why Dave was suspicious of them, but then it didn't take much to make Dave suspicious.

I took a ride up the Thorofare toward Deer Creek Pass just to see some new country and to locate a hunt camp that was a bit of a mystery to all the other outfitters in the area. Most of the outfitters interacted with each other professionally and even socially from time to time. They would bicker and argue about hunting in each other's territory and would tell on each other to me just like little kids. This one camp, however, was a total unknown to the other outfitters, Bragonier, and me. It was the Hidden Valley, or Lost Valley Camp, I can't remember, but it was located off the main trail to Deer Creek Pass in a high, rim-rocked mountain valley that was no more than a couple of thousand acres. I located the camp easy enough, and at first impression, it looked like any other hunt camp. The camp was very neat, clean, and seemed to have more social amenities than most. There was a tent set up as a bath house with a couple of fancy bathtubs. One tub I could understand, but I don't know of any hunting buddies that like to bath together. There was a large fire pit in the middle of the area with logs around it for people to sit and visit and a large table loaded down with about any kind of booze that a person could ask for, and good booze, too. There was no sign of a meat rack or any evidence that there were any rifles in camp. In most camps, there are always rifles around, and every saddle has a scabbard for a rifle. I saw none of this in this camp. There was also a clothesline strung at the edge of camp that was loaded with all sorts of sexy female undergarments.

I hailed the camp, and a man about my age came out of the cook tent along with two very attractive young women. Now, I should mention that I had been in the mountains for a while, but the gals were lookers. I stayed in the saddle and visited for a while, sensing that my presence was not really wanted. While we visited, I saw a couple of other attractive women in and about camp. I should mention that females are very rare in the hunt camps, except for an occasional wife that accompanies her husband on a hunt or a few cooks on occasion. This camp was loaded with at least five that could easily be Vegas showgirls. I did not see a hunter or guide in camp, but it was the middle of the day so they could have been out hunting.

I visited for only a short while before heading back to the park, more suspicious than ever. I suspected that there was very little, if any, hunting done out of that camp. For one thing, guides from other camps never encountered any guides or hunters from that camp. Bragonier said that they rarely checked any game at the check station. With their hunting record, he did not understand how they got clients, but according to records, they most always had a full camp.

It was rare that I ever encountered anyone inside the park, but on occasion, I did run into a few hunters. Most were just out sightseeing, fishing, or lost. I did run into some that had loaded weapons that I suspected were hunting though, and these, I confiscated their weapons and charged at them with possession of a loaded firearm in the park. It was a real pain in the ass though. It was a two-day ride out for me, a day in court, and a two-day ride back in, so I was gone from the boundary for almost a week. The US Magistrate in Mammoth, the honorable James W. Brown, was an old man that thought that a twenty-five-dollar fine was a big fine. I would go through all the effort to take someone to court, and he would give their weapon back and give them a fifty-dollar fine.

The first encounter I had with Judge Brown was early the first year I was in the park working at East Entrance. A kid from Cody on a motorcycle approached the East Entrance but stopped when he saw that he was going to have to pay two dollars to enter. He turned his bike around and headed back in the direction he had come until he thought he was out of sight. I caught a glimpse of his bike as he headed through the woods around the entrance station. I gave chase in my patrol car and pulled him over a few miles inside the park. I wrote him a ticket for vehicle off established roadway and arranged a court date.

Being my first court case, I spent hours and hours preparing my case; I had measurements, pictures, and diagrams showing his route of travel around the entrance. When I was on the witness stand, Judge Brown asked me what made me an authority on what the established roadway was. I didn't know exactly how to answer him and felt that I was the one on trial. After a long pause, I said, "Well, your honor, I kind of thought it was where they put the pavement." He got red-faced, dismissed the charges, and threatened to find me in contempt of court if I got smart with him again.

I caught a moose poacher one fall that had made an honest mistake and shot a monstrous moose about a mile inside the park. The state of Wyoming had changed their regulations that year concerning nonresident hunters in the wilderness area around Yellowstone. In previous years, the only way a nonresident could hunt in this area was with a guide. This year, they changed the regulation so that they could hunt these big wilderness areas as long as they were with a legal resident. Chick Henry, the guy I caught, was a farmer from Morganfield Kentucky who had a friend from Gillette, Wyoming. Chick had drawn a moose permit for the Bridger Lake area and arranged for his friend to pack him in. The friend rounded up a string of out-of-shape horses from the flatlands around Gillette, but not as many as was needed to pack in for that many miles. They came in over Eagle Pass after having spent the first night at Eagle Creek Meadows. The stock was played out by the time they climbed to the Meadows, but the next day, they had to climb to the pass and then make it all the way to the Bridger Lake area, another seventeen miles. Chick said that they nearly lost some of the stock before they even got to the pass. A couple of the pack horses that were too heavily loaded, staggering and stumbling along on a trail, could kill you if you made a bad step. It was almost dark by the time they got into the Thorofare area on their way to Bridger Lake. They saw what they thought to be boundary markers in a straight line across the valley. Thinking that they were outside of the park as soon as they were south of these markers, they set up camp in a grove of trees. What they had seen was the trail tags marking the South Boundary Trail; the boundary was about a half a mile farther south. The next morning, Chick got up at daylight and shot a large bull standing in the meadow just outside of their camp. I was east of their location a couple of miles when I heard the shot. It was hard to judge the direction of a shot down in the valley because of so many different valleys coming together, but since I was directly on the boundary when I heard the shot, I knew it was very close to the boundary. I rode along the boundary until I located Chick and his party in the process of dressing out the moose.

I rode up and introduced myself and just left it at that. Chick, who was a real talker, took over the conversation and told me all about how he killed the moose from camp, showed me where their camp was, and told me about all the trouble they had coming in over Eagle Pass. I let him talk on since he was so proud of the moose, and I really hated to break the news to him. He was just devastated when I informed him that he was still inside the park. I even rode with him to show him the park boundary that was plainly marked as boundary only a half mile farther down the trail. I placed everyone into custody and confiscated the entire camp—moose, rifles, tents, horses, and all. I had the four of them accompany me to Trail Creek, where we were met by our Woody Jones with a patrol boat. Woody and I took one of the hind quarters of the moose from the forks of a sawbuck saddle, dropped it to the ground, and drug the hind quarter to the boat at the dock. Chick's grandson, a big stout, redheaded, sixteen-year-old kid, 6¢1² or 6¢2² and about 225 pounds, grabbed hold of the other hind quarter, lifted it up off the forks on the sawbuck saddle, and then carried the hindquarter to the boat. Woody and I just kind of looked at each other, and one of us commented, "Let's not piss him off."

All the hunters, the moose, and all the gear went out on the boat that night, but I stayed at Trail Creek and brought all the stock out the next day. I can't remember exactly how long the pack string was, but I know I had a string of about a dozen or more animals. It was a mixed herd in that they were not used to being together, so I had a lot of minor uprisings to settle the entire twenty-five-mile trip, and none of Chick's animals had ever been loaded into a stock truck.

Chick was going to plead guilty, so we went right to court the day after I came out of the backcountry. We went before Judge Brown at Mammoth, and Chick was such a likeable, smooth-talking old con man that he had everyone, including the judge, feeling sorry for having to inconvenience him. The judge asked him how he pleaded, and Chick, in his most country manner said, "If Ranger Wilcox says I was inside the park, then I know I must have been." He rambled on for about five minutes or so explaining the circumstances and how sorry he was and on and on. When I took the stand, the judge asked me if Chick was inside the park when he shot the moose and if I thought it was an honest mistake, to which I answered, "Yes," but did not elaborate.

Judge Brown fined Chick five hundred dollars and returned all the property that I had confiscated, even the gun—a mere slap on the wrist. Had this case been tried in State Court, it would have cost him a minimum of $2,500, loss of the moose, the gun for sure, and loss of hunting privileges for at least five years. After the trial, Chick was thanking everyone for being so nice and kind and treating them so well, etc. The judge was just eating it up, so Chick asked him, "Say, Judge, can I still have the moose?" Judge Brown didn't even hesitate when he said, "I don't see why not. Ranger Wilcox, return the moose along with the rest of Mr. Henry's property."

I looked at the judge and was just getting ready to protest when Mernin intervened and drug me off by the arm. Later that afternoon, I was sitting in the Ranger Station at Lake when Chick came in and asked if I could pack out the head and cape the next time I came out of Thorofare. We had to leave the head and cape at the sight where they had camped. The moose was so large that we did not have an extra animal to pack the head and cape on. I told Chick, as nicely as I could, that there was no way that I would pack the head out for him and that the judge should never have given the moose back to him. I accused him of being a con man, at which he just grinned at me and said nothing else.

It was probably a good thing that I caught Chick and his party and made them go to the lake because I don't think that his stock would ever have been able to have gotten back over the pass with the added weight of the moose, even if he left the head and cape. I really liked that old con man and got a Christmas card from him every year for about ten years.

By the time I returned to the Thorofare, everyone had already heard about how easy Chick had gotten off and gave me hell about it. The hunters in these camps were paying $150–$200 a day for ten days just to be able to hunt a moose, so they wanted one of the parks bargain moose. On several occasions, when Judge Brown was out of the park for vacation or something else, I would have to go into Cody to federal court. Judge Day was the magistrate, and he would usually fine someone that I had caught with a loaded firearm in the park $250 and keep their gun.

I guess in the years I worked, I rode more new country than any ranger that had worked the Thorofare ever had. For one thing, most rangers worked Thorofare only for one fall because the isolation got to them. I worked it for ten years, and my bosses let me ride into the Thorofare from every trailhead that had a trail headed to Thorofare. I guess the wilderness area I covered was at least eighty to ninety miles square, and this is not counting the area inside the park that I rode in the summer.

One summer when I was working bear management, my boss needed to mark some backcountry campsites up in Pelican Valley around Fern Lake, Tern Lake, Wapiti Lake, and Mirror Lake. That area had been one of the most famous trout fishing areas in the U.S. earlier in the century. Outfitters had permanent fishing camps along Pelican Creek and used to bring fishermen in by horseback on a daily basis. Park regulations were not as restrictive in those days, so I guess they were not limited in the number of people or stock that they could have in camp as they are today.

I wanted to get up there to try my luck with the trout, so I volunteered to find good locations for the new campsites, mark them, locate them on a topo map, and write a detailed description of how to find them. Fern Lake Patrol Cabin also needed some work, so I was given a week to accomplish everything. A seasonal ranger named Chuck

Lomas, who was a vice principle from Dearborn Michigan, went along to help me. Chuck was no horseman or backcountry man, but he was great company because he knew more jokes than anyone I have ever met and had a great knack for telling them, and even better, Chuck was a great fly fisherman.

We headed up the valley by Pelican Cone on up Pelican Creek to the patrol cabin near Fern Lake, which we found to be in dismal shape. Fern Lake had gotten very little use since the big fishing camps had stopped coming into the park. We were the first rangers to have visited the cabin in several years, and it showed. There were two or three windows that had broken glass in them, which we replaced that afternoon. The cabin desperately needed a good, thorough cleaning and straightening up.

Chuck and I rode hard every day, locating the old campsites used by the outfitters decades earlier, many of which still showed the effects of over-use and abuse. You could still easily see the fire pit, which we obliterated before we left and evidence of old rope scars where horses had been tied to trees. The old rope scars we could do nothing about, but the circular holes they pawed around the trees while tied there we filled in with dirt. By the time we finished with the sites, they looked much better, and hopefully in a few more years, the sites would be hard to locate.

We also located and marked about a half a dozen sites over the entire area and were still able to get in a little fishing, but not much. The reason that the outfitters and fisherman had abandoned the area was due to the fact that there were no fish. The disappearance of the fish was not caused by over-fishing but by the appearance of a new thermal activity that had not existed in the area. There was some thermal activity up Broad Creek, where Whistler Geyser is located, and up Shallow Creek. I think that's the name of that little creek above Wapiti Lake. I don't know which of these was responsible for destroying the fishing, but I guess runoff from them changed the temperature or chemistry of the water.

After about five or six days, we left Fern Lake Patrol Cabin and rode up to Mirror Lake on Mirror Plateau and then up onto Specimen Ridge to the Petrified Forest there. I had heard about the ridge, but this was my first chance to see it. There were petrified tree trunks sticking up out of the ground and lying all over the ground. Geologists say there are twenty-seven separate layers of them. We did not have long to spend as we had a lot of riding to do before dark. We rode over far enough to look down into the Lamar Valley and then headed south until we picked up Raven Creek. We followed it back down into Pelican Valley to Pelican Springs Cabin, where we were going to spend the next several nights.

Chuck was in bad shape when he got up the next morning at Pelican Springs. He had saddle sores on his knees and thighs that were bleeding, and he said his ass was just as bad; I took his word for that though. I had ridden so many miles in the past few years that it got to where I never really paid any attention to distance. We had left Fern Lake at first light and had ridden hard all day, arriving at Pelican Springs about 10:00 p.m., so I guess we were in the saddle the biggest part of seventeen hours and had covered between thirty and forty miles. Chuck didn't really ride, he just sort sat in the saddle and let his horse dawdle along, and then he would have to trot to catch up with me. But in true Lomas style, I was treated to a barrage of horse jokes all night.

Chuck stayed around the cabin for the next few days, taking care of the repair and cleaning while I rode back up Raven Creek to establish a few campsites. I saw a fair amount of grizzly sign on Raven Creek but did not get sight of any. It took me a couple of days to finish my work on the campsites by which time Chuck had recovered enough that we took the last day and did nothing but fish Pelican Creek. We were lucky that we had only a five-mile ride out to the trailhead; much more than that, and Chuck would have had a tough time.

One day during the summer, we got a report at Lake Ranger Station of a dead mule beside the trail near Park Point Patrol Cabin. I was sent in to confirm the report and found the mule in question about five miles down the trail below Ten Mile Post trailhead. The mule was lying in the timber about ten feet off to the east side of the trail in a stand of tall thick timber. The mule was going to create a real hazard for hikers on this heavily traveled section of trail by attracting bear to the carcass.

The mule belonged to a party of local fisherman that had come in the day before headed to the upper Yellowstone for a week or so. The green broke mule was evidently giving them problems and would not stay in line in the pack string. It sounded to me as if they had him in the wrong place in the string. According to the equine pecking order, if you put a less dominant animal in front of a more dominant animal, you have insulted the honor of the more dominant animal, and he is going to take it out on the less dominant animal. The less dominant animal will spend all of its time looking behind him trying to avoid the wrath of the dominant animal and not paying any attention to the trail or watching its step. I learned this lesson well in my first year.

Another contributing factor was with the way our trail crew brushed the side of the trail. When they had to cut one of the small saplings on the side of the trail, they would just slash it once with a brush hook about a foot or so above the ground. This would leave the stump sticking up with a sharp end on it. I had complained several times about the danger of not only an animal but a hiker falling and impaling himself on one of them.

After talking to the owner of the mule, I found out that was exactly what happened. The mule, not watching the trail, had tripped and fallen on one of the stumps. The owner said the mule jumped back up onto his feet, but blood was squirting out, so the owner knew that the mule was going to die quickly. He said he dismounted as quickly as he could and cut the cinch loose from the pack saddle so he could get the mule off the trail before it died, but the mule only made it a few feet before it bled out.

I was stuck with the problem of how to get rid of the mule though. We considered butchering the mule into quarters and packing it out as you would an elk or moose, but that would still leave the gut pile. I guess I should also mention that the weather had been exceptionally warm for Yellowstone, so the mule with its guts still inside was starting to get pretty ripe. I was having flashbacks to when we had to dig all those dead bodies up in Nam.

The decision was made to take it out by chopper, but this also created problems. With a combination of the high elevation, warm temperatures, and the 850–900 pound weight of the mule, the chopper would not be able to lift the mule straight up out of the trees. We had to clear a long strip of timber so the chopper could take off with him. The chopper came in early the next morning while it was still cool, but it was still barely able to get him out.

Another trip Mernin sent me on during the time when I was working bear management was up to Jones Pass, north of the East entrance. The trailhead for this trail was near Pahaska Tepee, which was originally Buffalo Bill's old hunting lodge on the Shoshone River, about a mile east of the Entrance Station. The trail outside the park was well maintained by the Forest Service and well used by hunters. The trail inside the park had not even been cleared or marked since the 1940s or 1950s. Mernin was convinced that there was a lot of encroachment into that area of the park during hunting season because that area had not been patrolled in decades.

Mernin wanted me to clear the trail enough that it could be ridden well enough to allow access to the pass with minimal difficulty and mark the pass with a big fancy Entering Yellowstone sign. Actually, there were two passes in the area. The Bear Creek trail forked on the Yellowstone side of Jones Pass, and another trail followed the ridgeline a mile or so to Crow Creek Pass. Both passes were on Mount Chittendon, but outside the park the trail, over Jones Pass, went down Jones Creek on the north side of Silvertip Ridge and the trail over Crow Creek Pass, and went down Crow Creek south of Silvertip.

Action Jackson went with me on this trip, and it was a good thing because the lower part of the trail was covered with so much downed timber that we seldom were in the saddle. From where we cut a log from the trail, we could usually see another one a short distance on up the trail. We cleared about four or five miles that first day, and the worst was behind us, for by midmorning on the second day, we were getting high enough that the timber started to thin quickly. Knowing that there would be no water or grass near the pass, we decided to establish our base camp a mile or so down from the pass at the edge of the timber. We had no problem locating and marking Jones Pass, but the there was no sign of the trail to Crow Creek Pass. We had to reestablish the trail based on its location on a topo map. We put trail tags, marking the trail and another sign at the pass. It set in snowing on us before we finished, and before we got to base camp, there was a good four inches of snow. This was mid-August, but it might as well have been mid-October from the weather. Bob and I spent a miserable night before packing up the next morning and heading down out of the mountains to the Pelican Valley, where it had only rained.

As long as we were having no bear activity, I was free to take these backcountry trips with the justification that I was looking for bear or sign in that particular area, but when we started to have bear in the campgrounds, I had to take care of it. We had a yearling black bear start coming into Fishing Bridge Campground, killing and eating dogs during the day when the owners were off touring the park after leaving their pet chained in camp. I set a couple of traps in the locations where a dog had been taken, but uncharacteristically, the bear did not return to those sites.

This went on for a couple of days until the bear lifted a baby from a play pen by the head. Grandma came out of the trailer with a broom and chased the bear away after it had dropped the baby. The baby suffered only minor scratches, but the bear had signed his own death warrant. I took the 30-06 from the Ranger Station and went after the bear. It was last sighted leaving the Fishing Bridge Campground and headed across the road into the trailer village. I eventually located the bear in the woods on the edge of the trailer village, but a crowd had started to gather, so I was afraid to shoot for fear that someone might be in the woods looking for the bear. I called in a couple of other rangers, and a couple of maintenance men came to help. After they got the crowd back, I shot and killed the bear. As the bear's body was being dragged to the trap behind my truck, I heard a little boy crying to his dad because I had killed the bear. I overheard the dad reassure the boy that we did not kill the bear that we had just put it to sleep. I was walking along behind the bear and noticed that the bear was leaving a trail of blood. Not wanting to cause the boy any further anguish, I started dragging my foot to obliterate the blood trail.

Another time, I received the report of a man in a certain campsite at Fishing Bridge Campground that was up in a tree with a bear. I located the incident easily because of the crowd of about a hundred people gathered in the campsite. Sure enough, there in the top of a lodge pole pine was a man. About ten feet below the man in the same tree was a yearling black bear, and surrounding the tree was this crowd of over a hundred people. As soon as I was able to get the crowd away from the tree, the cub jumped down and was gone like a shot, never to be seen at Fishing Bridge again. The man that had been in the tree reported that the cub had chased him up the tree, but after talking to several witnesses it appears as if they had both picked the same tree to climb.

Most likely, what happened was that the cub wandered into the campground and gathered a crowd of people around him; he became nervous when the people completely surrounded him and started to run for the nearest tree. The man that was between the cub and the tree thought that the bear was after him, so he started to run to the nearest tree. The crowd kept pursuing the bear, the bear kept running for the nearest tree, and the man was already climbing, so the cub just followed him up the tree. The people mobbed together under the tree, taking pictures and such, preventing the cub from making his escape until I arrived and spoiled all the fun.

Black bear usually tended to be daytime bear or early evening bear, very bold and non-aggressive. It did not bother them at all to come into a campsite while all the occupants were seated at the table eating and just join them.

A grizzly is usually a nighttime bear, shy, and elusive but very aggressive. They usually waited until the campground was asleep for the night and slipped around on the outer edges of the campground. The first indication that we might have a grizzly starting to work the campground was when we started to get reports from campers that their ice chest had been stolen during the night, particularly if their campsite was located on the outside of an outer loop. I would go to the site and walk out into the wood. If it were a grizzly, I would find what was left of the ice chest about a hundred feet or so in the woods. Most chests, if they had a strong latch on them, would be totally destroyed, but chests that were easily opened would usually have little, if any, damage. Quite often, an ice chest that I returned to an owner would be a treasured item if it showed teeth and claw marks. I would often enhance the marks if they were minor, a trick I learned from an old maintenance man named Blue Evans. Blue was an old Montana cowboy philosopher of legendary proportions in Yellowstone. We were after a griz one night and had forgotten a rope needed to drag the bear to the trap after it had been tranquilized. Blue borrowed a brand-new hemp rope from a visitor, but as it turned, there were enough of us that we just carried the bear to the trap. Dragging the bear didn't work very well anyway since there were so many downed logs that you had to lift the bear over anyway. I gave the rope back to Blue to return to the owners, and he took the rope and smeared it in the bear shit that had been kicked out of the trap. I asked, "What are you doing?" Blue casually replied in that slow cowboy drawl, "Them folks would be awfully disappointed if they thought we didn't use their rope." I went with Blue to return the rope and offer to pay for it, but they wouldn't hear of it. That stinking, shit-covered rope had become a treasured belonging. As Blue was fond of saying, "Just trying to make people happy."

Late one summer, we started to get reports of ice chests being stolen at Bridge Bay campground, so I went over to take a look around. As soon as I parked, a guy came up and asked if I was aware of the bear that had been coming into the campground around 2:30 a.m. According to that guy, he had been awakened the last two mornings by a bear trying to break into the bear-proof trash cans. The bear would beat and bang on the trash cans a little, but being unable to get in, it would leave.

I brought a trap into the campground after everyone was asleep and set it near the bear-proof cans. I decided I would stay and watch for the bear to show up. About 1:30, I began to hear banging noises farther up in the campground, which would start and then there would be a five- to ten-minute pause. Each time the sound would get closer until right on schedule, about 2:30, the bear just seemed to appear from out of nowhere. It was a huge grizzly, long, lanky, and tall. It began to work on the trash cans but quickly gave up and located the trap. It quickly cleaned up the chum I left outside the trap but was very leery about entering the trap. It would start to go in and then back out, walk around the trap a time or two, and then go a little farther into the trap.

Finally, the bear stretched as far into the trap as it could reach keeping one hind foot on the ground. The bear was so long that it could reach the bait bag hanging from the trigger. It took the bait bag in its mouth, and with a quick jump backward, it tripped the trigger but caught the door with its leg before the door could go all the way down, and the door had to go all the way down before it would latch. The griz kind of wriggled and squirmed its leg and butt until it was able to get out of the trap. It reminded me of a woman trying to get out of a tight girdle. The next night, I would be ready.

I followed the same routine as the previous night, except this time, I had tied a rope to the trigger and had parked my car close by. Things started to happen right on schedule as the night before. Then during what seemed to be an exceptionally long pause in the action, I rolled down the window of the patrol car and hung my head partially outside so I could hear better. I heard a sound as if something was scraping the pavement as it walked. I looked to my left and was staring eye to eye with the grizzly that was walking by my car that had the window open and me with my head sticking out. There could not have been more than two feet between the bear and me. He stopped, turned his head to face me, and just stared in my direction. I don't know if he was actually staring at me or just in my direction. Either way, I could hear him breathe and smell his breath; he was that close.

After a few seconds, he ambled off in the direction of the trash cans and trap. He beat and banged on the cans for a few minutes, and for a while, I thought he was going to be able to tear the concrete block that the cans were attached to out of the ground. He finally gave up on the cans and moved to the trap. He cleaned up the chum on the ground and started to enter the trap. When he got stretched out as far as he could, but before he was ready to grab the bait bag and jump back, I jerked the rope that I had attached to the trigger. The big, heavy door came down on the bear's leg, just above the ankle, but the door had to go completely down before it latched, so the bear started to raise the door again. I jumped out of the car with a nightstick and jammed it through the heavy steel grating of the back door. The bear had lifted the door a foot or so before I got the nightstick in place.

Upon seeing me, the bear jerked its leg free and charged at me, letting the door drop into place where the safety latch caught. The bear hit the door with such force that the front end of the trailer came up off the ground. At the same time, he hit the end of the trap; he huffed real loud, snapped the nightstick off in its mouth, and blew snot all over me.

I stood leaning against the trap for a few minutes so my legs would quit shaking and I could walk before hooking up the trap and hauling him to the maintenance area, where we stored them until they were transplanted.

I think I have already mentioned that the weight of a bear is hard to guess, and that in the dark, they look larger. And if they are charging you, they look larger still. Well, this bear had charged at me in the dark, and it filled the trap from end to end when it stretched out. I made my log entries that night and guessed the bear's weight at 425 pounds. When I left the bear at the maintenance compound, he was trying to destroy the bear trap from the inside out, beating, banging, chewing, and bellowing all the while. You could hear him over the entire maintenance and housing area.

I went home and had just fallen asleep when Dale Nuss called me on the radio. In his gruffest voice, he ordered me to come get that bear and park it under my window for the night. Dale's apartment was closest to where I had left the bear.

By the time I got the bear relocated to the ranger station, it was daylight. I didn't bother going back to bed, so we could transplant the bear early. He was still raising all kinds of hell in the trap, and I was afraid he was going to injure himself, if he hadn't already. I hated to trap grizzly for that reason; most of them fought the trap so hard that they would quite often break teeth, and an animal's health depends, to a large degree, on the condition of its teeth.

The secretaries from the ranger station wanted to see the bear, so I took them out to see it. The bear had settled down a little, but they still approached the trap timidly and tried to stand a good distance back. It's dark inside the trap, which prevented them from being able to tell anything about the bear. I told them they would have to get right up to the rear door to get a good look. I knew what was coming when all three of the girls got right up to the door with their faces only a few inches away. The grizzly charged at them like he had charged at me, hit the end of the trap at full speed, and blew snot all over them. I felt a little guilty for having set them up, but it was so damn funny.

They jumped back so quickly that they fell all over each other, knocking each other to the ground, while still trying to crawl away. I would never have thought that those sweet ladies even knew such language as they used on me. I guess my laughing was what really made them mad, but it would have been funny to anyone. It was a long time before I dare asked one of them to type one of my reports.

The grizzly, a large bear, had never been handled before because he had no ear tag. The biologist office told us where to transplant him, and the chopper was on its way. All we had to do was tranquilize him, take all our measurements, and put in an ear tag. My weight estimate looked right, so we darted him for 425 pounds. The bear went under quickly but quit breathing by the time we got him out of the trap. We gave him a shot of the antidote and tried CPR on him but with no effect.

The grizzly's body was sent to Montana State University for autopsy, and the results made me feel a little better for having overdosed him. He was a young bear and should have been in his prime but had no body fat whatsoever, so it was doubtful if he would have survived hibernation. He should have easily weighed 450 pounds, based on the size of his frame, but it only weighed 195 pounds. The reason for his poor condition was from infections in two different wounds. A three-eighths-inch cable was embedded in a festering wound around one of his front legs, and the wadding from a shot gun wound was found embedded in another festering wound in his neck.

The cable most likely came from a snare used by Idaho Game and Fish. A grizzly had been working a lambing area outside the southeast corner of the park. Idaho Game and Fish had snared it, but it chewed through the cable. There is no telling where the shotgun wound came from though, most likely from the sheepherder whose lambs he was eating.

Another grizzly incident that ended in disaster for the grizzly happened in Fishing Bridge Campground. It was late summer, and the campground was scheduled to close the next week. Every night, just before dark, a ranger in a patrol car would drive through every loop in the campground, stopping twice to give the campers a bear warning over the car's PA system. It usually went something like this: "Good evening, ladies and gentlemen. This is a park ranger. Due to the increasing frequency of both grizzly and black bear in this campground, campers are required to store all food, cooking utensils, and ice chests inside of your vehicles when not in use. You must not store food, utensils, or ice chests in your tent. Failure to store these items properly is a violation of park regulations and will result in a fine. Thank you for your attention and support."

If we were able to keep all the food and ice chests stored, any bear that came into the campground would usually not find any food and would leave without causing any problem. However, if they found food, you could bet that they would be back the next night. Most of the time, people never even knew when there had been bear in their campsite if everything was stored properly.

There was a group of two young Japanese couples tent camping in G-loop at Fishing Bridge who spoke little, if any, English, so the bear warning given by the ranger was misunderstood that they must put their ice chest inside their tent at night, which they did. About 1:00 a.m., a grizzly sow with three new cubs entered their campsite. The sow ripped open the tent and dragged the ice chest outside where she and the cubs proceeded to dine.

Somehow, the two couples were able to get into their car, which is where I found them when I arrived. They were peering out of their vehicle at the remains of their tent as these three cubs played tug of war with it. Their eyes pleaded with me to do something, but the sow was nowhere to be seen. I was not about to do anything until I knew where she was, and even then I was not sure what I could do. The cubs drifted out of the campsite in a few minutes to wherever the sow was. I gathered up what was left of the people's belongings and loaded it into their car for them, since they were not about to get out of the vehicle. Within minutes, they were headed to the Lake Hotel for the night.

I spent the rest of the night patrolling through the campground looking for the sow but never got a look at her. I was hoping to get a weight estimate so I could tranquilize her the next night. The next afternoon, we had people on foot patrol contacting every campsite, making sure that they understood the bear warning and that everything was stored properly. I went to work about midnight and parked in the campsite where the oriental couples had been the last night. I was going to mix the tranquilizer when I was sure of her weight. We also had several other rangers standing by to help with the cubs when we got her down.

About 1:00 or 1:30 a.m., a yearling grizzly cub came into the site but only stayed for a minute or so. Then immediately following the departure of the yearling, the three cubs came into camp with the sow close behind. I assumed that the yearling was her previous year's cub still trying to hang around mama. The sow and three cubs stayed for only a few minutes before leaving, but I had a good weight estimate, so I would be ready the next time she came in. She didn't show up in that site again.

I sat there until around 2:30 a.m. when I heard this bloodcurdling scream from somewhere in the next loop. I drove directly over to H-loop and was circling through the loop when I noticed movement in one of the pull-through sites. I swung into the site at the rear of a travel trailer with my headlights shining off into the trees. There in my headlights was the sow dragging a man in his underwear off into the trees. I drug the shot gun from its case as I exited the patrol car and racked a shell into the chamber. At the sound of me racking a shell into the chamber, the sow left the man and charged at me. I was barely able to get back inside the vehicle before she was on the hood slapping at me through the glass. I saw the victim moving and trying to get to his knees, but the sow also saw him and left me to charge at the injured man. This time when she got to him, she took his head into her mouth and then beat him with her front legs and paws; she did not use her claws though. It was as if she was just giving him a spanking for bad behavior.

I knew I had to do something, so this time when I got out, I knew where all the campsites were, so I could get a clear shot. The first time I got out, everything happened so suddenly that I did not have my bearings as to where I could shoot because I was right in the middle of the campground with campsites all around me.

I planned to make her charge at me again, and as soon as she did, I was going to drop her with the shotgun; there was no time for the tranquilizer gun. As I approached her, she started to charge at me but then swerved off to the right into the trees.

I could hear the man moaning softly, so I knew that he was still alive and that I needed to get to him as quickly as I could. Those forty to fifty feet that separated me from him were, I believe, the most difficult I have ever taken. Not knowing where that sow was or what direction she might come charging from, I finally reached the victim, a man about sixtyish. I expected to find him in shreds and bleeding profusely, but he had few noticeable injuries. One of his ears was hanging by just a little flap of tissue and his tongue was sticking out of a hole in his cheek. I remember picking pine needles from it. Other than that, I don't remember any other visible injuries except he was already starting to show bruising where the sow had beaten him.

Another ranger arrived about this time and the ambulance from the hospital shortly after. I stood guard while the victim was given first aid and then transported to the hospital. Several other rangers showed up and were assigned the task of patrolling the campground continually to keep the sow out of the campground. I was assigned to be the lead investigator on the case.

Based on my interviews of the family, the victim's name was Mike, a frequent Yellowstone camper from Salt Lake City. Mike and his wife were camped in their travel trailer, along with their daughter and her husband, who were in the same campsite, staying in a pickup camper. They had been gone from the campsite all day, having arrived back at their site sometime after 10:00 p.m. The son-in-law said that they had turned a rubber life raft over the top of their ice chest to hide it from view.

They were awakened by the sound of the cubs fighting over the ice chest full of food. Mike came out of his trailer waving a fishing vest at the cubs to chase them away. The unseen sow attacked from nowhere, knocking Mike down at the steps of his trailer. The son-in-law came out of his camper carrying a Coleman lantern to assist Mike. The sow left the old man and charged at the son-in-law, who was just able to get back into his camper. The lantern was lying smashed at the door of his camper.

Instead of playing dead, the old man tried to get up and get back inside of his trailer. The sow caught him at the door and started to drag him off into the trees, which was about the time I got there. The old man was lucky having done so many things wrong with a grizzly and living to tell about it. He was transferred to University Medical Center in Salt Lake City, where he was treated for minor lacerations and extreme internal injuries. Less than a month later, he came after us for money. To think I risked my life for this guy!

We were able to keep the bear out of camp for the rest of the night while we laid plans for the next night. We closed down the entire back half of the campground, G, H, and I loops, and doubled our foot patrol in the front half to catch any violation concerning food storage. Oak Blair and I parked our truck in G-loop again and waited. Oakley was driving, and I was going to dart her when she came in.

About midnight, she came into range. I started to roll the window down, so I could stick the dart gun out for a shot. When she heard the sound of the window being rolled down, she charged at the truck. I had to drop the tranquilizer gun outside of the truck, so I could get window rolled back up. She was on the hood, on the top, and in the bed, slapping and blowing snot everywhere. Oakley had to start the engine and back out from under her, throwing her to the ground. She took off into the woods before I was able to reclaim the dart gun and get a shot. We sat there a while longer when we heard a bear trap slam shut in H-loop.

When we arrived at the trap, we could not see into the trap, so we did not know if we had caught the sow, a cub, or anything at all. As it turned out, we had not caught anything, and it was still baited. I reset the trap, and we decided to wait there just in case she came back. The next time she came in, I was ready for her. I had the window down and the dart gun outside of the cab already. When I shot, I saw the dart hit, but it didn't look like a solid hit. It hit at an angle, and oftentimes, it does not inject the entire tranquilizer if the dart does not hit solidly.

We had no way of knowing if she was down or not when we went searching for her a few minutes later. I used the tranquilizer sucostrin, which puts them down in a couple of minutes but only keeps them down for about five minutes. It was another of those real intense incidents that would get your blood to pumping. I have never felt so alive or focused as when I was in a situation like this. All of my senses were more acute, and I was ready for anything.

It took us a couple of minutes to locate her. A short distance inside the timber, and luckily, she was completely out. I touched her eyeball and got no response. If she were starting to come out from under the drug, she would have blinked. We tied a rope to one of her hind legs and started to drag her to the waiting trap. By this time, we had a lot of help, but it still took time and considerable effort to get her limp body over and around logs. When I checked her reflexes again, she snapped at me. I picked up a stick about an inch and a half in diameter and two feet long and offered it to the sow in place of my arm or leg. She halfheartedly snapped it and was chewing on it the rest of the way to the trap. We got her inside the trap and dropped the door not a minute too soon either, but now, we had three cubs to capture.

The cubs stayed around the sow pretty close, so we didn't have to hunt them down, but capturing them was a real challenge. The cubs were heir to a proud bad ass tradition. Even though they weighed only about fifteen pounds, they knew they were grizzlies, and grizzlies are the baldest of the bad. I remember one time I was hauling a grizzly cub down the road in a trap when I came upon a roadside black bear. The instant the adult black bear caught sent of the grizzly, it took off into the woods at a dead run. It didn't wait around to see what size the grizzly was. We got two of the cubs tranquilized and in traps all right, but we only had three traps in the area. One had the sow, which was awake and raising hell by now, and the other two traps had a cub a piece in them, who were also beginning to get pretty active. I had tranquilized the third cub but did not have a place to put it, and it was starting to come around. I told Oak on the count of three to lift the door of one of the traps that already had a cub in it but only about a foot. I grabbed the cub by the hide on it shoulders and ass and started to swing it back and forth as I counted. The cub, by this time, was fighting like a wild cat, claws and teeth flashing. On the count of three, Oakley opened the trap, and I threw the cub in with its sibling, just before being ripped to shreds. As the saying goes, one of us needed some relief!

The next day, we tranquilized all of them and transplanted them to the north edge of Two Ocean Plateau. That's just what I need in Thorofare, another crazy grizzly. Normally, a grizzly that injures someone would be put to sleep, but being so late in the season, the biologists' office reasoned that most of the campgrounds would be shut down in less than a week, and the sow would be going into hibernation in less than a month. If she returned the next year, she could be put down, but at least, the three cubs would be old enough to take care of themselves.

We had to make two trips, taking the cubs first and laying them together while still drugged. We brought the sow on the second trip and lay her a short distance from the cubs. After giving all of them the antidote, we hovered above them in the chopper to make sure they were all right. The cubs came out of the tranquilizer first but were just milling around at the edge of the plateau, not knowing what to do.

When the sow came out of the tranquilizer, it was instantly. She jumped up and headed down over the edge of the plateau. It appeared as if the cubs and the sow were headed toward each other, but they got in heavy timber, so we lost sight of them. Twenty-four hours later, I trapped the sow in Fishing Bridge Campground in the same place where we had tranquilized the cubs the earlier. I guess she was so stoned when she came out from under the M-99, a morphine derivative; she was not alert enough to detect the presence of her cubs. The last place she remembered them was at Fishing Bridge Campground. She traveled from the plateau and all the way around the lake in less than twenty-four hours.

We flew back out to the plateau, and sure enough, there were the cubs, lying there waiting for their mother in the same spot that we had dropped the sow. We tranquilized and flew the sow back out to the plateau and placed her near the cubs. This time, we tied one leg of the sow to a tree so at least she would have to be alert enough to chew the rope into. The cubs came to her as soon as we lifted off in the chopper. It was something to see the cub and sow's reaction upon finding each other.

A few days later, I was headed into Thorofare for the fall and had no further dealings with the grizzly family that year. However, less than two weeks after their last transplant on the plateau, the sow showed up in one of the campgrounds in the northern part of the park, and again, she injured a visitor. I only heard about this part of the story, but according to the story, a motorcyclist pulled into the campground late one evening. He didn't even bother to pitch his tent but just rolled out his sleeping bag on the ground. During the night, he was awakened by something stepping on his feet. When he sat up, he saw the cubs at the feet of his sleeping bag. The sow cuffed him with her paw, and she and the cubs took off. The motorcyclist suffered only minor injuries, probably because he was inside of the sleeping bag and made no effort to fight her or escape.

The sow was destroyed and the fifteen-pound cubs were radio-collared and transplanted. The three cubs went into hibernation together, survived the winter, but two of the three starved to death in early spring. It had been such a mild winter that there had been very little winterkill of elk or deer, and carrion is what the bear depend on when they first come out of hibernation before the plants green up. The third cub survived by feeding off the carcasses of its siblings. That summer, the cub was poached by someone, and its radio collar buried up in Hayden Valley. The radio transmitter signal stopped moving, so the biologists' office wanted me to see if I could locate the collar. I eventually found the collar buried just barely an inch or so deep but found no sign of the cub.

The chief ranger, Bud Esty, had been a ranger almost as long as there had been a Park Service and most of that time in Yellowstone. He had been removed from the day-to-day operations of the park for so long that he was not aware of the poaching problem we had in the interior of the park. To Bud, the boundaries were the places we needed to worry about, and up to this incident, you could not convince him that we had a problem in the interior.

There were several reasons for the problem, some caused by policy and others caused by the high rate of unemployment during the winter months. The permanent rangers could not take leave or go to any training during the busy summer season, which sounds reasonable until you look at the whole picture. During the summer months besides the two permanent rangers in an area, there would be from half a dozen to twenty or more seasonal rangers, many of which had far more experience than many of the permanent rangers. During the off-season, there were no seasonal rangers except during the snowmobile season. That time period from September, October, and part of November, and then again in April and May, the roads were open throughout the park, but most of the field rangers were either gone on leave or at a training session of some kind. It was during this time when most of the poaching occurred. The road from Cooke City to Gardner Montana runs right through the middle of the winter range of the Bighorn Sheep in the entire northern half of the park. It was not unusual to see two or three full curl Bighorn rams lying near the road. The poachers would shoot a ram, drop a man off to cut the head off, and picked it back up later. The entrance stations were not open during the off-season, so they would just drive back out of the park.

The same thing was done with elk and bison in different areas of the park. After this cub was taken, I convinced Bud of the problem by locating the carcasses of three bison in the Lake sub-district that had the heads removed, which is a good indication that they had been poached. I started to work a lot during the off-season, filling in for a permanent ranger that was gone. There were times when I would be the only ranger on duty in the entire southern half of the park with hundreds of miles of road to patrol by myself. After I graduated from college, I started working during the winter snowmobile season. The first year, I was working out of Old Faithful, and my entire life has never been the same since, for it was during this winter that I met my future wife, though I didn't know it at the time.

I had started working in early December, a couple of weeks before the park officially opened to the public. My duties were to be snowmobile patrol of the roads and ski patrol around the area. I had never been on a set of skis before, but if you can walk, you can cross country ski.

About the middle of December, the concession employees arrived at Old Faithful. There were a few facilities open on a limited basis at Old Faithful and none elsewhere in the park, except at Mammoth Hot Springs, where Park HQ was located; the road was kept plowed all year. At Old Faithful, there was overnight lodging, food, and drink at the Snow Lodge. There was also a snack bar, snowmobile fuel, post office, and visitor center available.

Before the Snow Lodge opened for the season, it always served a practice dinner, and all Park Service employees were invited for a free meal; in other words, we were their guinea pigs. Marve and I went over to the Lodge for the dinner but decided to have a drink in the bar first. The bar was packed.

When we entered, and at the bar were these young ladies, one sitting and the other sitting on her legs on the bar stool with her ass stuck out. It was the nicest ass I had ever seen, before or since. I poked Marv, pointed at her, and made some comment about her having an ass like a Montana Mare. Marve took one look at her from the rear and said, "Oh, that's Dee Ann. I'll introduce you." Dee Ann was working as a cocktail waitress that evening, along with serving as head waitress, but Marve invited the two ladies to join us for a drink after they had finished their shift.

Dee and the other girl, Marion Dow, Dee's best friend, joined us in the bar after the dining room closed at 10:00. We had a drink, played cards, and visited until about midnight. Dee was the most beautiful woman I had ever seen. Her dark brown eyes were perhaps her most striking feature, other than her ass, that is. They were so mesmerizing that I tried to avoid looking into them. We shared many similar interests, and she was a lot of fun to be with.

If I would have known the effect that this encounter would have on the rest of my life, I might have given a little more thought before I started to make the Snow Lodge a nightly routine. I had already decided that I was a confirmed bachelor; I liked my lifestyle, being free to come and go as I pleased. Give me an hour's notice, and I would have all my worldly possessions, saddles, panniers, skis, guns, and sleeping bag, loaded in the back of my truck with still plenty of room to sleep, my canoe strapped down on top, a full tank of gas, and I was off on another adventure.

Our relationship started slowly, and it's probably a good thing that it did because I did not want to get involved in a lasting relationship. I had found my life's calling, I thought, and I had seen how difficult Yellowstone was on relationships. The long winter isolation was more than most wives could stand for more than a couple of seasons. By the end of that first winter, we were just good friends with no romantic ties to each other. Dee was not planning on returning to the park for the next summer, so I thought that we would probably never see each other again, which is one of the sad things about Yellowstone. People drift in and out of your life so quickly; about the time you really get to know and like them, the season is over and they go back home.

That first winter in the park was a whole new experience for an ole southern boy from Arkansas. I spent a lot of my time either riding snowmobiles or working on them, and it seemed that the two times were proportional to each other. I began to get the knack of staying upright on my skis and being able to get up when I crashed. The first time I crashed, I thought I would never get up; I flopped around and fought it until the snow was pretty well packed down. I skied several miles almost every day, mostly around the geyser basins and up to the falls.

There were thousands of snowmobiles that came into Old Faithful each day, most of them from West Yellowstone Montana at the West Entrance. Some of the snowmobilers stayed at the Snow Lodge for the night, but most just made the southern loop and returned to West Yellowstone. Snowmobilers were a different breed than the summer visitors. They drank from the time they got up in the morning until they went to sleep. They really liked the flavored brandies, especially blackberry. I caught a group of about fifty people from a snowmobile club from Minnesota skinny dipping in the Fire Hole River between Old Faithful and Madison Junction. It was a beautiful sunny day with the temperature somewhere in the twenties, but the water in the Fire Hole River is about the temperature of bath water. Some of them would get out of the water and then dive into the snow, then back into the water. I just kind of watched for a while and thought it best if I just ignored the situation and drove right on by. I'm sure they were half-drunk, judging from their actions, and one drunk is hard enough to deal with; I didn't even want to think about dealing with fifty.

I loved the drive along the Fire Hole River during the winter with its large concentration of thermal features. There was such a contrast between the hot water and steam from the geyser basins. The river was not only ice-free but warm because of the runoff from the geysers and hot springs, so many water fowl stayed in the river all winter. There was always several pair of Trumpeter Swans along with many species of duck swimming in the river, along with elk grazing on the algae mats in the water. Large numbers of bison roamed through the steam of the geyser basins covered with sheets of ice where the steam had frozen on their fur. It is one of those special scenes found only in Yellowstone, and there are many more.

There were also snow coaches carrying passengers bound for Old Faithful that entered the South Entrance each morning. There were also coaches that made the southern loop each day. All of these people stayed in the Snow Lodge at night. They were generally a little older and wealthier than the average snowmobiler. Walter Cronkite, the news anchor, was at the Snow Lodge on New Year's Eve but got so drunk that he had to be taken to his cabin before midnight. To quote Cronkite, "And that's the way it was December 31, 197?"

I don't remember which winter season that this event occurred, but I remember that it was when Bob Mahn was stationed at Lake. Bob was a stoutly built ranger from Ohio that had a very unusual way of talking due to the speech therapy he had when he was young. He told me no one could understand a word he said until he started school and received therapy. Because of the slow drawn-out way he spoke, many people thought he was dumb, but it was just the opposite; he was exceptionally smart and a hell of a likeable guy.

I headed out from South Entrance by snowmobile an hour or so before daylight on my way to meet Bob at Lake. It was better than twenty below at South when I started out, but the northern part of the park was giving better than forty below for a low, and I was headed north about forty-five miles or so. I could not make up my mind if it was better to drive fast and freeze to death quickly or drive slower and drag out the misery longer. Either way, the wind chill had to be from eighty to one hundred degrees below zero.

I made it to Lake just as the sun was beginning to come up. When I pulled up at Lake Ranger Station, I was not even able to get off the snowmobile for a while. It took a long time to get my legs straightened enough that I could walk on them, and they just would not work right. It took about an hour of drinking hot coffee and warming up in the station before I was able to continue on to Sylvan Pass to shoot down avalanches, which was mine and Bob's objective for the day.

We loaded five or six rocket rounds and the gun on Bob's sled and headed for the pass, twenty miles to the east. I have forgotten the caliber of the rocket, but it seems as if it was about 120 mm. It was a beautiful day, clear, still, and warming fast. The road to Sylvan Pass and East Entrance was lightly traveled, so the snow was in great shape, and we made the pass in good time. The view from the pass was stupendous or orgasmic as Clement was fond of saying, with the entire Absorka Range before you and the plains stretching on forever.

On the south side of the road right at the pass was an elevated platform, about twelve or fifteen feet above the ground. There was no snow on the ground right at the pass because of the wind that kept it blown free. We parked our snow machines at the base of the platform, unloaded, and mounted the gun. Sylvan Pass was cut deeply between two towering peaks with barely enough room to get a road between them. During a storm, the wind would cause the snow to build up on the peaks to tremendous depths. Even though there was only a small number of snowmobiles that came into the park from the east entrance, we tried to keep the pass safe of avalanches; but from the pass toward the entrance was just one avalanche shoot after another. To make matters worse, the road just sort of hung to the side of a sheer cliff most of the way. It was probably the most dangerous stretch of road, not only in Yellowstone but in that entire stretch of the Rockies.

Bob Mahn was killed there a few years later while working out of East Entrance. It seems as though he reported that he was headed for the Pass in a storm to check road conditions. If the conditions got too dangerous because of avalanche danger, he would close the road until we could shoot them down. Bob was never heard from again, and his body was not found until the next summer. He either missed the road during a whiteout or an avalanche took him over the side. Either way, the results were the same. Bob was a newlywed when it happened.

On this occasion though, Bob and I shot about three or four rounds at the ridgeline on the north side of the road, which looked to have the worst buildup of snow, but very little snow was released. With the next round, we heard that rumbling sound, which indicated that we had triggered an avalanche somewhere, but we could not see it.

Bob was pretty clumsy and accident prone to boot. One fall in Thorofare, Bob had been sent in to help me remove a large, dead tree standing in the corral, which was leaning toward the barn. We figured out where to notch the tree so it would miss the barn when it fell. Everything went as planned except that the tree was hung up in the fork of a green tree next to the barn. I started cutting the tree into about eight-foot sections so that they could be skidded down to the cabin and cut up into firewood. We had the tree in sections, all except for a short piece about eighteen inches long that was wedged tightly in the fork of the dead tree. I walked down to the cabin where the stock was tied to get a mule so we could start skidding the logs to the cabin. All of a sudden, I heard Bob yelling in a real panicked voice, "John, saw, saw!"

I ran back to the coral and found Bob standing on a log with his hand stuck in the fork of the tree where that short piece of wood had been.

Evidently, Bob had reached up and pushed the block out, and the fork in the tree had closed on his hand. I grabbed the chainsaw, and luckily, it started with the first jerk of the rope. There were only a couple of inches between Bob's gloved hand and the bottom of the fork of the tree where I needed to cut and relieve the pressure on Bob's hand. I was real nervous about cutting so close to his hand, knowing how bad chainsaws are to jump and how much damage they can do with just a slight bump. I cautiously eased the chain into the wood until I could feel the tree starting to bind on the bar of the saw. I killed the engine and worked the blade out of the cut, and using an ax as a lever, I was able to get Bob's hand out.

The whole ordeal had lasted for only a few minutes, but Bob was about to blackout from the pain by the time I got him loose. His hand swelled up almost instantly and turned black. Bob said the hand was numb for over two weeks. I don't know if he broke anything, but I can't see how it didn't. It was just a good thing that he had on a pair of heavy work gloves. Bob never griped or complained about it; his only comment was, "You know, that's the second time that has happened to me."

Bob also had the distinction of being the most prodigious eater in a group of hardworking young men that had missed too many meals. Me and Scotty could really put away the food, particularly if we had been drinking. Scotty and I would often go into the Elk Horn Café after we had closed down the Cowboy Bar around 2:00 a.m. and order a dozen eggs and a pound of bacon apiece. It would come with about a pound of hash browns and about a half a loaf of toast. It was all I could do to finish the meal, but Scotty would still be looking to see if I had anything left for him to finish. I'm sure Bob could even outdo Scotty, and Bob didn't care what it was. One night at Trail Creek, I watched him put away a whole big pan of some kind of experimental casserole that one of us had tried. The experiment failed the test badly except with Bob. After we had finished a big meal and were cleaning up the dishes, we told Bob to take the casserole outside and dump it somewhere, so it would keep the bear run off. I watched Bob standing outside with this big pan of casserole cradled in his left arm shoveling it to his mouth with a spoon as large as a small shovel. There was none left when he brought the pan back in, and there had to be a couple of gallons of the stuff. The worst part was that he farted like a pack mule for two or three days.

Just before the end of the winter season, Marve and I took a ski trip to Mary Mountain Patrol Cabin. The trailhead was located between Norris Junction and Canyon Village. This was a good choice for my first outing being that it was only seven or eight miles in from the trailhead with very little elevation gain. I had not mastered the art of skiing uphill yet, but there were enough hills to give me a lot of practice. We skied across the Central Plateau on the Plateau trail to Mary Mountain and Mary Lake where the cabin set on its west shore. It was a great trip, good food, drink, and friends. The bullshit was knee deep in the cabin by the time we left. Marve had packed steaks, baking potatoes, salad, and all the fixin's. I had packed the beer, whiskcy, and snacks. It just doesn't get any better than that.

The next day, we skied down Nez Perce Creek on the Mary Mountain trail to the road between Madison Junction and Old Faithful, where we caught a ride on the Thiakol road groomer back into Old Faithful. Part of the trail we skied on was actually an old road that had been cleared across the plateau by General Howell so he could get his cannons through the timber while chasing Chief Joseph and the Nez Perce Indians back in 1876 or 1878.

A couple of years after Crazy Horse and the Sioux had defeated Gen. Custer at the Little Big Horn, the Nez Perce and Chief Joseph refused to stay on their reservation in Washington State. They had heard about the Sioux escaping into Canada after defeating Custer and decided to join the Sioux in Canada. Their path brought them through Yellowstone, which was already a park, having been created in 1872. The Nez Perce captured some park visitors on the Yellowstone River in Hayden Valley and kept them captive for several days before turning them loose unharmed. General Howell was chasing them from the west, and two other armies were closing on them from the south and east.

The Nez Perce, on their Appaloosa horses, would get so far ahead of Howell that they would think he had given up the chase. The Nez Perce would stop to rest and hunt for a while since they had women, children, and all their belongings with them. Howell would catch up after a couple of weeks, a skirmish would occur, and the Nez Perce would take off again.

This happened several times before the Nez Perce reached the safety of Canada, or at least they thought they were in Canada, but they had stopped a few miles short. The three armies converged on them at the same time, defeating them, and made them walk to the Oklahoma Indian Territory.

To make a long story short, the Appaloosa horse nearly became extinct before a few were discovered in Oklahoma. They became very sought-after for a long time, and there is even an Appaloosa Horse Club today. I'll bet you are beginning to wonder where the old fool is heading with this story. Well, the Appaloosa Horse Club decided they would retrace the route that the Nez Perce had taken on their flight across Washington, Idaho, Wyoming, and Montana. The only way the Park Service would give them permission to cross Yellowstone with such a large group was with a ranger.

What better ranger could they choose than one that had already traced what I thought to be the course they would have taken through the park, based on historical records provided by Dr. Mary Marh, a close friend in the biologist office at Mammoth, and plain logic as to the best route to take where no records existed? Besides that, I was the only ranger riding an Appaloosa.

Those people sure knew how to travel, as long as you didn't care how far you traveled. I don't think we were ever on the trail much before noon and had to make camp in time for happy hour. I don't think we ever covered ten miles on any day, but we covered it in style.

I know this story doesn't fit in with the winter season, but thinking of that Nez Perce trail down from Mary Mountain jogged my memory. I can still see the opening through the timber that Howell's Army cleared through the thick Lodge Pole Pine.

Shortly after I arrived back in the park for the summer season, Dee sent me a letter stating that she had decided not to go to Radiology school but to return to the park instead. I should have started to become suspicious at this concerning her motives but was just anxious to see her again. It worked out well that she had been transferred to the Lake area for the summer. I didn't know until later that she had asked for the transfer so she and I would be closer, nor did I know that she, Marve, and Scotty were conspiring behind my back to get us together.

I don't guess I resisted very hard because by the summer's end, we were pretty well a steady item. There had been a couple of other girls that I dated on occasion, but nothing serious. I didn't think Dee knew about the other girls, but she made Marve take her to Canyon Village, where one of them worked so she could get a look at her. Dee let me continue to think that she knew nothing about the other girls. She made no demands on me nor was she possessive toward me. Gradually, I was spending more time with her and less with the others, until, without realizing it, I was not seeing the other girls.

I didn't think about how deeply involved we had become, but in the back of my mind, I knew that I was hooked and so did my buddies. I started getting teased about being henpecked and whipped, but I didn't care. I was enjoying being with her as I had never enjoyed anyone's company before. From this point on, it's not just my story, but mine and Dee's.

Dee decided that she would return to college at Utah State in Logan, and I went to work out of Mammoth for Craig Johnson. The reason that I ended up in Mammoth was because of the unusual weather conditions that year. We had early deep snow followed by a warm spell. The snow had melted down to about six inches of slush when it turned cold as hell, changing the six inches of slush to six inches of ice. Not even the bison could paw through it. By late December, large numbers of elk were leaving the park along the Yellowstone River. On any given night, there would be two or three thousand head of elk in downtown Gardiner and Deckard flats.

The State of Montana decided to open a late elk hunt and issued four-day permits to anyone that applied. Deckard Flats, just outside the north entrance to Yellowstone, was a relatively flat, treeless area about a mile or so wide and long. Each hunt would start at daylight on Thursday morning; the elk would be everywhere. At first light, the shooting would start, causing the elk to run first this way and then that, where they were shot at again. It was a slaughter that lasted until dark Sunday, by which time most of the elk had been slaughtered. By Thursday, another herd had drifted out of the park, so the slaughter started again.

I was sent to Mammoth to ski the boundary during the hunt to prevent encroachment and to kill the wounded animals that had gotten back into the park. The trail was red with blood for a couple of miles up the Black Canyon of the Yellowstone. I actually worked out of Crevice Creek patrol cabin on the north boundary, and it was not what I was used to with regard to patrol cabins. Mernin would not have tolerated its condition. The cabin was in such poor condition, structurally and aesthetically. The cabin floor was so buckled and unleveled that the door would not open but about halfway. There was very little in the way of cooking utensils, condiments, or tools. I had to ski in with everything, including food, since there were no winter rations.

The cabin sat on the north side of the Black Canyon of the Yellowstone in fairly steep terrain, so I had to use caution concerning avalanches, particularly with that layer of ice at the bottom. Many times when I would be skiing along on a side hill, the snow in that area would just slump downhill suddenly and scare the shit out of me.

After each hunt, I would have to ski up the canyon to kill the wounded elk. I would spend the night in a cabin down in the canyon. I can't believe that I have forgotten the name of that cabin. I can see it well enough in my mind and the trail leading up to it. The trail was on the north side of the narrow gorge with a suspension bridge leading over the river to the south side where the cabin was located a short distance up stream where the canyon widened a little. The next day, I would ski out of the canyon and across the flats to the road from Mammoth to the North East Entrance and Cooke City.

I repeated this routine for a few weeks when a bigger problem arose. The northern herd of bison also decided they would leave the park. I was headed out onto Deckard Flats at daylight one morning when I saw five big bulls grazing off in the distance. After checking in with Dale Nuss, he told me to try to herd them back into the park, which, surprisingly, I was able to do. What made the problem worse with the bison is that Montana is a brucellosis free area, except for the bison in Yellowstone. Brucellosis is also known as Bang's disease, which causes domestic cows to abort their fetuses. It has no effect on bison cows, but they are carriers. The Department of Agriculture wanted Yellowstone to round up all the bison that were carriers and destroy them, estimated at between eighty and ninety of a herd that numbered about 1,600 animals. The Park Service refused to even consider it but compromised and agreed to kill any bison that got within a mile of the park boundary if it could not be herded back up into the park.

I was able to drive them pretty well as long as they were in the timber, but when we reached a meadow, the bulls would just stand there as if daring me to come out of the trees onto the meadow. I was able to get them a couple of miles back up the canyon by dark, but by daylight, they were back on Deckard Flats again. This time, however, the local ranchers had heard about the bison being out of the park and complained to the Department of Agriculture, who in turn complained to the secretary of the interior, who complained to the director of the Park Service, who complained to the superintendent of Yellowstone, the chief ranger, district ranger, and sub-district ranger. Finally Craig Johnson, the sub-district ranger that I was working for at the time, ordered me to shoot them. I used a 375 H&H Magnum rifle, a rifle designed for hunting elephant and rhino. I have been kicked by cows, bulls, horses, and mules and have shot almost every weapon ever made when I was in the Corps, but I have never had anything kick like that rifle.

I gained a healthy respect for Indian squaws as we began to skin and butcher the bison. We had everything we needed to make it easier, but it was still a tremendous effort. We had a truck with gin poles and a winch to pick the animal up or move it. We had a truck set up as a field butcher shop with every kind of saw and knife available, and it still took a crew of a dozen or more men all day just to field dress the five bison.

The park contracted a helicopter to help me keep the rest of the herd driven back farther into the park. Bob Schullinger was the owner and pilot of the chopper and had been doing contract flying for the Forest Service for many years. That first morning I reported to the LZ and saw the chopper, I was more than a little skeptical about whether that chopper would be able to fly with both of us or not. I had been used to large military choppers, and even the choppers the parks contract in the summer were much larger. This thing looked like those little Bell choppers used in the movie *Mash*. To make things worse, there was a set of jumper cables running from Bob's truck battery to the chopper battery. Bob fired it up and yelled for me to unhook the jumper cables and get in. Like the fool I am, I did as I was told, and as I buckled myself in, I noticed that the Plexiglass bubble had been duct-taped in several places.

As we headed up the canyon, I was glad that the chopper was no larger. It looked as if the tips of the rooters were only a few feet from the canyon on each side. I sure was relieved when we spotted the herd, and Bob dropped me off with my skies. I pushed the bison through the timber, and Bob would pick them up with the chopper and drive them across the meadow. When they entered the trees again, the chopper was useless until I could catch up and drive them through the trees. If it was a large meadow, Bob would fly back for me. He would hover a foot or so above the ground, and I would just sit on the bar that was the landing gear with my skis still on my feet and hang on. Bob would fly a few feet above the ground all the way across the meadow and drop me off near the trees.

We got so good at herding the bison that we eventually were able to push them all the way up and out of the canyon onto the flats. Once they got out onto the flats, we could do nothing with them except keep them scattered. By the next morning, the herd would be halfway down the canyon again, and we would start the process again. Believe it or not, the chopper flew perfectly, but we had to jump it each morning.

I really gained a lot of respect for Bob's flying ability as we flew up the canyon each day, but at first, I was scared to death. As we flew, I was constantly hanging out of the door opening, looking straight down through the trees; it was the only way you could spot the bison in timber. Bob would do the same thing on his side and appeared to be paying no attention to where he was flying, and like I said, the canyon was so narrow that there was little room for mistake. I would yell at Bob to keep his eyes on the road and let me look for the buffalo.

Bob and I became good friends over the duration of the winter and would usually meet in Gardner a couple of times a week for dinner and drinks. One night after having dinner at the Town Saloon in Gardner, we went out to the bar for an after-dinner drink and visit. The Town Saloon was the Park Service hangout and the nicest of the seventeen full-time bars in Gardner. I guess I should mention that there was only one part-time church in Gardner; it was open only from June through August. Other than some of the park people, Gardner was populated by nothing but poachers and seasonal maintenance employees drawing unemployment compensation.

The bar in the Town Saloon was an L-shaped affair with about a dozen bar stools down its length and four stools at the end near the dining room. Bob and I settled in on the two middle stools at the end of the bar since the only open stools were those at the end. We were having our first drink when two young ladies came into the bar and sat down by Bob and me. The bartender came over and told the two girls that if he had to call them down again, he was going to throw them out of the bar. I guess that they had been in earlier and had been pretty loud and obnoxious; both of them had obviously been drinking considerably.

The gal sitting next to me started telling me how she had just gotten back into town after having been in Reno working as a show girl; I thought to myself she was more the stripper type. I could see her sliding up and down on one of those poles; she had the body for it. She began to talk about her silicone implants, and remember, this was in the mid-1970s when implants were a new procedure. Jokingly, I told her that from what I could tell, she had gotten her money's worth.

We were joking around when in a very casual, matter-of-factly manner she asked me if I knew anyone that would be willing to pay $100.00 for some love. I jokingly replied that old country boys were used to paying no more than $20.00 for love or freebies when they could get it. When I said freebies, she went wild and started cursing me at the top of her lungs. You dirty mother f—in s.o.b., etc., etc. I don't think that I have mentioned it, but the bar was full of park people, like the chief ranger and his wife, the district ranger and his wife and family, and most of the secretaries from HQ.

The bartender yelled for both of the girls to leave and pointed toward the door. At that, Nora, that was her name, headed for the door, cursing the bartender as she headed down the length of the bar. As Nora got about halfway down the length of the bar, the bartender said for her not to ever return. Nora paused and gave him a hateful look, and then told him, "Well, go f—k yourself, and this c—t too!" as she slapped the woman seated at the bar directly in front of her on the back. The woman slapped was the bartender's wife, and I guess there was bad blood between her and Nora, something in the past. As Nora turned and headed for the door again, the bartender's wife reached over the bar and grabbed a tall bottle of Galliano and gave it a back hand sling at Nora.

The bottle missed Nora, hit the carpeted floor, bounced up, and shattered the glass in the front door without breaking the bottle. Nora bent over, showing her ass in her little mini-skirt, picked up the bottle, and threw it back at the bartender's wife, but she also missed her target. The Galliano bottle wiped out several dozen glasses, a half dozen bottles of booze, and the mirror of the back bar when it hit. Everyone at the bar had ducked down below the bar when Nora cut loose with that bottle. As Bob and I peeked up over the bar to see if she was gone, we could see everyone in the bar looking at us. Bob and I just sat back down on the floor where we were hidden and had a good laugh until Doug, the bartender, peered over the bar at me and asked what in the hell had I done that set her off.

Just before the start of the winter season, Marve, Scotty, and some other friends met Dee and me in Jackson for some fun before we split up for the winter. It was in Jackson during this trip that I finally realized how much of my life now evolved around Dee. I had to face the fact that knowing her had totally changed my priorities; I no longer wanted to be the good times bachelor but was ready to become domesticated. It was during a romantic moment at the Antler Motel while we were at Jackson that I asked Dee to marry me, and after leaving Jackson, we went to Salt Lake City so I could ask her dad for permission. The rest you know.

The reason I mention this here is to point out how Dee was already changing my life. Six months earlier, I would not have given the incident a second thought, but now that I was engaged, my first thought was what Dee would think. I decided I had better call Dee in Logan and tell her what had happened, because I knew she would hear about the incident eventually. As it turned out, she had already heard, but I was able to convince her that I was innocent of any wrongdoing other than being in the wrong place at the wrong time.

For days after the incident, Bob was not safe to fly with; we would be flying along when he would start laughing hysterically and say that it was more excitement than he had seen in years. Bob and I had a lot of good times that winter just flying around over the northern part of the park chasing bison.

Bob had one of the local artists, Scotty Chapman, make a painting of him and his chopper herding bison up the canyon. I complained because it did not show me hanging on to the running gear for dear life. He had Christmas cards made from the painting and would send Dee and me one every year until he was killed in a helicopter crash several years later.

The story I heard about his crash was that it happened while he was conducting a rescue of some climbing victims from the side of a cliff. No one knew for sure what happened, but somehow, he got his rooters into the side of the cliff, causing him to crash. I can't think of a more fitting way for him to go. He was a damn good man and friend.

A minor incident that I have forgotten to mention that happened that winter occurred near that cabin down in the Black Canyon. I was skiing along the trail and came around the sharp, blind curve that was at the approach to the north end of the suspension bridge. Lying at the end of the bridge in the middle of the trail just soaking up the sun was a huge mountain lion—the first I had seen in all my years in the park.

If you have ever tried to turn around in a pair of cross-country skis, you know that it is not an easy task and requires a little time. I am sure I set a personal, if not a world, record. I don't know where the cat went and didn't really care as long as it was different from mine. That cabin may be Crevice Creek; if so, I don't remember what the one up above the canyon was called.

At the end of the season, I spent a few days with Dee in Logan before going back to Arkansas. Marve had gone to law enforcement school in Brunswick, Georgia. Dr. Steve Clemente, that's right that degenerate had become a full-fledged PhD, had been at some University in Florida to present a paper, and I had just arrived in Arkansas. Marve and Steve were going to come through the airport in New Orleans within hours of each other, and neither had to be back to work for several days, so we decided to meet in the Quarter for a few days.

We had a room in The Hotel Charter on the corner of Charter and Bourbon Streets in the French Quarter. It was a nice old hotel with open courtyard that included a bar and restaurant. The restaurant only served one meal a day, breakfast, but they served it until late afternoon.

We did all the normal tourist things for New Orleans; we had dinner at The Court of Three Sisters, drinks at Pat O'Brien's, chicory coffee and beignets at Café de Monde, of course jazz at Al Hirt's club, and Preservation Hall, where all the old-timers played. While roaming up and down the Quarter, we passed by a Frederick's of Hollywood several times. After having several drinks as we roamed up and down to different clubs, we decided to drop in at Frederick's for a peek.

There were very attractive young ladies in their modeling lingerie, and one was even modeling a G-string and pasties. Marve and Steve dared me to buy a set and send to Dee as a souvenir of my trip to New Orleans. Well, who can turn down a double dog dare from his buddies, so I bought her a set and mailed them the next day; the box was about as big as a match box, but a little deeper.

I was sure that Dee would get a good laugh from the present, but it kind of backfired on me. We had talked over the phone about the type of ring she liked, and I secretly bought the ring and was planning to take it with me when I went back to the park in the spring. Well, a little package from me about the size of a ring box arrived at Bill and Helen's house addressed to Dee. Women being what they are, Helen jumped to the conclusion that it must be the engagement ring and called Dee at school. Dee's curiosity has always been legendary, but this was more than she could stand. She drove in from school so she could open the little box in front of the whole family. Yep, you guessed it, the G-string and pasties. Did I know how to impress future-in-laws or what? In spite of everything, the wedding was planned for November 20, 1976.

That summer, which was the bicentennial year for the United States, was filled with all kinds of ceremonies in almost every town. Cody, Wyoming, was no exception. The highlight of the celebration was the presentation of a commemorative Winchester model 1894 30–30 by the Winchester Corporation to The Duke, John Wayne, and the presentation of their entire firearms collection to the Cody Museum.

The presentation was made during the July 4th rodeo with The Duke riding around the arena waving his rifle, a familiar scene from *True Grit*. It was a wild weekend in Cody, with over 20,000 visitors there for the festivities, most of them hippies, bikers, cowboys, and rednecks. It was an ideal mixture for a riot. As Dee and I were driving down Main Street on our way to our motel on the east side of town, a huge crowd of young, disorderly drunks had spilled out of a bar and were fighting on the sidewalk and street. Dee and I were stopped at the stoplight in front of the bar when the cops and fire truck rolled in and went to hosing down the crowd; the riot was on. One of the cops whacked a long-haired hippie on the head, knocking a chunk of scalp with long hair from his head. The chunk of scalp flew all the way out to where we were sitting and landed right in front of my truck. Almost instantly, an Indian or at least he was dressed like an Indian, grabbed the piece of scalp by the hair, held it up, and let out a war cry, just before the cops dropped him. We were finally able to make our escape and managed to get to the motel without further incidents.

We had tickets to see the Nitty Gritty Dirt Band, who were in concert that night at the rodeo arena. This was the first Fourth of July that I had not worked in all my years in the park. I was looking forward to getting away because the motorcycle gangs descended on the park for the Fourth. One gang from somewhere in Idaho always camped in Bridge Bay Campground because they liked the way I treated them, but they were a real pain in the ass. I never had much trouble from them, but the potential was there if you didn't handle them right. There was a picnic area between the upper and lower loops in Bridge Bay Campground that because of its location was never open. I would usually open this picnic area and put the motorcycle gang in there. That way, they were isolated from the other campers and could stay up all night drinking, doping, and raising hell all they wanted to without disturbing anyone else.

Anyway, like I said, I was looking forward to getting out of the park for a couple of nice quiet days off, but Cody was worse than anything in the park. As Dee and I entered the rodeo grounds just before dark, I was recognized by one of the sheriff's deputies who asked where I would be sitting because they might need my help before the night was over.

I knew what he meant for you could feel the tension in the air; one event could set off another full-blown riot. Luckily, Dee and I were seated in the middle of a small group of the only sane people in the entire arena. I don't remember who the opening band was, but they were not good enough to gain the attention of all the drunks and dopers. The crowd that was down in the arena in front of the grandstand was shooting bottle rockets at those of us in the bleachers. The drunks and dopers in the bleachers were throwing beer bottles at those down in the arena. This went on for quite a while, but as soon as the Dirt Band started to perform, everything settled down, and we had a pleasant evening.

The ceremony on the fourth went off without incidence since most of the drunks and dopers were still sleeping it off at noon. We returned to the park early on the fifth since Dee had to be at work before the noon meal was served at The Lake Hotel where she was the food and beverage manager. I checked in at the ranger station to find that John Wayne and his family were going to be having a picnic at Bridge Bay, in that same picnic area that I had the motorcycle gang in. I had to get rid of the gang immediately, but I knew that I had to find some way to get them to want to leave. As I was driving to Bridge Bay, a radio communication from West Entrance caught my attention. Scotty was notifying Park HQ that there was already a minor riot going in West Yellowstone, Montana, in one of the bars.

I suddenly knew how I was going to get rid of my gang. The leader of the group, a huge, dark-complexioned, longhaired psycho that had a voice that reminded me of a growling dog, got all excited when I casually mentioned the big riot in West Yellowstone. Within thirty minutes, he had all hundred or so of bikers headed in the direction of the West Entrance.

We had security set up all around the picnic area and campground for the Wayne picnic. It was a real pleasure to meet The Duke since I had grown up watching his movies and had seen *The Sands of Iwo Jima* at least a hundred times while I was in the Corps. It was a little sad, though, because even though he was still a big stout man, you could tell that he was not well. His mannerisms were just exactly what you saw in his movies, and he acted as if he was pleased to meet us.

The park routinely received a lot of celebrities, politicians, and foreign dignitaries coming to the park for one reason or another. Pat Nixon, Gerald Ford, Jimmy and Amy Carter, Jim Guy Tucker and family, who was the attorney general and future governor for the state of Arkansas, and all kind of lesser self-aggrandizing bureaucrats were among the politicians that came through while I was there. There were scores of foreign dignitaries coming through continually, particularly when Yellowstone had its Centennial Celebration in the fall of 1972; luckily, I was in Thorofare and missed that mess. Besides John Wayne, we were visited by Clint Eastwood and Allie McGraw, James Garner, and many, many others that I can't even remember.

Vice President Gerald Ford had worked as a seasonal ranger in Yellowstone as a young man, and his son was working up in the northern part of the park as a seasonal ranger while Richard Nixon was president. The Secret Service came and picked him up in the middle of the night, so we suspected something was going on. The next day, Nixon resigned from office, and Ford was sworn in as president.

A couple of years later, when Ford was running for re-election, a picnic was planned by our chief ranger, Bud Estey, who had been also a seasonal ranger at the same time that Ford was here. Ford had worked in the Canyon Village area, so the picnic was planned for Artists Point on the rim of The Grand Canyon of the Yellowstone.

Nuss called me in one day and, in his typical gruff manner, told me I was going to help with security for the president's visit. Helicopter One would be coming in low over a grass-covered ridge on the east side of the canyon. The Secret Service wanted security on that ridge, so I was to take Apple and patrol to the ridge. Dale asked if I carried a saddle gun, and I told him I carried a 30–30 saddle carbine, but this was not a large enough caliber for him, so he gave me that damn 375 H&H Magnum that I had used on the bison to carry on my saddle. He also gave me three boxes of ammo and sent me to the range to make sure it was sighted in. I squeezed off the first round, and it was dead on at one hundred meters. That damn rifle was older than I was and was designed for men a lot tougher than me. There was no recoil pad or anything else to ease a shooter's pain. It even had a metal butt plate, and when it recoiled, it just knocked the shit out of you, no matter how tightly you pulled it to your shoulder. My shoulder was still throbbing when I squeezed off the second round. I guess I jerked a little because the second shot was a little low and to the left, a good indication that I had anticipated the shot and flinched. This second shot hurt a lot worse than the first, but I decided that I had better shoot another round just to make sure that it was me and not the rifle that had caused the miss. As bad as I hated to, I squeezed off a third round, which was so far off target that it hit the 2 ′ 6 board, which was the target framework. The target exploded as if it had been blown up by a bomb and splinters of wood rained down. That shot had brought tears to my eye, and I would not have shot it again unless it was in direct defense of my own life. To hell with the president; he was on his own.

A friend of mine, Don Yestness, was about twelve or fifteen years older than me and was another of those characters I have known. I have to give you a little of Don's history to paint a picture of who Don was. Don had been a middle school principal somewhere in California. He was caught up in the rat race in suburbia when he noticed that his neighbor had just installed an electric garage door opener, which had just come on the market and was expensive. It really bothered Don that he could not afford to buy a door opener. Every time he would drive up and see his neighbor's door opener, it would depress him. One afternoon as he pulled into his drive, he stopped and just sat there looking at that door feeling depressed. All of a sudden, he thought to himself, "What do I need with a garage door opener? What do I need with a garage door, or a garage, or a house?" Don said that he got out of his car and walked off with nothing but what he had on his back.

Don moved to Colorado and took a job on the ski patrol at a new ski resort, Vail. During the summer, he started working as a seasonal ranger in Yellowstone in the summer. Each winter, he would return to Vail. Don was a very competent, people-smart ranger, so I bet he was a good ski patrolman. Don eventually became head of the ski patrol at Vail. As head of the patrol, he was required to ski along with all the prominent politicians that had condominiums at Vail. Teddy Kennedy and Gerald Ford were just a couple of them. After a day of skiing, he would be invited back to their condominium for a drink, so Don was on first-name basis with both Ford and Kennedy.

Plans were made for a reception committee made up of the secretary of the Department of Interior, regional director, park superintendent, and seasonal ranger, Don Yestness, to greet the president as he disembarked from the chopper. Don had been working for years as a backcountry ranger at Shoshone Lake and had gone a little rustic, with a long hair and a beard. He didn't even have a full uniform, but we all loaned him what he was missing, and after currying him down a little, he was fairly presentable.

So the stage was set for the big picnic; The Rim Drive was closed to the public, and a sweep of the entire area was conducted. Apple and I were on the ridge by first light, patrolling the meadow and sweeping the tree line for any movement. Eventually, two identical choppers came in real low directly over the ridge I was on and dropped down onto the parking lot below. It's a good thing that there was no threat to the president because Apple went wild when those two monstrous choppers suddenly came over the trees directly above us; I had my hands full saving my own life from that damn Appaloosa.

I finally regained control of Apple about the time that the president was climbing down the steps of Helicopter One. I saw the secretary of the interior nudge the regional director and ask him who the guy on the end was, meaning Don. The regional director then nudged the park superintendent and asked who Don was, and the superintendent just shrugged as if he didn't know either. As President Ford approached them, he went right straight for Don and greeted him as if they were long-lost friends. The look on the face of the other three in the party was priceless; who the hell is this guy anyway?

About fifteen minutes and a million dollars less in our park budget, the president was off for somewhere else. We then got to go down and finish off the food. It was interesting visiting with the Secret Service agents though.

President Carter also came on a fishing trip to the park, and I was involved more directly with his trip. I should have known something was up six months earlier because one of my old bosses, Dick Davis, with Barber Bridge Builders called Larry Barber to find out what I was up to. It seems that the FBI had been checking up on me; I guess for a security clearance. Dick told Larry that he did not know what I was up to, but he didn't tell the FBI a thing.

Carter's chopper set down in a meadow at the end of the south arm of Yellowstone Lake. Two marines snapped to attention at the foot of the ladder and stood there unmoving the entire time that the chopper was there. I should mention that standing at attention all that time would be no problem anywhere else, but in Yellowstone, the mosquitoes are so thick in the marshy areas along the lake that they swarm you in clouds. These guys had so many mosquitoes on them that you could scarcely see their hands and faces, and I never saw the two move a muscle, twitch, swat, or anything. The guards at Buckingham Palace would have been proud.

The area of the lake that we were fishing was in the extreme lower end of the south arm and was designated as an area for hand-propelled craft only, row boats or canoes. We had two row boats with the president and his guide. I believe Woody Jones, one of our boat rangers, was doing the rowing. The president had brought some hotshot fishing guide from DC with him.

In the other boat was the president's daughter, Amy, John Scott acting as her guide, and me rowing the boat. John Scott had been raised on Yellowstone Lake. John's father was a professor of humanities and department head at the University of Nebraska. He and his family came to Yellowstone every summer. John's dad worked repairing boat motors for YP Company which operated the boat and marina concession in the park. When John was little, he helped to dock and clean boats after their use. He eventually worked his way up to fishing guide and then was hired by the Park Service as a boat patrol ranger on Yellowstone Lake. If there was one piece of water that John knew how to fish it was Yellowstone Lake. A few days before President Carter arrived in the park, John set down and tied up some flies, which he knew would catch fish that time of year on the lake.

The day of the fishing trip was a typical beautiful Yellowstone day, or as Don Yestness would say, "Just another shitty day in paradise." The president and his guide were not catching a thing while Amy and John were taking a nice cutthroat trout with almost every cast. After about thirty minutes of this, the president's boat came rowing over, and the president asked what we were using. John gave him a few flies, and then he also went to catching fish. A couple of hours later, the president was gone, and things returned to normal in the park, if there was such a thing as normal in Yellowstone.

Dee and I were married on November 20, 1976 in Salt Lake City. Neither of us had to be back to the park until mid-December, so we spent most of the month on our honeymoon. We spent our wedding night at Park City, which was little more than an old ghost town in those days. There was not much there except the old hotel and a bar and restaurant. It had not yet become a ski and vacation resort.

After our stay in Park City, we headed down to the Four Corners area, where we camped along the way and hit all the sites in that area. From there, we stopped by the north rim of the Grand Canyon, Brice Canyon, Zion, and Cedar City. We spent one night in Las Vegas before heading to Death Valley, where we spent three or four days. I had been offered a winter job with the Park Service in Death Valley, but I declined because they did not have married housing. I had only been married a few days, and already I had to rearrange my priorities.

From Death Valley, we went into Yosemite for a couple of nights and then finally on to San Francisco, our original destination. Dee's maid of honor, Marion Dow, was from the San Francisco area, and we stayed with her for about a week while we visited the city. Of all the cities I have ever been in, San Francisco had to be the strangest. I guess some people like that sort of place, but it was not to my liking: I couldn't wait to get out of there. We eventually drifted back to Salt Lake City and stayed with her folks for a few days and then back to the park for the winter.

I was working out of the South Entrance for Jerry Mernin again, and there was also a new ranger by the name of Dwayne McClure. Dwayne was very intelligent but just not cut out for Yellowstone. He would have done well in a historic site or a battlefield but was not suited for the isolation of Yellowstone. He was like a boy scout when it came to being prepared. His pack always weighed a hundred pounds because he carried every gadget ever made but just didn't have the wilderness or survival skills. He had developed a drinking problem during the course of the couple of winters that he was there. I had to cover for him a couple of times, and I even sent him home from the ranger station a couple of mornings when he showed up smelling of peppermint schnapps and noticeably drunk—and he was my boss. Dwayne was killed a few years later in a canoe accident on Yellowstone Lake on his day off. I often wonder if he was drunk when it happened, but Yellowstone Lake never gives up its dead; the water is so cold that your life expectancy is only about five minutes before hypothermia kills you.

At this point, I am going to relate another story that happened not because it belongs here but just because I was reminded of it because of Dwayne's drowning. It involved a troupe of Eagle Scouts from somewhere in Utah, I believe. There were five or six canoes of them, one canoe with two adult leaders and four or five canoes with two scouts in each canoe. They were on a two-week backcountry trip on Yellowstone Lake and were all experienced canoers but not accustomed to such cold water or its danger.

They headed down the east shore of the lake and stayed in close to shore as required by the Park Service regulations. They camped for the night a few miles below Park Point Patrol Cabin and planned to canoe across the southeast arm to their next campsite on the promontory. The conditions on the lake were fairly predictable most of the time—calm in the morning with winds rising from the west by 9:30 or 10:00 and getting stronger throughout the afternoon. If the Boy Scouts stayed with the east shore of the lake, they would be fighting the wind all afternoon, but if they crossed the arm early in the morning to the promontory, a strip of land between the south and southeast arms of the lake, they would be on the leeward side of the promontory and out of the wind.

For some reason, they were late getting on the water that morning and were scattered all the way across the arm. The first canoes made it all right, but the last three canoes got caught by the wind and capsized, killing all but one of the canoers in the last canoe. That canoe was not much more than a quarter of a mile from the east shore when it capsized. One of the two boys was a competitive swimmer with

Olympic aspirations and used to cold water, so he made it back to the east shore of the lake.

It was late afternoon before we received word of the accident and was almost dark before we were able to locate the survivors that had reached the promontory. Our boat rangers searched for survivors in the water and along the east shore but called it off until daylight.

At first light, I was headed down the trail along the east shore of the lake on Apple, just in case a survivor had located the trail. In less than an hour, I had passed Park Point and located the camp they had vacated the morning before. The boat patrol rangers, Woody and John, had already located the survivor and were transporting him to the hospital at lake. He was suffering from severe hypothermia, not just from the cold water, but he was only wearing shorts and a T-shirt when the accident occurred, and the night time temperature had dropped into the upper thirties. To make things worse, the boy had encountered a bear and had to spend the night in a tree.

The survivor was transported by chopper to the University Medical Center in Salt Lake City for treatment. A year or so later, we got word that the boy's body temperature never returned to normal and that he had died almost a year after the accident.

We would usually have several drownings every summer, and all of them were because of the cold water. I usually did not get involved with most of them, but another incident occurred while I was out on the lake with John Scott one day. I don't remember the occasion, but there were also a couple of secretaries from not only our ranger station but from several other stations as well. Come to think of it, they were on an orientation tour of the campsites along the lake shore. Mernin had sent me along to point out the merits of each campsite to them since they would be the ones recommending and assigning campsites. We were in the twenty-foot Bertram down in the south arm when the call came about a drowning on the north shore of the lake.

The boat we were in was running poorly and would not get up on plane, so Woody Jones, who was in the twenty-five foot Bertram and not far from us, came by to pick up John Scott to help him work the drowning. I was left with the disabled twenty footer and all the secretaries down in the south arm of the lake. I thought to myself that I was in a pretty good spot when Nuss called me and wanted me to head to Steamboat Point on the north shore as fast as I could to assist with the search for the body. The engine would run pretty good at about half throttle, but if you tried to open it on up, it would die. It took us better than an hour to make the twenty miles to Steamboat Point. As usual, the body was never found.

As related to me by the wife of the victim, her husband and five- or six-year-old son, along with her husband's brother, had taken their small rubber raft out to a large rock, Pelican Roost, a short distance from shore to fish. The brother had come back to the shore in the raft for some reason, leaving the father and son on the rock. The wind came up, and the brother was unable to paddle the raft back out to the rock against the wind. The father told his son to sit on the rock until he returned and dove into the water to swim to shore so he could help his brother paddle the raft out to the rock. According to the victim's wife, when her husband hit the water, he never came up, and the water in that area is over thirty feet deep. The cold of the water could be such a shock that it literally would put many people in shock immediately, and as usual, we never recovered the body.

Now, I will get back to what I was telling about that first winter season, but I will probably diverge from it again as my memory remembers some other event. If I don't relate it when I remember it, I will have forgotten it in about five minutes.

Dee was working at the Snow Lodge at Old Faithful for the winter as food and beverage manager. We did not even have the same days off, but I would snowmobile over to Faithful on my days off, and she would ride to South Entrance on a snow coach on her days off.

It was a good winter with plenty of snow and good skiing. I took a couple of ski trips that winter to shovel the snow from the roofs of the cabins and to take snow readings. I guess that all the snow readings are probably taken by remote now, but in those days, we had to ski in and take a snow sample with a core drill. We would first measure the depth of the snow and then take the core into the cabin so we could melt it and see how much water was in the sample. Being used to snow in Arkansas that had high water content, I could not believe that we could melt eight feet or more of snow, and it would contain only a few inches of water.

We would usually take a week every month to take our readings at Harebell Cabin, Fox Creek Cabin, and Heart Lake Cabin. Sometimes, we would take a ten-day trip and go on in to Thorofare and out to Lake across the frozen lake. I could never get used to skiing across the lakes. The ice would be creaking, groaning, and cracking all the while we were on it. I also knew that there were thermal features in the lake that prevented the ice from being very thick in some areas. It was very unnerving for me.

When Dee and I first arrived at South Entrance, we had made no arrangements to get our winter supply of food before the park closed to automobile travel at the end of October or the first of November. After that date, the only way to get anything into the park is by snowmobile. Most people that are going to winter in will make a trip to town just before the park closes and buy several thousand dollars' worth of food, toilet paper, paper towels, dish detergent, and, of course, plenty of booze.

Dee and I had to turn around as soon as we got to the park and go back to Jackson for some winter rations and supplies. Mernin brought his snowmobile and dog sled down to Flagg Ranch to meet us and help transport our supplies. Flagg Ranch was as far as the road was plowed and was where we left our automobiles parked. Even though the road was plowed, there was always a six or eight inch thick layer of hard snow pack on the road and parking lot where we left our vehicles.

I remember one time when Dee and I decided to go into Jackson for the weekend, which we tried to do about once a month or so, we snowmobiled down to Flagg Ranch and pulled into the parking lot where we had left our vehicle over a month ago. There was no sign of the vehicles anywhere, just large humps of snow. I did not remember exactly where I had parked my vehicle, so I had to search each hump of snow. I finally found a forest green vehicle I thought was mine, but after about fifteen minutes of shoveling, I realized I was shoveling out the wrong vehicle. From then on, I always marked my vehicle with a tall snow stake.

From Flagg Ranch, we had about a seventy-mile drive over snow-packed roads to Jackson. Going to town was so much effort that we went very seldom, but when we did go, we got a room at the Antler Motel for the night. The lady that owned the Antler always gave Yellowstone people a very low rate.

I remember one time when Marv, Scotty, John Scott, and I rolled into town after having been stalled in an avalanche in the Hoback Canyon for six or eight hours. It was around 10:00 p.m., and all her rooms were occupied except the four-bedroom presidential suit. We ended up staying there for the night for $16 total, $4 apiece. Not all Park Service people got that good a rate, but she liked us.

We had all been to Pinedale, Wyoming, where Scotty was building a cabin, and were on our way back to the park when we came upon a large avalanche that had just come down across the road. It must have covered about 150 feet of roadway and was twelve to fifteen feet deep. To get to Jackson by any other route would involve a drive of several hundred miles and many hours over snow-packed roads. We decided to just wait it out since the skip loader was already there and removing snow. We were sitting on the tailgate of his Blazer watching the snow removal when Scotty drug out a new fifth of Rye Whiskey and handed it to me. I removed the lid, took a big gulp, threw the lid out into the snow, and handed the fifth to Marv, so you know what kind of shape we were in when we got to Jackson.

I guess I got sidetracked again, didn't I? Back to Dee and I going to Jackson. A person from the park could not just go to and come from town without stopping at every residence in every area of the park to pick up any outgoing mail and see if they needed us to pick up anything for them. If we started to town early, it would be midafternoon at the earliest before we arrived, and then we had all these shopping lists for everyone.

All the merchants in the surrounding towns knew the park employees and would always save covered boxes to put our purchases in since they knew we had to transport everything on a dog sled behind snowmobiles.

It was almost impossible to get fresh vegetables back into the park. We would put fruits and vegetables in an ice chest to try to keep them from freezing, but if you had very far to go inside the park, you would have to put something hot in the ice chest. I was never able to get bananas home without them being frozen.

I would usually hang gallons of milk with bungee cords from the rack on the back of the sled. I lost a gallon from the back one night but didn't realize it until we got to the cabin. I immediately went back looking for this white gallon of milk lying in the white snow. I found it frozen solid when I ran over it at about 45 mph. It was like hitting a boulder, and it caused my snowmobile to turn over, breaking the windshield and pitching me off into the loose snow off the side of the road.

That winter, there were three of us rangers at south, Jerry Mernin and his wife Cindy, Dwayne McClure, and me and Dee, when she was there. Most of the time, one of us was on our days off, so usually, there were two of us working every day. One of us would keep the ranger station open until noon for the incoming snowmobilers and then spend the afternoon skiing the trail up to the hot springs.

We had to watch the hot springs closely to keep the employees from Flagg Ranch and the ski resorts in Jackson Hole from swimming in them. The hot water dissolved minerals out of the rock and deposited the minerals in very delicate patterns around the edge of the pool. Swimming in the pools destroyed the mineral deposits.

Swimming was permitted in the runoff channels from the springs, and the springs were far enough in the backcountry that skinny dipping was not illegal. It was not at all unusual to encounter a dozen or more skinny dippers in the runoff channels.

That first year I was married, it was my turn to ski up to the hot springs, and Dee was at South Entrance for her days off, so I skied by our cabin to see if she wanted to ski with me. The weather was not very good that afternoon, though with moderate snowfall and blustery winds. It was one of those afternoons that I would just have soon stayed in the area since I did not expect anyone to be out and about at the hot springs. Dee decided to stay home and read and take a nap before starting dinner.

I skied back through the housing area until I picked up the trail to the hot springs. Even though it was snowing pretty hard, I could make out fresh ski tracks on the trail headed toward the hot springs. The trail paralleled the runoff channel all the way up to the hot springs, and at one spot just below the hot springs, the trail climbed up a slight rise above the runoff channel. As I skied up onto the rise, I saw three sets of skis and ski poles sticking up in the snow, along with three packs and three sets of clothes. I could not see anyone but heard voices from the direction of the runoff channel.

I skied over to the edge of the rise until I was overlooking the runoff channel. The warm water of the stream created a fog that covered the air immediately above the stream, and as I peered into the fog, my first thought was, "What are all these baldheaded guys doing swimming in the stream?" Just then a gust of wind parted the fog like Moses parted the Red Sea, and I realized that what I had seen were not baldheaded men at all but was three naked, large-breasted young ladies lying on the backs in the runoff channel. The stream was only about sixteen inches deep at that location, so there was no hope of getting hid in the crystal clear water. They were not aware that I was present, so I took my time before greeting them. I thought about closing one eye to save it in case I was struck blind but figured what the hell, I would risk it.

I listened to them chatter about their boyfriends for a little while before I said, "Good afternoon, ladies." They did not appear to be very concerned about my presence and merely set up in the stream and casually covered themselves with their arms. But one of them did not have large enough arms to cover everything. She was one of those gals that you could tell had large breasts from looking at her back.

One of them asked me if I was coming in and sounded not the least concerned if I was. I kind of mumbled something that I am sure sounded real intelligent like, "No, I forgot my towel." I tried to carry on a conversation for a few minutes but quickly decided that I had better ski on before they decided that I was a total retard. As I tried to ski on up to the hot springs, I was having a hell of a time navigating. I was having trouble keeping my ski tips from crossing, and I just could not seem to keep both skis going in the same direction.

I eventually made it back to the ranger station without injuring myself. While having a beer with Jerry and Cindy at their kitchen table, I told them of the encounter, but I made the mistake of doing it while Dee was there. She made the accusation that the only reason I went up there was to see these gals' tits. Never mind that I tried to get her to go with me or that it was my time to go; I had planned the whole thing. I had not planned it, but it was well worth the butt chewing.

We did not get mail delivery into the park during the winter but had to pick it up at the post office at Moran, Wyoming. There was not really much at Moran except the post office, which serviced the entire area. Anytime someone went to town, they would pick up everyone's mail and bring it back with them, so mail delivery was very infrequent.

Our first Christmas together was a rough time for Dee. She was from a large family, and her mother always had had large traditional Christmas celebrations. Dee had never been away from home on Christmas before, and here, she was wintered inside Yellowstone with no TV, only one radio station, and a new husband. To make matters worse, the presents from neither her family nor my family had reached us. I went out on the park boundary and cut a tree, and we made our own decorations like stringed popcorn and painted pine cones. Dee did all right until Christmas morning when all we had under the tree was my present to her and her present to me. Gift opening lasted about one minute, and she broke down in tears. I felt so sad for her but did not know what to do.

Jerry and Cindy came by a little later with presents, and Dee recovered. I actually don't think the presents had been bought for her, but Cindy was such wonderful person that I suspect she wrapped up some of her personal things for Dee because I was sure that I recognized some of the stuff. Marv also came down to have dinner with us and brought gifts, so we really ended up having a nice Christmas. Every Christmas since that first one, Dee always buys so many gifts for everyone that the presents are stacked several feet high around the tree and take up half the room. I complain about it every year, but I think it goes back to our first Christmas, and she is not about to change.

The road crew started to plow the park roads about the first of April, but they start in the northern part of the park, and we were at South Entrance, so we were the last to get plowed out. The south side of the park received the deepest snow in the park. The storms would come in from the south and dump most of their snow on the south slope of the Yellowstone Plateau before reaching the top. At South Entrance, we would typically have about six to eight feet of snow pack at the height of the season, but just north of the entrance in the Lewis River Canyon, twenty feet of hard-packed snow was common.

When the road crew started to plow from Grant Village to South Entrance, they would use a rotary snow blast that could handle snow ten feet deep. From Grant to Lewis Lake, there was from four feet at Grant Village to about six feet at Lewis Lake, but from there through the Lewis River Canyon, they would have to take a dozer and push the top ten or twelve feet of snow off into the canyon so they could use the snow blast on the bottom ten feet. It was not at all unusual for us to get four feet of fresh snow in one night at south.

This was the reason that one of us shoveled snow every morning, just to keep the roofs of the buildings from caving in from the weight. By the end of the season, the snow was up to the roof, and our cabin was just a lump in the snow. I would snowmobile over our roof to let Dee know I had returned to the area for the evening and would be home in about an hour after cleaning and fueling the snowmobile.

We would usually ski up to Jerry and Cindy's for a beer and a glass of hot spiced wine. The amount of booze that was consumed during the course of the winter was amazing, even though we never drank much at one time, except for Dwayne; we sure went through a lot of it. A good indication of how hard the winter had been was by counting the number of empty bottles of booze (beer cans and bottles were not counted) that we loaded into the trash truck when it arrived in the area after the roads had been plowed out. We had no trash pickup during the winter, so we just stored our trash in a building about the size of a typical garage, and then everyone helped load it. The area that had the most empties had bragging rights for the year.

I am not sure if this is the right year or not for this story, but it was Christmas day when I got a call from Mulberry that my father had passed away on the evening of the 24th. I was not surprised by the news because when I had seen him last in November, he was really down. He had been in the hospital earlier that year and had to stay with my sister, Mary Ann, and her family until he was able to return home.

Medically, Dad was all right, but as he talked I could tell that he was tired of being sick and was ready to die. He told me that for years, he had been fooling himself into thinking that if he could just get over the latest illness he was having, he would be all right. But then there was always another illness, as with this latest one. He was quiet for a couple of minutes before he looked me in the eye and said that when a man's daughters had to wipe his ass for him, it was time to go. He continued by saying he was tired of it and just wanted to lie down by Marge's side. Margie was my mother, but Dad always called her Marge.

Dee was with me on this trip, and I was glad she was since it was one of the few times she met my dad. When we left his house and were headed back to the park, I told her that I would never see Dad alive again because he would not make it until spring because he had given up.

I hate to admit it, but Dad remains a mystery to me even today. He was a bigger than life giant to me as a child, and an unemotional, honest, virtuous, fair-minded, and utterly predictable enigma to me when I got older. He was very broad-minded about many things but stubborn and hardheaded about others. As an example of his stubbornness, you may have wondered how the farm got divided as it did. Dad called in a surveyor to divide up the farm and gave them instructions as to how he wanted it divided. But instead of dividing it from the county road, Dad had it divided according to the south section line. He was convinced that the road should have originally been built on the section line and that one day the existing road would be moved to the section line. Since they won't even grade the road, I can't imagine that it will ever be moved, but if it ever was, the property would be laid out perfectly. The way it is, nothing works out well with the existing road. Dad possessed such clear common sense most of the time, but when he got something in his head like the problem with the road, no amount of arguing would convince him otherwise.

Dad never left home, or at least until he started getting sick; even his barber would come to the house to cut his hair and visit. A lot of the old men in the neighborhood would come over to visit with him and argue politics and religion. They would get louder and louder and finally get mad and storm out in a huff. I have heard Dad tell them that they are crazy as hell at least a hundred times. The next day, they were back again, and it was the same thing.

I flew home for Dad's funeral and to be with the rest of the family for a few days. It was a strange feeling knowing that dad was gone. I felt as if I was an orphan, even though I had not really depended on him for anything since I was about sixteen years old, and I saw him so seldom, but his death left a void in my life that I still feel today. It was different when Mom died several years earlier; even though I had always been much closer to her and missed her terribly, as long as Dad was alive, I still had someone I could count on if I needed help. With both of them gone, I had no one to turn to for help or advice; it was now up to me alone to make a future for my family and me.

The trip back to the park was a mess from one end to the other. As I was setting in the plane ready to leave Denver for a direct flight to Jackson Hole, the luggage carriers came back out and started to unload some of the luggage that they had just put on the plane a few minutes earlier. I saw my bag being taken off. The fuel truck also came back out, and we took on more fuel.

The pilot announced that the airport in Jackson Hole was shut down because of the weather, so we were going directly into Salt Lake City. Luckily, Dee's family was in Salt Lake City, so I at least had a place to stay. Bill picked me up at the airport, and I spent the night with them.

The next morning, I called the airport to check on the status of my flight and was told that Jackson Hole was open again, so I would be able to get out that day. Bill dropped me off at the airport and left since I was sure I would be flying out that day. I checked in at the ticket counter, was cleared through security, and was sitting at my gate waiting for my flight to be called, when it was announced the Jackson Hole was shut down once again because of blizzard conditions and cold temperatures. I felt bad about being gone from the park so long with conditions so bad because Mernin would have to handle everything since McClure was gone somewhere.

There was a little group of four of us that were determined to get into Jackson that day, so we cashed in our tickets and rented a car and drove into Jackson in a blizzard in near whiteout conditions with the temperature better than twenty below all the way until we got near Jackson, where it got cold. Now remember that my luggage had been taken from the plane in Denver, so all I had with me was my carry-on bag; most of my cold weather clothing was in my luggage, wherever it was. It was my good fortune that I had left my snowmobile suit in my truck at the airport along with mittens and my packs, cold weather boots that have a heavy felt liner in them. I called Mernin, and he brought a snowmobile down to Flagg Ranch and left it for me. It was so cold that I could not even get the crank rope to move an inch; Mernin had to drive down and pick me up.

The next morning, we got word of a group of winter campers from a wilderness survival organization, National Outdoor Leadership School, NOLS as it was known, that were camped in the area of Heart Lake. The night time temperature had dropped to more than forty below, and there was concern for the safety of the group. Even though they were well equipped and had experienced leaders, such extreme conditions could be dangerous or even fatal if something went wrong, which always seemed to happen.

There was no place I would rather be than in the wilds somewhere when conditions were good, but at times like this, it was as if Mother Nature was suffering from PMS and at her most disagreeable. Mernin headed into Heart Lake looking for the party and found them without much effort. I have never been out in more hazardous conditions. I think I had on every stitch of clothes that I owned and wished I had more. You had to keep skiing continually just to keep warm. Every time

I would blink my eyes, my eyelashes would freeze together, and quickly my goggles would frost up on the inside from my breath.

We found the group easy enough, and most of the dozen or so members were all right. Three of the members, however, were suffering from varying degrees of frostbite of toes and fingers. Mernin said that it was not as if they had done anything different or wrong, that individual differences in circulation could account for it under such extreme conditions. We started helping them ski out to the road, but the going was slow because of their frozen feet.

After a few miles of skiing, their feet began to thaw because of the exertion, and the pain set in. I felt sorry for them because there was nothing we could do for them. It wasn't like when I was in Nam and I could just shoot them full of morphine; they just had to tough it out.

We had to dig snow caves and spend the night, but their feet refroze during the night, which we learned hit better than sixty below at Old Faithful and better than fifty below at South. Even though we were dug in well below the surface where it was warmer, it was still a cold, miserable night, and I had an expedition sleeping bag rated for forty below.

We headed out again the next morning and finally reached the trailhead by late afternoon. Mernin sent me ahead to stop the snow coaches headed to South Entrance from Old Faithful. We knew that they would be warm and had room to transport injured persons much better than on a snowmobile and sled. We managed to get the injured to the hospital in Jackson, but at least, three of the group lost toes. It was the first real severe frostbite that I had seen. Their toes were swollen and black. I guess between my Marine Corps years and my Yellowstone years, I encountered about every kind injury, from torture to frostbite and everything in between.

Dee and I were both stationed at Lake again that summer, with her as food and beverage manager at the Lake Hotel. I was still working as the bear specialist in the district when needed and did patrol work when not. As soon as I reported for work that year, Mernin and I were sent up to Glacier National Park for a seminar on bear management. All the bear people were there from all different agencies and even zoos, but there were few of us with grizzly experience. I was kind of in an elite crowd, the Craigheads from U of Montana that were now working on a project in Alaska, Mernin and I from Yellowstone, Oak Blair, who had just transferred to Glacier and another guy I don't remember from Glacier, and a few others I can't recall. The rest of the crowd were black bear people. It was a good seminar with a lot of good hands-on training and sharing of ideas and problems. I got a chance to try my hand at shooting at a target with a tranquilizer gun from a moving helicopter, which proved to be more difficult than it looked.

Dee and I spent most of our days off going outside the park just to get away from the crowds. One of our favorite places was the Sunlight Basin, an isolated area just east of the park between Cody and Cooke City, Montana. There was a gravel road of about sixty miles or so that crossed the basin and came out on the highway twenty-five or thirty miles north of Cody. About halfway across the basin, there was a small wilderness campground on a small stream. The camp was in the shadows of the Absorka Mountains that made up the east boundary of Yellowstone. The entire basin was made up of just a few large ranches and government land, so there were very few houses or anything else.

Another of our favorite places was up in the Bear Tooth Mountains, also out of the northeast entrance of Yellowstone, between Cooke City and Red Lodge, Montana. We would drive up near Bear Tooth Pass to Bear Tooth Lake and camp. As a matter of fact, I am sure that it was at Bear Tooth Lake that Nathan was conceived in the back of my Toyota pickup.

Both of these areas were all but deserted, a far cry from the horde of people a few miles away in Yellowstone. It has probably changed a lot by now because Cooke City and the Sunlight were just beginning to show the first signs of development.

There were all kinds of good restaurants in the most out-of-the-way places scattered around Wyoming and Montana. Dee and I made a point of seeking out these places to eat. Every little town and wide spot had a bar, usually the old saloon, that served an excellent steak and prime rib at a very reasonable price.

Several years before I met Dee, I stumbled onto one such place while prospecting for gold near South Pass and Atlantic City, Wyoming. South Pass was the lowest and best route across the Rocky Mountains on the Oregon Trail. Gold was discovered just east of the pass, and the boom town of Atlantic City appeared overnight as a result. It was a typical boom town story except that Atlantic City has the history of being the first town in the United States to give women the vote.

When gold prices fell, the mines closed down, and the town died out pretty well. There were only two businesses in the entire town, the general store and the hotel, but all the old log buildings were still there, including the jail, blacksmith shop, and many others I can't remember.

There was a restaurant in the old log hotel, so I dropped by to see if I could get a bite to eat. I was expecting to find a typical greasy spoon restaurant, but I was shocked when I was met at the door by a man wearing a tuxedo and a lady in an evening gown. Since I had been panning for gold all day, I was dressed in muddy, wet jeans, flannel shirt, and hiking boots. I could see that the entryway to the hotel had been restored to all of its original glory. I half-expected them to slam the door in my face for the way I was dressed, but the man in the tux escorted me to the bar for a drink since I was going to have to wait for a table. He and I were the only humans evident for about thirty miles in any direction, but I was going to have to wait for a table, but what the hell, I always enjoy a drink before dinner.

I was left alone in the bar, which gave me a chance to look around. The bar had also been restored and was very elegant with red silk wallpaper and fancy chandeliers. Hanging in frames all over the walls were newspaper and magazine articles from all over the US praising the quality of the food and ambiance of the Atlantic City Hotel. Several articles gave a brief history of Atlantic City, the hotel, and its most recent owners. I have forgotten most of the story except that the owners were from New York City and were big in the corporate world. She was a big executive with some advertising firm, and he had a similar type position, but I can't remember the type of firm. On vacation one year, they had been to Atlantic City and loved the area. They were both fed up with the corporate world and were looking for something different. When they discovered that the old hotel was for sale, they decided to buy and restore the hotel and open a gourmet restaurant as both of them were gourmet cooks.

When I was escorted to the dining room, I was the only diner except for one other table of about twelve women, a gourmet cooking class from some college back east. The dining room was just as fancy as the rest of the hotel and such a contrast from the rugged, weathered logs of the exterior. After having drunk most of a bottle of wine, I struck up a conversation with the ladies at the other table and found that the restaurant was only open on weekends during the summer, served dinner only, fifteen guests an evening, and everyone ate the same thing. I was beginning to wonder why I had not received a menu or had my order taken. The table setting was as elegant as everything else. I had never seen so much silverware in my life; it was strung out on both sides and above the plate for a nearly a foot. All during the meal, which was several courses, I had to keep looking at the ladies to see which tool they were using, but I finally figured, what the hell, I was not ever going to see any of these people again, and they probably already had me pegged as a low brow anyway. So I just used one fork and enjoyed my meal. I tend to be pretty simple of taste, if you hadn't guessed that by now, and favor meat and potatoes, but the meal was excellent. At first, I thought I would go hungry because the portions were so small, but they just kept coming, course after course for hours. I crawled into my tent that night very contentedly, having found a little gold that day and having had memorable meal, never mind that I had spent a lot more for dinner than I was likely to make with a week of panning. I slept like a baby.

I think that one of the things that attracted me to Dee was that she also loved to roam around and find unique out-of-the-way places to visit and eat. On our honeymoon, she found some obscure national monument, Hovenweep, that had just been created. We had to travel about fifty miles by gravel road in the middle of the night across an Indian reservation to find the place and were the only people there. We got caught in the middle of a stampede of wild horses out on the reservation while trying to find the place. It turned out to be an interesting set of Indian ruins, completely different from those at Mesa Verde National Monument.

Another place I would drive hundreds of miles out of the way to eat was in the small town of Hudson, Wyoming. It was located in the old historic saloon, complete with the original bar, back bar mirror, and bullet holes. Sweelers was the name of the place, and they served the best steaks I have ever eaten, and every little town out there served good steaks.

Just after I had gone into Thorofare for the fall, I was making my nightly communication to the Lake Ranger Station when Mernin relayed to me that Dee had been to the doctor that day and was pregnant, or as Mernin had said, "The rabbit died." I don't even remember what my reply was, but I am fairly certain it was something really dumb.

By that winter, Dee was starting to show considerably, and by the end of winter, she was so large that she could hardly fit on a snowmobile, but then she was starting her last month. We came out before the roads had been plowed in the middle of April, and Nathan was born on May 16.

I had been trying to gain permanent status with the Park Service for about seven or eight years by this time, but there was a hiring freeze on government jobs during this time. To make things worse, affirmative action was at its peak, and nothing but minorities or women were being hired to replace vacated positions. I was the wrong color and sex even though I had received excellent recommendations from all of my supervisors and was highly recommended for permanent employment by all of them. Having the baby had put us considerably in debt, about $1,700 as I remember, so I decided not to go back to the park that summer but work construction at home instead.

We did go back to Thorofare that fall and took four-month-old Nathan with us. Dee had a carrier that was like a backpack, except it fit in front, that she would put Nathan in. Her horse, Dusty, was very calm and dependable, so I didn't particularly worry about them getting hurt, as long as we stayed on the trails. We would feed Nathan just before we headed out, Dee would mount, I would hand Nathan to her, and she would zip him inside the pouch. My parka and riding slicker were large enough to go around Dee and Nathan both, so even in bad weather, he was warm and dry. Every two hours, he would start fussing, and we would have to stop so Dee could nurse him. As soon as his belly was full, he would fall asleep as we headed down the trail.

The worst thing was the diapers that had to be washed almost daily. There is no way we could have used disposable diapers; they were too expensive, and it would have taken an entire mule train to get that many diapers in and back out of the backcountry. I had a clothes line strung for about one hundred feet or so, and it was always strung full of diapers. Poor Dee washed a bunch every day, and this was in a wash tub on a rub board.

There were a lot of times when I needed to cover a lot of country or rough country that Dee and the baby would stay at Thorofare while I went elsewhere. Many a night, she and Nathan stayed at Thorofare by themselves while I was at Fox Creek or Eagle Pass. She would always shutter the windows and bolt the door so she was safe enough, but I am sure it was a little unnerving for her though she never said anything.

By mid-October, the weather had started to get bad enough that I took them up to Trail Creek, and John Scott came in with the patrol boat, breaking ice for the last half mile or so, to pick up Dee and Nathan. I returned to Thorofare for two or three more weeks.

The entire fall, Nathan did not have a sniffle, sneeze, or anything. He loved to sit out in the yard in his backpack carrier and watch the Grey Jays and Ravens come in to eat the table scraps I had left on a stump. Even though he could barely hold his head up, he would snap his head around to watch them come and go until he fell asleep.

That winter, we were at the South Entrance again with the Mernin's, and Cindy just fell in love with Nathan. I began to realize, though, that having a baby had altered our lifestyle tremendously. Dee was no longer able to just come and go with me as she had been before, and due to the extremely cold temperatures, she was stuck in the cabin most of the time. We were not free to just go into Jackson and spend the weekend as we had been before.

Dee was interested in pursuing a career in nursing, which she could not do with us in Yellowstone. By the end of the winter, I decided that if I was going to continue to work for the Park Service, it would be better for the family if it was in a less-isolated park.

I applied and was accepted in a seasonal ranger position on the Buffalo National River in northern Arkansas. I worked out of Buffalo Point as a patrol ranger. Four days a week, I would spend most of my time in the campground or hiking one of the trails. There was such a mileage restriction on our vehicles that we could only cove the roads once a shift; the rest of the time, we were just parked somewhere.

The weather that summer set all kind of records for continuous day of over one hundred degrees, and the nights cooled off very little until a few hours before daylight. One ranger was assigned the duty of canoeing down the river from Buffalo Point to Rush, a ghost town about five miles below the point. There were all kinds of old abandoned lead and zinc mines along the river. The days were so hot that most of the rangers did not want to get out of the air-conditioned car or ranger station and would make any excuse to avoid having to canoe the river. They quickly learned that I would trade duty with them, so I spent almost every day on the river canoeing. I would spend a lot of the time picking up trash along the shore and prowling through the mines. The mines were always cool, so I would canoe until it got real hot, and then go a little way back in one of the numerous mines and cool off for a while.

I was even able to con my way into a three-day float from Buffalo Point down river to its confluence with the White River at Buffalo City. Don't let the name fool you; there was nothing but a few houses at Buffalo City, which you reached by river or gravel road, if you could find it. My justification for the trip was to check on the small elk herd that had been introduced into that lower Buffalo wilderness area a year or two before and no one had seen since. There had not been anyone that patrolled the lower river since they had been introduced.

It was a great trip, even though the water was low and the weather was hot. I was lucky in that the hot dry conditions caused the elk to stay near the river, and I got sight of them late one evening coming down to the river's edge for water. If it had been a normal year, I might never have got to see them.

I camped each night on the gravel bar, ate fish, and saw no one. It was as if I had that whole little section of the world to myself. The last day, I started to see John Boats coming upstream with smallmouth fisherman from the White River, but that was only the last few miles. I have always wanted to repeat that trip but have not yet.

I enjoyed the park, but the rangers I worked were totally different from the guys I had worked with in Yellowstone. No Mernin, Marv, Scotty, Jackson, or anyone I felt I cared to get to know. I guess because Yellowstone was so large and isolated and everyone lived inside the park; the park just consumed you. Buffalo River was the opposite; no one lived in the park except for a few seasonals, and it was an eight-to-five job to most everyone. There was just not the same camaraderie that I had become accustomed to in Yellowstone.

The thing that really bothered me, though, was the fact that I was separated from my family. Dee and Nathan were living in my dad's house, or I guess I should say my house on Georgia Ridge, and I was living in a trailer at Buffalo Point. I would drive home on my days off, about four hours one way, but by the end of the summer, I decided I would not be separated from them again if I could help it.

Mom and Dad's old house was pretty primitive; there was only one electric circuit in the entire house and only one receptacle. Everything else was plugged into drop cords that ran from each light. To make a cup of coffee, I would have to unplug the 1950s' model frig. The electric circuit had been added a few years after Dad had built the house in 1947. There was no electricity available on the ridge until about 1949. I spent most of my days off sorting through and getting rid of Mom and Dad's stuff that had not already been claimed by my brother and sisters. What was left was mainly just junk, but still it was hard to throw it away.

My summer on the Buffalo ended my Park Service career; I realized that other than Yellowstone, Glacier, and a couple of other large western parks that were exceptions, most parks were like the Buffalo. What really helped convince me to give it up was that I had already had the best job in the Park Service and that everything else was not going to measure up and that with permanent status would come all the paper work. Mernin was rarely able to get out into the field because of his administrative duties. All the good jobs were seasonal jobs, but the pay was not sufficient for a family to make ends meet, and eventually, kids need to be able to go to school. So at the end of the summer of 1980, I decided it would be best for my family if I tried other employment that paid a little better.

John, Dee, and Nathan at Thorofare 1979

Real Life

After leaving the Park Service, I took a job as a policeman in Mulberry. I was one in a two-man police dept. The Chief, Randy Chastain, was an old high school buddy of mine. He had graduated the year ahead of me, but we had played on the same ball team together. Since there were just the two of us, we worked twelve-hour shifts, and on the other days off, we also were on call twelve hours. I did enjoy the work even though it was very difficult for me since Dee worked at night at the hospital as a scrub in surgery. When I was on call, I had to find something to do with Nathan if I got called out. It was costing me more in babysitting than it was worth.

On one occasion, I was working alone when I received a call from the Franklin County Sheriffs Dept. They requested that I go out on the interstate at Exit 24 and set up a roadblock to apprehend a kidnapper being chased by the sheriff. I decided there was no way in I was going to try to set a roadblock on the interstate but that I would watch for the suspect vehicle and give chase if found.

I had been setting for just a few minutes when the suspect vehicle went speeding through. I pulled in behind the suspect vehicle doing about 80 mph. When the suspect became aware that I was behind him, he picked up the speed to 100-plus mph. We were speeding along in the west-bound lane, but the traffic was pretty light, so I didn't push him any faster, but the Franklin Co. Sheriff, who was very old school and had been in office for several decades, went flying around me, and I was doing 100-plus.

The sheriff pulled up alongside the suspect vehicle and tried to force the suspect off the road. The suspect and sheriff crossed the median into the east-bound lanes headed west into oncoming traffic. I stayed over in the west-bound lane running along beside them. At this point, things started to happen real quickly, the sheriff started shooting at the suspect vehicle, and the suspect slammed his vehicle into the side of the sheriff's vehicle, causing them to lose control of their vehicles. Both vehicles came to rest in the trees on the south side of the interstate right of way.

I continued on a short distance to the next exit. I knew there was a gravel road that ran parallel to the interstate a short distance through the trees where the suspect had crashed his vehicle. I had driven down the gravel road about a half mile when the suspect walked out of the woods with his hands up. I cuffed him and notified the sheriff that I had his suspect in custody. The sheriff replied, "Bring that S.O.B. up here to me where I can do the same thing to his head that he did to my vehicle."

I loaded the suspect into the back of my vehicle and drove back to the Sheriff's location. By this time, there were about fifty law enforcement vehicles on the side of the interstate. There were at least two state troopers, cops from Alma, Dyer, Mulberry, Ozark, and deputies from two counties.

The suspect showed no visible injuries when I turned him over to the Franklin Co. Sheriff, but the sheriff pulled a sap from his back pocket and went to beating the suspect on the head. I have never seen so many cops disappear so quickly, I included. I was not going to interfere because there was little doubt that I would have to fight the sheriff to stop him.

That next week, I noticed an article in the *Spectator*, the weekly paper printed in Ozark, reporting the incident of the kidnapper's arrest. Near the end of the article, it was stated that the suspect was in the hospital being treated for extensive facial injuries sustained in the crash.

A short time later, I resigned my position as a patrolman for Mulberry P.D., due mainly to the babysitting issue, and went to work for a construction company.

Dee Ann started working as a scrub tech, at Sparks Hospital in Ft. Smith, and entered the nursing program at West Ark College in Fort

Smith. It was during this period that our second child, a little bald-headed, brown-eyed girl, was born, which we named Sarah Dee.

I was working in Okla. City at the time, building hangers at Wiley Post Airport when Dee called me and wanted me to come home because she felt as if she was about to go into labor.

I left OKC just before noon and drove in as fast as I could, breaking about every traffic law on the books. When I walked in the house, Dee was sitting in the floor, playing Pac Man and visiting with a friend that had come over to stay with her until I arrived. Dee told me I had plenty of time to clean up before we headed to Sparks Hospital in Ft. Smith. We headed to the hospital but had to stop for fuel since the truck was on empty after my trip from OKC. Dee said she was feeling fine, but by the time we got back on the interstate, she grabbed my leg and said I had better hurry. I just did get her to the hospital in time, but Sarah was already born by the time I had Dee checked in and got upstairs. This was perfectly all right with me. When Nathan was born, I was in the delivery room during the ordeal and took unbelievable verbal abuse from my wife. Labor and delivery is no place for the fathers who need to be in the waiting room passing out cigars.

After the birth of Sarah, Dee Ann started her nursing profession at Sparks Hospital, working in surgery, where she continues to work today.

The economy was very slow at this time, and there was little work in the construction industry, so we decided that it was time for me to return to school to get a teaching certificate. I entered the Teacher Ed. Program at the University of the Ozarks at Clarksville, the same school I had graduated from about a decade earlier with a B/S degree in Biology.

This time, things were different. For one thing it did not bother anyone that I was a veteran and I had no interest in college life. I was there for one thing, to get a degree as fast as I could.

It took me a full year to receive my certification and find a job. I started my teaching career working a half day at Mulberry High School and a half day at Alma Middle School. Eventually, I was employed full-time at Mulberry, teaching both Jr. High and Sr. High Science.

A few years later, our third and final child was born, a bald-headed, blue-eyed little girl named Jessica Ray.

From this point forward, life just became a blur. Dee was working long hours on the night shift at the hospital and had various part-time jobs. I was teaching full-time, driving a bus route morning and evening, plus ball trips two to four nights a week.

In my spare time, I started remodeling and adding onto my dad's house, which had been left to me with his passing. Dad had started building the house in 1947 but had never finished. There was no electricity on the mountain in 1947, so what little electricity there was in the house when we moved in had been added after 1947.

There was one circuit in the entire house with only one receptacle. There was on overhead light in each room with drop cords strung wherever needed. To make a pot of coffee in the morning, I had to unplug the refrigerator. By today's standard, the house would not have been livable but over the course of twenty-plus years, Dee and I built a very comfortable home, doing all the work ourselves as we could afford.

I had never planned to teach more than a few years as I still had hopes of returning to the Park Service, but I found that I enjoyed teaching so much that I was hooked.

There are advantages and disadvantages to teaching in your home town, particularly such a small town. I had gone to school with the parents of most of my students, and in my later years, I taught their kids. I knew their family history, and they knew mine.

I taught nearly all the science seventh through twelfth grade, so the poor kids were stuck with me for five or six years, but this gave me the advantage of knowing exactly what they had been taught before.

When I first started teaching, there were no real standards. You just showed up a couple of days before the start of school, cleaned your room, and helped cut the grass or whatever else needed to be done.

There was no maximum class size. My first seventh grade class had nearly fifty students. After the first couple of days of class, the principal came into my room and asked if I had enough desks. I told him I wasn't sure because I had not been able to get them all seated yet.

Paddling was a common way of dealing with discipline, especially in lower Jr. High. It was a rare day that I didn't have to paddle many of the seventh and eighth grade boys, and I don't mean one at a time. There were times when I would have all of them out in the hall. By the time they were in the ninth grade, I rarely had to discipline them. I know there is a lot of controversy over this form of discipline, but in my later years, the attitude of parents had changed so much that I did not paddle, but I never had the control of a class that I did in the early years.

I had little trouble dealing with the boys. Most of their activity involved burping, farting, cussing, or fighting. These things I understood and could deal with pretty effectively. I had an outside door, and I would move them outside until they shaped up. It was my feeling that a fight where there was no bloodshed was not a fight, but just an argument.

Girls were a different matter though; there was always an emotional crisis of some kind that I had to try to deal with. Notice I said I tried to deal with the crisis, but I am afraid I was not very effective. The boys would have a fight, and five minutes, they would be over it; girls would hate each other forever.

If I am remembered as a teacher for anything, it will probably be for my field trips. I went on a field trip to an Indian museum when I was in the second grade, and I can still see the displays today. I fell in love with museums and field trips at that young age.

I always took every class on at least one fieldtrip every year. I tried to take every student, but in the later years, the behavior of some students was so poor that I had to start leaving some at school.

I never had a problem getting permission from the administration, maybe because I was a bus driver and always drove my own trips. I took classes to Memphis, Little Rock, Tulsa, Oklahoma City, and Kansas City. We went to caves, science museums, art museums, and electrical power plant (nuclear, coal–fired, and hydroelectric).

The trip that the students enjoyed the most was what the students named the Death March. I required each student in the seventh and tenth grades make a leaf collection near the end of school. I wanted it to be made of native trees, and I wanted the students to see the trees in their native habitat, not just in someone's yard. I found the best way to do this was to take them to the mountains.

I would drive the bus loaded with students and parents to the top of White Rock Mountain, where we would hike six miles of the Ozark Highland Trail down to Shores Lake, gathering leaves on the way. This is a beautiful trail with a great diversity of trees and geologic features. I could show the students examples of most of the things they had studied in both life and earth science.

At about the half-way point, the trail crosses a creek with a good water fall. We would always eat lunch and swim for about an hour at this point. It would usually be about 3:00 p.m. before we reached the lake where the bus had been left for us.

Depending on how many classes I had each year, I took from two to four trips down this trail each year for nearly twenty-five years. Most trips I had nearly as many parents and former students who would come along, but they were no help identifying the leaves. My brother, Don, and brother-in–law, Isaac would usually go along to help the students identify the trees, as they knew as many or more trees than I did.

I have been told by many students that the Death March was one of their best memories from their high school years. I have to admit that it is one of the things I miss the most since I retired. I have hiked the trail by myself since I retired, but it is not the same without the enthusiasm of a mob of kids. A large number of the students had never hiked a trail through the wilderness in their entire life.

It's hard to condense thirty years of my teaching career as I have so many good memories of the teachers I worked with and the outrageous stories of the students I taught. I think it's best to sum up the thirty years by saying that day to day, I never knew what was going to happen next. If thing got quiet, I knew they were up to something.

One Final Note

Since I wrote this biography, I have received word from Cindy Mernin that her husband Jerry had passed away suddenly last winter. Jerry and Cindy figured prominently in my life during my Yellowstone years.

Jerry has become a legend in the Park Service and was a mentor for me and many others. No, mentor is not a good enough description for my relationship with Jerry; he was my hero, and dear friend. It's not many people who are lucky enough to get to work so closely with a person of Jerry's character. I have known many outstanding men throughout my life, but Jerry is the giant among them. I think Jerry was the reason that I didn't have the same feeling for the job after I left Yellowstone.

A memorial service was held for Jerry at Lake Ranger Station, on the Shore of Yellowstone Lake, the summer of 2012. Dee and I attended and got to see Cindy and many other old friends we had worked with.

Cindy honored me by requesting that I escort her on one last trip into the Thorofare Country to spread his last remains. I have long dreamed of getting back into the Thorofare, where I worked boundary patrol for so many years. I just wish it was for a different reason.

I will end with a Jerry Merninism, of which he had many.

"Be careful of the company you keep."

The End

Made in the USA
Lexington, KY
04 December 2014